Educating slow-learning and maladjusted children

Educating slow-learning and maladjusted children: integration or segregation?

David M. Galloway
Carole Goodwin

Longman
London and New York

Longman Group Limited London

*Associated companies, branches and representatives
throughout the world*

*Published in the United States of America
by Longman Inc., New York*

© Longman Group Limited 1979

First published 1979

British Library Cataloguing in Publication Data

Galloway, David M
    Educating slow-learning and maladjusted children.
    1. Slow learning children 2. Remedial teaching
    3. Problem children – Education
    I. Title II. Goodwin, Carole
    371.9'2 LC4661 78–40867

    ISBN 0–582–48914–8

Printed in Great Britain by Richard Clay (the Chaucer Press) Ltd, Bungay, Suffolk

Contents

Acknowledgements

We gratefully acknowledge the help we have had from colleagues in writing this book. In particular we are indebted to Sir Edward Britton, former General Secretary to the National Union of Teachers, Mr Robin Hedderly, Principal Educational Psychologist to Kirk Lees Education Committee, and to Mr David Loxley, Principal Psychologist to Sheffield Education Committee, for their helpful criticisms of the manuscript.

We are indebted to the following for permission to reproduce copyright material:

The Journal, *Behavioural Psychotherapy* for extracts from the article 'Application of Behavioural Analysis and Behaviour Modification in School Psychological Service Practice' by David Galloway; Her Majesty's Stationery Office for a table from *Education Statistics for the United Kingdom* by D.E.S.; The Journal, *Therapeutic Education* for extracts from the article 'Research into Learning and Behaviour Problems' by David Galloway.

Disclaimers

Introduction: Why concentrate on the ESN(M) and the maladjusted?

Categories of handicap

The categories of pupils requiring special educational treatment are laid down by statute (Ministry of Education 1959). The Warnock Report (Department of Education and Science, 1978) has recommended a new system to replace categorisation by handicaps, but until this is implemented the following are recognised in England and Wales:

(a) blind pupils;
(b) partially sighted pupils;
(c) deaf pupils;
(d) partially hearing pupils;
(e) educationally subnormal (ESN) pupils;
(f) epileptic pupils;
(g) maladjusted pupils;
(h) physically handicapped pupils;
(i) pupils suffering from a speech defect;
(j) delicate pupils.

Since the Education (Handicapped Children) Act 1970, the ESN category has informally been split between the ESN(M), or moderately mentally handicapped, and the ESN(S), or severely handicapped. In this book we are concerned principally with the ESN(M) or slow-learning child.

The two anomalies

The ESN and maladjusted categories stand out from this list because the handicap is not defined primarily on medical grounds. Many of the children concerned do suffer from some form of medical condition which may have contributed to their difficulties; nevertheless, it remains true that the handicap itself is not defined on medical grounds in the same way that applies to other categories. Instead, the handicap is defined on educational and/or psychological grounds. Throughout this book we use the term 'medical' handicaps to include all children within the eight categories defined on essentially medical grounds. These children could be said to have educational difficulties *because of* their medical handicap. For the ESN the handicap *is* the educational difficulty. Similarly, some medically handicapped pupils are said to have emotional or behavioural difficulties resulting from the frustration caused by their handicap. For the maladjusted the emotional or behavioural difficulty *is* the handicap.

There is another sense in which the ESN and the maladjusted differ from the medical handicaps. Although a depressing number of children with medical handicaps still seem to escape early detection by the routine maternity, child welfare and school health screening services, it remains true that objective tests are available for detecting handicaps. They may be difficult to apply with a recalcitrant infant and the picture may further be complicated by changes in the level of handicap from day to day, for example in cases of catarrhal deafness; nevertheless the criteria for detection and definition are well defined compared with those available for assessing children who are thought to be ESN or maladjusted.

The fact that some psychologists still use intelligence and personality tests in the assessment of these children does not invalidate our argument that the selection criteria are essentially subjective. The tests themselves, as we shall see later, are notoriously crude and unreliable. A more basic point is that the test results cannot prove that the child should be regarded as ESN(M) or maladjusted. Low scores on intelligence and reading tests have to be interpreted in the light of the child's present circumstances and previous history. If he has missed most of his education through illness, we cannot expect him to have made much progress in reading. Similarly, if the organisation of his class has been disrupted by frequent changes of teacher, we will not be surprised if this is reflected in the results of so-called personality testing. By comparison, the assessment of medical defects is relatively straightforward.

'Hidden integration' of the ESN(M) and maladjusted

The Warnock Report not only reflected public concern about the education of the handicapped, but has itself generated an enormous amount of publicity on the subject. Much of the discussion has focused on the question of integration: should handicapped children be educated in separate special schools, or given special facilities in ordinary schools?

This overlooks the fact that integration has always been a fact of educational life for the majority of pupils who might be described as ESN(M) or maladjusted. As we shall see in Chapter 2, the existing special schools cater for no more than a small minority of children with severe learning difficulties and behavioural or emotional problems. The rest remain in ordinary schools. Indeed, before the 1944 Education Act maladjustment was not recognised as a handicap in its own right, hence there were no maladjusted children! In fact, of course, the children existed but were not labelled maladjusted and generally remained at their ordinary schools. Although they are now categorised as handicapped it remains true that the majority of children who could be described as maladjusted remain in ordinary schools. The same applies to the ESN(M). This raises a fundamental issue on which the Warnock Report, to its credit, was absolutely clear, namely that children cannot be divided into separate groups of the handicapped and the non-handicapped. Nevertheless, in planning future facilities it is obviously essential to ask whether the minority of children selected for special education in special schools fare better, educationally and socially, than the much larger number who remain in ordinary schools.

The needs of the silent majority

Compared with the eight categories of medical handicap, the ESN(M) and the maladjusted have attracted relatively little attention from the public at large. As they constitute by far the largest groups of children in special schools – and the majority, as we shall see in Chapter 2, have always remained in ordinary schools – this must be a matter for some surprise. The bulk of discussion both before and since publication of the Warnock Report has focused on the educational needs of children with medical handicaps.

One reason is depressingly clear. Children in every other category of handicap are supported by powerful pressure groups of parents and voluntary organisations which are independent of the established special school system. The pressure for integration has not on the whole come from teachers in special schools; with a few notable exceptions they have argued powerfully against it. Instead it has come from parents or voluntary organisations of, or concerned with, handicapped people. Almost by definition, the ESN(M) and the maladjusted lack this sort of support; they seldom come from homes where the parents are sufficiently articulate to organise themselves into a self-help group to promote their children's interests. This is not to undervalue the commitment or ability of teachers in special schools; we are simply pointing out that there are other possible points of view, and these are seldom heard in the case of the non-medical handicaps.

Special needs of the slow-learning and the maladjusted

We have argued that there is less public support for assimilating special schools for the ESN(M) and the maladjusted into the mainstream of the education system, than exists for the medical handicap. Conversely, the pressure against integration is greater in the case of these groups. Yet whatever the arguments for or against the integration of children with medical handicaps there is also a powerful case for educating ESN(M) and maladjusted children in ordinary schools rather than in separate schools.

This is a recurring theme throughout the book. We argue that the existing system should be called in question for at least three reasons;
1 It has developed in an *ad hoc* manner with insufficient attention to its immediate goals or long term objectives.
2 Its effectiveness has not been adequately evaluated, but most of the available research suggests that ESN(M) and maladjusted children may do as well, or better, in ordinary schools than in special schools.
3 In the long term the separate special school system cannot benefit ordinary schools, since it focuses attention and resources on a rather arbitrarily selected minority which might otherwise be used to raise the quality of education for a much larger number of pupils.

Readership

This is not principally a book about teaching methods. In the early chapters we describe the historical background to the present facilities for children who could be labelled ESN(M) or maladjusted and demonstrate the inadequacy and inconsistency of their facilities for many of the pupils concerned. A critical summary and discussion of research on the results of special education is followed by a chapter in which we examine the theoretical issues involved in the successful integration of slow learning and disturbing children in ordinary schools. Children only attract labels like maladjusted or disturbed when they are disturbing to their teachers or, less frequently, their parents. This remains true whether the child disturbs the adult by his withdrawn behaviour or by his physical aggression. Of course, there are some withdrawn children who do not disturb adults because their unhappiness goes unrecognised; often they sit at the back of the class and are regarded as no problem by busy teachers in a large school. Yet these children would not have been recognised as disturbed or maladjusted either. A recurring theme is that the term 'disturbing' implies a recognition of the child's effect on us, while the terms maladjusted and disturbed misleadingly imply some quasi-medical state within the child. (We have reluctantly retained the term maladjusted in the title of the book because of its greater familiarity). The middle of the book describes innovations in Scandinavia (Ch. 5) and this country (Chs. 6–8) and discusses the practical lessons to be learnt from them. Finally we look in detail at the administrative procedures and practical resources needed if the ESN(M) and the maladjusted are to be educated successfully in ordinary schools.

We hope that this book will stimulate discussion among teachers in special and ordinary schools. It should be of particular interest both to teachers responsible for planning remedial education or pastoral care in their schools and also to education psychologists, school medical officers and advisers who have responsibility for the education of any slow-learning or disturbing children. It will also be of interest to social workers and to sociologists interested in the processes which result in some children being regarded as 'problem' and in constructive ways in which this problem of labelling may be faced.

Chapter 1

The development of education for ESN(M) and maladjusted children

A. Historical overview

Special education up to 1944

When considering presentday provision for ESN and maladjusted children it is salutary to remember that as recently as 1890 the Lunacy Act stated explicitly: ' "lunatic" means an idiot or person of unsound mind', thus confusing mental illness with mental deficiency. In his excellent book on education for the handicapped from 1760 to 1960, Pritchard (1963) shows that the distinction was in fact quite widely recognised by doctors and educationalists, though apparently not by parliamentarians, by the end of the nineteenth century. It had even been recognised as early as the reigns of Edward I and II when the idiot, or born fool, *fatuus naturalis,* was contrasted with 'the person of unsound mind, but with lucid intervals, *non compos mentis, sicut quidam sunt per lucida intervalla.* . . . The difference was of practical importance, since if a man was found by the Imposition to be a lunatic the Crown sequestered his property only during the period of his lunacy, whereas in the case of an idiot the Crown entered into the permanent possession of the property.'

Free and compulsory education came to England with the Elementary Education Acts of 1870, 1876 and 1880. These Acts made no provision for dull children or children with learning difficulties and behavioural problems. A process of rapid natural selection led to their sinking or simply remaining at the bottom end of the lowest classes. Many schools reacted to this situation by creating a Standard O taught by pupil teachers, since the few qualified teachers were needed for the more 'normal' children. Into Standard O sank not only the 'feeble-minded' but also the physically handicapped, partially sighted and delicate children who could not cope with an ordinary class curriculum. Pritchard notes that with ages ranging from eight to thirteen, 'together they stagnated'.

Nevertheless, by the early 1890s pressure for special provision for feeble-minded children was growing. A subcommittee of the Charity Organisation Society (1893) supported the principle that a large number of children needed special education outside the ordinary Board schools, and argued that the school boards, and not voluntary bodies, should be responsible for establishing the proposed special schools. They also suggested that school boards should be made responsible for providing residential care where necessary. The Charity Organisation Society's recommendations had been anticipated by the Medical Superintendent at the Royal Albert Asylum,

G. E. Shuttleworth (1888), who made unfavourable comparison between the limited provision in England with that in less wealthy countries such as Germany and Norway. Pressure on the London School Board also came from within when the Chairman of the Subcommittee on the education of the blind and deaf, Major-General Moberly, persuaded the Board's School Management Committee in 1890 to accept a proposal to open a special school for 'feeble-minded' children (Education Department, 1898). This proposal was not accepted, but in the following year the School Board agreed to open three experimental 'Schools for Special Instruction' in the poorest areas of the city. Staff–pupil ratio was not to be above the unthinkably generous level of thirty to one, and children were to be nominated by the head teacher of their ordinary schools as 'intellectually weak, poorly endowed with perception, memory, reasoning, etc', a phrase borrowed from Klemm's (1891) book *European Schools*. Before admission each child was to be examined by a committee consisting of an inspector from the School Board, the Board's Medical Officer and the head teacher of the receiving school.

In view of the bitter controversy which bedevilled special education for the next eighty years (and is only being satisfactorily resolved in the 1970s) it is of particular interest that the criteria for admission were primarily educational. This was true both of the London School Board's first three schools and of the Milton Street Board School in Leicester where a classroom was made available in 1892 for twelve feeble-minded children. Here, children were selected by a Mr H. Major, a Leicester School Board Inspector, who used a reading book, not to see whether the child could read but rather whether he could explain what was happening in the pictures and answer questions about his environment (Education Department, 1898). Another feature of the London schools which is of interest as the first official recognition of a recurring theme was that appointments were initially for five years only, as the Board thought it important that teachers should be able to return to work with normal children.

At this time it was feared that the strain of working with feeble-minded children for a prolonged period might harm the teacher's physical or mental health; more recently the concern has been that a prolonged period in a special school could lead to a lowering of standards, and that a refresher year with normal children might help teachers retain a sense of proportion, and realistic educational objectives (Ministry of Education, 1954; Department of Education and Science, 1973a).

By 1896, four years after the opening of the Hugh Myddleton School in London, 900 children were attending twenty-four special schools. At the same time schools or classes had opened in Bradford, Birmingham, Nottingham, Bristol and Brighton, and thought was then being given in official quarters to the needs of children who were retarded as well as simply backward. Dr Alfred Eichholz, first Medical Inspector to the Education Department suggested that children requiring special education should be classified into three groups:

1. Those with pronounced mental deficiency.
2. Physically defective and epileptic children.
3. Children who were 'physically and morally healthy – but backward'.

He considered the third group to be very numerous and stated that many should be able to return to their ordinary schools. This conception of some special schools as remedial establishments aiming to prepare children for return to ordinary schools anticipated the emphasis on rehabilitation in special education today. In 1898 the Education Department's Departmental Committee on Defective and Epileptic Children published its report recommending that provision of special education should, when necessary, be compulsory. (Under the 1870 Act parents could place their children beyond the jurisdiction of the school Board by exercising their right to select a voluntary school; owing to anxiety about the stigma attached to special schools, this led to the voluntary schools having more defective children than the Board Schools.) The Committee suggested that classes should not generally exceed twenty, and that all heads and the majority of assistants should be qualified. Many of the Committee's recommendations were subsequently endorsed in the 1899 Elementary Education (Defective and Epileptic Children) Act, but the Education Department did not accept the principle that local authorities should be obliged to provide special schools. Consequently the Act merely permitted local authorities to make provision for their epileptic and mentally and physically defective children. In the following ten years just over a third of the 328 local education authorities used their powers.

This was in part due to the appointment in 1904 of a Royal Commission on the Care and Control of the Feeble Minded. The Commission heard evidence from the growing eugenicist lobby influenced by the belief of Sir Francis Galton that mental and moral deficiency were, like physical characteristics, hereditary. This was supported by Dugdale's (1877) study of the Jukes family in which he claimed that over 400 of 700 descendants of five mentally defective sisters named Jukes were criminals, prostitutes, or paupers. In addition the developing intelligence test movement held out little hope that the feeble-minded could become self-sufficient; although Binet and Simon (1904) had argued that the feeble-minded should be taught to read and write, they nevertheless remained pessimistic about attempts to educate many of them. Finally, voluntary workers such as Mary Dendy and Dame Ellen Pinsent were arguing in favour of the lifelong segregation of the feeble-minded, thus obviating the need for day special schools, and were exerting considerable influence in the National Association for Promoting the Welfare of the Feeble-Minded, which was founded in 1897. Thus when the Royal Commission reported in 1908 it recommended that the 1899 Act should be amended to exclude mentally defective children who should henceforth be the statutory responsibility of local mental deficiency committees; local education authorities which had exercised their right under the 1899 Act to establish special schools for such children should either transfer them to the mental deficiency committees or continue to operate them under their direction.

Not surprisingly, the Royal Commission's report provided an active disincentive to local education authorities exercising their powers under the 1899 Act. Nevertheless the gloomy picture presented by the report had the positive effect of encouraging supporters of the existing schools to publicise their successes. As a result the Mental Deficiency Act of 1913 required of local education authorities (as opposed to simply empowering) that they should ascertain children aged 7–16 who were mentally defective. The only children who would be passed on to the mental deficiency committees would be those who were incapable of benefiting from education in a special school, in other words the group who would today be regarded as ESN(S). The following year the Elementary Education (Defective and Epileptic Children) Act made the 1899 Act mandatory as far as defective children were concerned.

The Act did not lead to the escalation of special educational provision that might have been predicted. In 1914 there were 13,563 children in the mentally defective schools, but by 1939 the number was still less than 17,000. There were three principal reasons for this lack of growth:

1. During and immediately after the First World War the country had other things to think about.
2. From 1924 to 1929 a committee chaired by A. H. Wood was investigating the educational needs of the feeble-minded, and local education authorities were understandably reluctant to use existing legislation to increase their provision when the committee might recommend a change in the basic structure of special education.
3. By the time the Wood Committee reported the United Kingdom was joining America and other European countries in the recession of the 1930s. In this climate no form of expansion could be contemplated.

The Wood Committee's first brief was to examine the incidence of feeble-mindedness, and the second to propose changes in the present system of educating feeble-minded children in the light of experience gained since the 1899 Act. The Committee's investigations into the incidence of feeble-mindedness are discussed in more detail in Chapter 2. What is important here is that the Committee, whose members included Cyril Burt and Ellen Pinsent, commented that existing special schools were catering for only one-sixth of the estimated number of feeble-minded children in the country and no formal provision was being made for the even larger group of retarded children who did not technically fill the criteria for certification as feeble-minded. This group was estimated to include about 10 per cent of the population, but could not under existing legislation be admitted to special schools as they were not mentally defective. The committee's recommendations, published as the Report of the Joint Departmental Committee on Mental Deficiency (Board of Education and Board of Control (1929), were that certification of the feeble-minded should be abolished, so that the feeble-minded and the retarded might be catered for in one comprehensive scheme. The report referred to children who were 'educable in a true sense' but could not benefit from an ordinary school; thus the group we would now know as ESN(S) was deliberately excluded. The committee hoped, however, that abolition of certification would remove the lifelong stigma attached to attendance at a school for the feeble-minded and enable parents to feel that they were being offered 'a helpful variation of the ordinary school'. With commendable farsightedness they hoped that rural areas and small towns would establish special classes (as there would be an insufficient number of children for a special school), but that even in the large towns there would be special classes for less severely retarded children in ordinary schools.

For a variety of reasons, notably the depression of the 1930s, the Wood Committee's recommendations did not receive statutory recognition until the 1944 Education Act. It is on this Act that the present structure of special education is based.

The 1944 Education Act

The 1944 Education Act was heavily influenced not only by the Wood Committee but also by the reports of the committees which inquired into the education of partially hearing and partially sighted children (Board of Education, 1938 and 1934). All these reports called for special schools to be incorporated within the main stream of the education system as a way to reducing the stigma attached to attending them. Section 34 of the Act placed a duty on every local education authority 'to ascertain what children in their area require special educational treatment', but other parts of the Act made clear that this need not be in special schools; indeed it was stated explicitly that special schools should be provided for children with serious disabilities, while those whose disability was less serious could be catered for in any maintained or assisted school. In practice this meant that special education could be provided in the ordinary classes of ordinary schools, not only in special classes of ordinary schools. The intention was laudable but, as we shall see later, it led to a number of anomalies.

Under Section 33 of the Act the Minister of Education (now called the Secretary of State for Education and Science) was empowered to issue regulations regarding the categories of pupils requiring special education with additional recommendations on the appropriate provision for each category. In fact, the 1945 Regulations (Ministry of Education, 1945) recognised eleven categories of handicap: educationally subnormal, blind, deaf, epileptic, partially sighted, partially deaf, physically handicapped, delicate, diabetic, children with speech defects, and the maladjusted.

Of these only the ESN and the maladjusted directly concern us here. The term 'feeble-minded' ceased to have any administrative significance, at least so far as school-age children were concerned, and children who were *retarded* in their educational attainments were included with the generally backward in the new concept of *educational* subnormality. In other words *any* child whose educational attainments fell significantly below the norm could be included, whatever his developmental level in other respects. As we shall see in more detail in the next chapter, this definition included some 10 to 15 per cent of the school population. Indeed, this proportion must have been included since the criteria for selection were to be relative rather than absolute, a point which is considered in more detail later in this chapter.

The 1945 regulations issued under the 1944 Act (Ministry of Education, 1945) placed a *duty* on local education authorities for the first time to provide special education for maladjusted children. Official recognition of the needs of the maladjusted had been granted in the 1930s in financial support for the pioneer Child Guidance Clinics; in addition the 1921 Education Act enabled a few conscientious authorities to pay the fees of maladjusted children attending voluntary homes or schools on the grounds that they were empowered by the rather vague wording of Section 80 to cater for children's health and physical education. Following evacuation of children from inner city areas during the Second World War the authorities became painfully aware that many could not or would not conform to the expectations and requirements of the families on whom they were billeted. Just as it took the Boer War to persuade the authorities that something must be done about the health of the nation's children (it was very inconvenient that only one in every three potential recruits was physically fit enough to be enlisted), so it took evacuation and billeting in the 1939–45 war to persuade them to recognise the needs of the disturbed, or perhaps simply disturbing, children who could not or would not cope with a 'normal' education or family life. Under the 1945 Regulations special schools and 'boarding homes' could be approved by the Minister.

The expansion of special schools since 1944

We saw earlier that there were still less than 17,000 children receiving education in what we would now call ESN(M) schools at the outbreak of the 1939–45 war. As an expensive resource, special schools naturally suffered during the war and by 1946 there were only 11,000 children in ESN schools. By 1950 the number had increased to just over 15,000 (in England and Wales). In the case of maladjusted children the increase in the post-war period was not so dramatic, though it has escalated subsequently. In 1944 there were no recognised schools and only a handful of children were being catered for under the 1921 Education Act. By 1950 nearly 600 children in England and Wales were being educated in special schools for maladjusted pupils. Figures from 1950 onwards are given in Table 1.1 (DES 1977):

Table 1.1   Full-time pupils by category of major handicap

	1950	1960	1965	1970	1974	1976
Maladjusted	587	1,742	2,904	6,093	11,583	13,653
ESN(M)	15,173	32,815	42,670	51,768	53,353	53,772

(Quoted by permission from: Department of Education and Science, 1977. *Statistics of Education 1976*, vol. 1. *Schools London:* HMSO.)

The figures show a startling rise in the quantity of provision available, and at least in the case of maladjusted children there is no evidence that this rise is being halted by the dramatic fall in the birthrate in the last few years. With this category of handicap demand has always increased to exceed the available supply of places.

At first sight, a curious feature of the increasing number of special school places available has been the remarkably steady waiting lists for such places. Although the number of ESN places doubled between 1950 and 1960 the waiting lists remained similar at around 12,500. A survey carried out in 1956 (Ministry of Education, 1961) showed that 19,000 children were thought by their local education authorities to need places in day ESN schools and a further 7,000 in boarding schools. By including the number of places already available and allowing for the expected increase in school population by 1965, the estimated total number of places needed became 54,000. This figure was virtually achieved by 1976. Bearing in mind that the figure represented a mere 0.8 per cent of all children in maintained schools, and that the definition of subnormality was intended to include educationally retarded children as well as those who would formerly have been certified as feeble-minded, it is not hard to see why the supply of children considered to need special education has escalated in proportion to the availability of places.

B.   Problems in assessment leading to recent developments

Limitations of assessment based on test scores

Parkinson's law states that the supply of work needing to be done increases in direct proportion to the number of people available to do it. That a variation of

Parkinson's law should operate in the field of special education is neither surprising nor in itself particularly alarming. The definition of educational subnormality was explicitly intended to be relative rather than absolute, since it included children who were educationally retarded for reasons *other* than intellectual dullness. A more fundamental point, which may or may not have been recognised by the architects of the 1944 Act and the subsequent Statutory Instruments and official circulars, is that the criteria for selection could not have been absolute on purely logical grounds. To recognise the significance of this point it is necessary to understand the meaning of an intelligence test score, or a score (such as Reading Age) on a test of educational attainment. Typically, intelligence test results are expressed in terms of an intelligence quotient (IQ); most test scores are based on a standard deviation of 15 points; by generalising from the group on whom the test was developed to the population at large, it is possible to predict the proportion whose scores fall within a given range. Thus 68.2 per cent of the population obtain scores which fall within one standard deviation of the mean (IQ 85–115); 95.4 per cent obtain scores within two standard deviations of the mean (IQ 70–130); and a mere 0.2 per cent of the population is expected to obtain scores which are over three standard deviations from the mean (above 145 or below 55). On this basis 2.3 per cent would be expected to score below 70, with the same number scoring above 130 on a test such as the Wechsler Intelligence Scale for Children. In the same way a Reading Quotient derived from a Reading Age $\frac{(RA \times 100)}{CA}$ gives an idea of the proportion of children obtaining scores in any given range, while the Reading Age is simply a rather crude statement of what the 'average' child on whom the test was standardised could cope with. The crucial point here, however, is that test scores, as any other measure of development or attainment, are based on the population at the time. If educational attainments improve across the country as a whole, this will *not* be reflected in 'better' test scores unless out-of-date tests are used. This is because test scores are merely variations from the norm and if the norm varies so will the test scores.

Yet problems in the use of test scores for selecting ESN(M) children go much deeper than this. The ESN(M) and maladjusted are the two groups of handicapped children for whom there is most confusion over the relative status of educational, psychological and medical reports. This question is highlighted by the breadth of the definition of the ESN child in the 1944 Act. Thus assessment as ESN(M) may mean that a child is very backward in all areas of development and needs specialised teaching of a sort that no ordinary school can be expected to provide; or that he is seriously retarded educationally due to prolonged illness; or that his educational retardation is due to learning difficulties associated with some specific perceptual problem; or that he comes from a problem family and is performing at the same level that one should expect of any child in similar circumstances.

It should be noted, incidentally, that we are only considering the group now regarded as ESN(M) since the ESN(S) only became the responsibility of local education authorities following the Education (Handicapped Children) Act of 1970. Superficially the problem has focused on the priority which should be given to globally backward children compared with the educationally retarded, since both were subsumed under the generic label of ESN. In her useful book *The Slow Learner,* M. F. Cleugh (1957) puts the problem succinctly:

Prior to 1944 the transfer to a M.D. school of Charlie who was a nuisance, but whose intelligence quotient was relatively high, could be challenged on the grounds that he was not mentally defective, but now (unless the circumstances were quite exceptional) he would be fairly sure to come under the ESN umbrella. It is excellent that Charlie's need for special help is recognised, but at the same time it is easy to fill the special ESN schools with Charlies and then for the Authority to sit back complacently and do nothing about other children whose need is greater.

Evidence that this occurs comes from the disproportionate number of boys in ESN schools; although boys vary more than girls at both ends of the intellectual spectrum, the difference is nothing like sufficient to account for the greater number of boys (nearly 32,000 in 1971 in England and Wales, against less than 21,000 girls); a boy who finds himself failing at school is more likely to show behaviour problems of the 'acting out' type than a girl, who is more likely to show her distress in withdrawn behaviour that can easily go unnoticed in a large class.

The ascertainment of ESN(M) pupils has been dogged by twin controversies:

1. That ESN schools are too often used as 'dumping grounds' for relatively bright, but difficult and educationally retarded pupils.
2. That selection is too often made on the basis of unreliable intelligence tests.

At first sight these two points seem unconnected, but as we shall see shortly they are closely related, at least in the case of immigrants. Cleugh (1957) argued strongly that ESN schools should not be used for the relatively able but retarded child, and ministerial pronouncements have tended to support her view. Thus, the report of the Ministry's chief medical officer (Ministry of Education, 1958) expressed concern that more children in certain schools had IQs over 80 'than might have been expected'. 'This selection for special school education of children with high IQs', the report continued, 'causes me to consider what becomes of the children with low levels of intelligence – particularly those who are on the borderline of educability.' The Ministry's 1961 Circular to local education authorities made a similar point, noting that while the majority of backward pupils could be given suitable education in an ordinary school, 'it is undesirable that severely handicapped children should be allowed to remain in ordinary schools'. The majority of head teachers of ESN schools, too, maintain that their schools are more suitable for the 'genuinely ESN' child than for the retarded pupil, and by this they generally mean those children whose score on an IQ test falls below 70 or perhaps 75.

When medical officers were largely responsible for selecting pupils for special schools the most important single item in the selection process was generally the Stanford-Binet Intelligence Scale. Special courses for medical officers were held at regular intervals, at which, among other things, they received training from psychologists in the administration of this test. This is not the place for a discussion of the relative usefulness of the Stanford-Binet Intelligence Scale and other IQ tests, though it is worth noting in passing that few educational or clinical psychologists would now consider it their first choice and many would consider it to be definitely contra-indicated for children over eight unless used for the purpose of comparison with other test results. The more fundamental point relates to the usefulness of intelligence tests as predictors of an individual child's capacity for educational progress.

It has been known for years that IQ is not a static variable and is vulnerable to a wide variety of influences. Among the less usual of these was described in a letter I received years ago from the head of a school for maladjusted children: 'No one would believe until I demonstrated it with controls that the IQ scores of pupils from an open air school could be lifted ten points or so by thawing them out on the hot-water pipes for half an hour before testing.' More seriously, performance on intelligence tests can be highly influenced by the child's physical and emotional state at the time of the test and by his confidence, or lack of it, in the examiner. All too easily an intelligence test can condemn a withdrawn child as a dull one, especially if the test used is one which depends, like the Stanford-Binet, largely on verbal responses. Similarly, an intelligence test result is something of an irrelevance for the socially or emotionally deprived child who has had little or no opportunity to talk with adults or play with other children before starting school. Among other requirements, intelligence tests expect the child to understand instructions, explain himself verbally, remember things verbally and visually, and demonstrate an ability to carry out abstract reasoning tasks. The child whose opportunity to engage in such activities has been restricted by culturally or emotionally impoverished home circumstances, or by erratic teaching at school, will naturally do badly on an 'intelligence' test. The fact is that IQ tests do not measure intelligence, but are rather tests of the child's *attainments* in certain somewhat arbitrarily selected skills. Another criticism is that many of the most widely used tests have a middle-class bias, and are therefore biased against working-class children. The best that can be said of them is that they are somewhat less influenced by school and family factors than tests of educational attainments in skills such as mathematical or reading ability.

Our argument is not that IQ tests are altogether without value, but that they should constitute at most only a small part of the total assessment process. In the past, and occasionally still today in authorities with inadequately trained educational psychologists, the decision has been made almost entirely on the basis of IQ score. Nowhere has this practice aroused more resentment than among West Indian immigrants. In his provocatively titled book, '*How the West Indian Child is Made Educationally Subnormal in the British School System*', Bernard Coard (1971), a former teacher in a ESN(M) school, quoted from an Inner London Education Authority report (ILEA, 1968) that 28 per cent of pupils in day ESN schools were immigrants, against only 15 per cent in the ILEA's ordinary schools; moreover, West Indians accounted for an unexpectedly high proportion of the immigrants in ESN schools. The same survey reported that nearly half the ESN schools regarded 20 per cent or more of their immigrant pupils as wrongly placed. Worse, although immigrants were four times as likely as white children to be regarded as wrongly placed, the number returning to ordinary schools was only slightly higher (7 per cent against 4 per cent). Coard argues that this situation arose largely from the inability of intelligence tests to allow for the influences of cultural bias, social class and emotional disturbance when used with immigrants. (This point is discussed in more detail in Chapter 2 in relation to a major survey of the intelligence and reading attainments of London children.) The same arguments apply to the use of IQ tests with non-immigrant children, since a majority of those put forward for special schools are not only working class, but also lack the experiences available in a nursery or a caring, stimulating home, and show a degree of behavioural or emotional disturbance. With a few notable exceptions the rate of return from ESN(M) to normal schools remains below 5 per cent. This could point to the excellence of initial selection, though, bearing in mind that they cater for around 1 per cent of the population, the relatively high IQs and educational attainments of many of their pupils scarcely support this view; alternatively it could mean that the schools are too reluctant to release their 'improved' pupils to ordinary schools; a third possibility is that ex-ESN school children may be unable to cope with ordinary school life after the protective atmosphere of the special school. Whatever the truth, evidence from national surveys (see Ch. 2) supports the belief of many special school teachers that the educational needs of globally dull children differ from those of their educationally retarded or relatively bright peers. If ESN(M) schools are to provide a long-term alternative to ordinary schools for the former, assessment must be a lengthier and more complex process than was possible when an intelligence test formed the major part.

Some teachers and some psychologists have tried to get round the limitations of IQ tests by developing observation schedules which are 'criterion referenced' rather than normative. Instead of giving the child a test and evaluating his scores against some statistical norm, the teacher compiles her own profile of the child through systematic observation of his performance in a wide variety of educational and social skills; the criteria are specified in a precise way, so that they provide a reference point for the teacher's observations. This is in fact no more than good educational practice, though it is depressing that so many teachers still prefer to rely on a traditional, and much more limited, battery of tests devised by psychologists. Nevertheless, the use of criterion-referenced assessment does not altogether overcome the problem that we raised in connection with test scores. They can give a more comprehensive picture of the child's strengths and weaknesses by focusing on social and emotional development in addition to the rather limited range of reasoning skills investigated by traditional intelligence tests, and unlike traditional intelligence tests they are child and classroom orientated in the sense that they give the teacher a base from which to plan future work with the child in the light of his specific problems. Yet the significance of a child's difficulties still has to be viewed against the performance of other children; to put it crudely, if half a class of six-year-olds cannot copy, or even recognise, their own names their teacher will perhaps review her teaching methods, while if Johnny is the only child who has not yet reached this stage she may wonder whether he needs more specialised help.

Problems in identifying maladjusted children

A similar argument applies to children showing signs of emotional or behavioural disturbance. With these children the norm is less precisely specified than is the case in educational skills since behaviour cannot so easily be tested. We saw in the Introduction that behaviour regarded as normal in one subculture within the United Kingdom would be regarded as deviant and abnormal in another. Children vary in their behaviour at least as much as in their intelligence and educational attainments, with the added potential source of conflict that working-class children brought up to accept one standard of speech, dress and behaviour frequently find themselves in schools with predominantly middle-class values. It is therefore predictable, without making any sort of judgement about the 'rightness' or 'wrongness' of teachers' expectations regarding normal behaviour, that a small minority will attract labels such as 'difficult', 'disturbed', 'delinquent', 'deprived', or 'maladjusted'. Just as a minority of children fall far below the average range in the skills measured by intelligence tests, so others will fall far below the 'acceptable' norm on the social emotional continuum. This is not a statement about their ability or their behaviour in any absolute terms, but rather an assessment of their performance relative to that of other children of similar ages.

Yet this does not take us very far. Assessment as maladjusted could mean that a child's capacity for normal learning and stable behaviour was seriously impaired by neurological or other constitutional problems; or that he was temperamentally unable to cope with the normal lessons and problems of ordinary school life; or that his teachers and parents had broken off diplomatic relationships so that removal to a special school became the easiest way out of the impasse; or that he was reacting to intolerable stress at home, or even at school, in a manner which, though disturbing for his teachers, could only be described as normal.

Thus with maladjusted children the problem of selection is if anything even more complex than with the ESN(M). It centres not only on the nature of the medical (in this case psychiatric) contribution to the assessment process but also on the meaning of the term itself and the possibility of special *educational* treatment. In spite of being both misleading and inadequate, selection of children for ESN(M) schools on the basis of an IQ score below 75 or 70 did at least have the virtue of simplicity. No such spurious luxury has ever applied to maladjustment.

Different classifications of maladjusted children are dealt with in more detail in Chapter 2 in relation to prevalence studies. Here we need only consider the Underwood Committee's (Ministry of Education, 1955) classification of the symptoms into six headings:

1. Nervous disorders ('to describe a disorder which is primarily emotional').
2. Habit disorders (such as bed-wetting, tics and some psychosomatic symptoms).
3. Behaviour disorders (in which the child becomes unmanageable or shows overt aggression).
4. Organic disorders (in which the behaviour problem is associated with physical illness such as meningitis or epilepsy).
5. Psychotic disorders (which 'might be simply and comprehensively described as conduct which is so profoundly disturbed that disruption of the normal patterns of development takes place at all levels, intellectual, social and emotional').
6. Educational and emotional difficulties (in which the 'maladjustment' is related to educational failure).

Leaving aside the descriptive nature of classifications which describe maladjustment in terms of the child's symptoms (as opposed to the child's frequently predictable, reasonable and 'normal' interaction with his environment) we can see that *no* behavioural problem could fall outside the Underwood net, a point covered in more detail in the next chapter. The popular illusion that some problems are 'behavioural' and others 'emotional' conveniently overlooks the fact that 'emotional' problems are invariably expressed in a variety of behaviours, such as not talking, avoiding other children, appearing frightened and so on. More importantly, one is entitled to ask how doctors (normally psychiatrists) could expect teachers to provide *educational* treatment for *psychiatric* (or at least behavioural) problems. With the growing involvement of educational psychologists since DES Circular 2/75 the position should have improved to some extent, as they should be more experienced in determining a child's educational needs. Similarly, the policy of gathering together in one small school children with such a motley variety of severe symptoms needs some justification. As we shall see in Chapter 3, evidence that children benefit from attending schools for maladjusted children is notoriously hard to find, so the widespread belief among head teachers of special schools that children with a variety of symptoms can help each other requires more supporting evidence than is available so far. Much has been written about the therapeutic regimes of different schools (Shaw, 1965; Lennhoff, 1960; Wills, 1960) without any clear consensus emerging about the methods of treatment or the form of school organisation which will help a certain child or group of children.

In her survey of children in schools for the maladjusted in Inner London (ILEA, 1965) Roe found that the most frequent reasons given by psychiatrists for admission to a residential school were primarily connected with the child's home: he was becoming delinquent, his parents could not control him, he came from a broken home, or his parents' unfavourable attitudes could not be modified. In contrast, breakdown at school due to overtly difficult behaviour or to excessive timidity or withdrawal were much more frequent reasons for admission to day schools for maladjusted children than home problems. Yet although there is obvious logic in placing children with unsatisfactory home backgrounds in residential schools and children with severe problems at the ordinary school in day schools, we still need to know in more detail what symptoms each group has in common that entitles us to apply the generic label of 'maladjusted' in order to educate (or treat) them together in a small school separated from their peers.

(Parents) feel in no position to ask whether there is any reputable research evidence that their schools help children — and when they do ask they are not always given a direct answer. All too often they are palmed off with hopeful platitudes, when what they want is concrete information about what the school will do to help Johnny get over his anxieties, temper tantrums, stealing or whatever (Galloway, 1976).

As long as this sort of vagueness remains, doubt will persist as to whether schools for maladjusted children have increased in numbers primarily for the benefit of the children who attend them or for the benefit of the ordinary schools from which they were removed. If the latter, they can certainly still be justified, but we should have greater honesty about their *raison d'être*.

Administrative procedures in selection

We have been concerned so far with the process which results in the demand for special school places fairly consistently exceeding the supply, and with the psychological and educational objections to various selection procedures. The justification for transferring a child to a special school following his failure to reach an acceptable standard of work or behaviour is another matter, which is dealt with in Chapter 3. Meanwhile we must look at some of the practical and administrative problems which have arisen since the 1944 Act in response to unease about the issues we have been discussing.

The Act abolished certification of 'mentally defective' or 'feeble-minded' children but retained the possibility for local education authorities to compel a child to attend a special school. Education has to be appropriate to 'age, ability and aptitude', so if an authority could only provide this in a special school it was logical that it should be given the power to fulfil its responsibilities. Section 34 of the Act stated that the medical officer who had examined the child should, 'if required by the parent or by the authority to do so, issue to the authority and to the parent a certificate in the prescribed form showing whether the child is suffering from any such disability as aforesaid and, if so, the nature and extent thereof'. This seems to be perfectly clear; the authority was empowered, but not compelled to request a formal certificate of ascertainment. Yet to make the point absolutely explicit, Section 34 continues:

Provided that a local education authority shall not require the issue of such a certificate in respect of any child unless the certificate is, in their opinion, necessary for the purposes of securing the attendance of the child at a special school in accordance with the provision of this Act relating to compulsory attendance at primary and secondary schools.

From this wording it is clear that formal ascertainment should have been needed only when a child's parents wished to resist the local education authority's decision to provide special education. Unfortunately many authorities ignored both the letter and the spirit of the Act by formally ascertaining *all* children as suffering from one of the statutory categories of handicap before placing them in a special school. Prior to 1944 medical officers could make the educational decision that a child should attend a special school by the simple act of certifying him mentally defective. For over thirty years after 1944 they continued in many areas to do exactly the same, signing the necessary certificate (Form 1HP) after completing Forms 2HP, 3HP, or 4HP (see below). Hence formal ascertainment replaced certification and the elements of compulsion and stigma remained largely unaltered in spite of occasional efforts by the Ministry to alter the situation. The problem arose to some extent from genuine confusion over the forms issued by the Ministry for completion by medical officers. The first of these, Form 1HP, was the certificate prescribed for use when the authority wished to enforce attendance at a special school. However, 1HP went further than the 1944 Act intended by calling on the doctor to make an educational judgement by certifying the category or categories of handicap in which he believed the child should be placed. The remaining forms were not statutory; they were Form 2HP ('report on a child examined for a disability of mind'), Form 3HP ('report by head teacher on a backward child'), Form 4HP ('report on delicate or physically handicapped pupil'), and Form 5HP ('handicapped children of parents serving in the Armed Forces'). A further confusing factor was the statutory nature of the medical examination; since the examination was one which imposed a legal obligation on parents it seemed anomalous not to complete the process by issuing the prescribed certificate if the results indicated a need for special education. Other, and perhaps less creditable factors were the genuine but misplaced belief of some doctors that they were the most appropriate people to assess the need for special educational treatment, with a corresponding reluctance to share this responsibility with the developing profession of educational psychology; some doctors seemed to feel anxiety about losing one role without gaining another. It is true that Section 34 expected that reports would be obtained 'from teachers or other persons with respect to the ability and aptitude of the child', but the formal medical examination took place all too frequently in the clinical isolation of the doctor's office in the Education Department – hardly a setting in which a backward and possibly a nervous child was likely to feel at ease. Access to Form 3HP ('report by head teacher on a backward child') was not a satisfactory alternative to seeing the child in his classroom and talking to his teacher. Even if this sort of discussion had taken place as a matter of course, the situation would still have been unsatisfactory since it would have implied a doctor's competence to make educational decisions, an assumption as unwarranted as would be a teacher's or educational psychologist's assumption that he could diagnose and treat a physical illness. The categories of handicap in which the problems raised by this situation were most acute were those of educational subnormality and maladjustment since these related most directly to the child's performance and behaviour in the classroom.

The problem was recognised both by educationalists and by senior medical officers. The Chief Medical Officer of the Ministry of Education suggested in 1958, for example, that recommendations on the admission of children to an ESN(M) school should be the responsibility of a panel comprising a school medical officer, a representative of the chief education officer, an educational psychologist and the head of the present and/or proposed school. In 1961 the Ministry of Education went a stage further by issuing a Circular to all local education authorities on special educational treatment for educationally subnormal pupils. The Circular recognised that the formal procedures set out in Section 34 of the 1944 Act were not legally necessary providing the parents agreed to a special school place for their child: 'There need . . . be no formality about the offer of a place in a special school if the child needs it or about his admission if the parents accept such an offer, although it is essential to ensure that the parents know that the minimum leaving age from a special school is sixteen.' (The latter was a piece of 'positive discrimination' in the 1944 Act which caused intense resentment among those it was intended to help; a majority of children in schools for ESN(M) and maladjusted children have always come from Social Classes IV and V, for whom another year of compulsory schooling increased what they often regarded as the stigma of special education.) Unfortunately Circular 11/61 went on to recommend that the medical examination prior to admission, which it rightly regarded as essential, should be held in the formal manner prescribed by Section 34. The effect of this recommendation was to reduce the influence of other suggestions in the Circular regarding the importance of teachers' views and those of educational psychologists; in many areas parsimonious or conservative authorities refused to appoint educational psychologists who could offer specialist advice on the educational needs of handicapped and problem children and left responsibility for selection (with formal ascertainment a frequent result) largely in the hands of medical officers. As a result it gradually became clear that the procedures for selecting children for special education needed a more radical overhaul. This was carried out in another Circular, issued by the Department of Education and Science in 1975, which set out to clarify the uncertainty which had arisen 'about the circumstances in which medical examinations can be conducted without formal procedures and about the status of examinations by an educational psychologist'. The Circular advised that formal medical examinations as prescribed in Section 34 should no longer be held except in the extremely rare cases where a parent resisted the local authority's decision that his child should attend a special school. This did not mean that medical examinations should cease, but simply that they should take place at an early stage in an informal atmosphere in which the child's needs could be fully discussed with his parents. Further, the Circular recommended that the medical examination should precede assessment by an educational psychologist, and that the educational psychologist should be the person responsible 'for conveying to the authority a recommendation about the nature of the special education required and where it should be provided'. The old Forms 1HP to 5HP were withdrawn and replaced by a new series: Form SE 1 (for completion by the child's teacher), Form SE 2 (for completion by a school doctor), Form SE 3 (for completion by an educational psychologist), Form SE 4 (a summary and return sheet describing the needs of a child requiring special education), Form SE 5 (containing the essential elements of Form 1HP, for use only when the authority wishes to enforce attendance against a parent's will), and Form SE 6 (an up-to-date version of Form 5HP about handicapped children of parents serving in the Armed Forces).

Circular 2/75 from the DES forms the administrative basis for the selection of children for special education today. Although it does not have statutory force, it has been implemented, at least in part, by most local education authorities. In theory, the effect is to ensure that decisions regarding special education are made on educational rather than medical grounds. In practice this is not always the case, as medical or ancillary resources are often based on special schools, so that the child must attend the special school in order to benefit from these resources even if his educational needs could be better met in an ordinary school. The circular has not overcome any of the problems concerning the use of IQ or personality tests in the selection process, nor has it resolved the anomalies and inconsistencies in the concept of maladjustment. What it has done is to broaden the scope of assessment processes and place greater emphasis on the child's educational needs, so that medical diagnoses are considered strictly in the light of their implications for the child's future teaching. This of course, means that children should be placed in special schools because the special school can offer them something more than an ordinary school, and not simply because they have a medical condition or an IQ below 70. Many educational psychologists and remedial teachers can think of cases where children whose IQs fall well below 70 have benefited from their local primary or secondary school, while others with IQs approaching the average range have benefited from an ESN(M) school.

The Warnock Report

In November 1975 Margaret Thatcher, then Secretary of State for Education and Science, announced that she proposed to appoint a committee 'to review educational provision in England, Scotland and Wales for children and young people handicapped by disabilities of body or mind, taking account of the medical aspects of their needs, together with arrangements to prepare them for entering into employment; to consider the most effective use of resources for these purposes; and to make recommendations'. The committee was established the following year under the chairmanship of Mary Warnock and submitted its report four years after that (DES, 1978).

As the first government report in the history of British education to inquire comprehensively into the education of the handicapped, the Warnock report is likely to have enormous influence on future policy and provision. The somewhat indigestible number of recommendations – 225 are listed in the summary – reflects the range of the committee's inquiry. We shall be returning to the Warnock Report from time to time in later chapters; at this stage we only need to discuss some of the early recommendations relating to the scope and definition of special education for the ESN(M) and maladjusted.

In the light of evidence on the incidence of learning difficulties and behaviour problems, described in the next chapter, the committee concluded that one child in six might require some form of special educational provision at any one time, and one child in five at some stage in his school career. Further, it was clear that medical handicap and educational handicap could not be equated in the manner implied by the statutory categories of handicap. From an educational point of view a pupil who has permanently injured his writing hand may be far more handicapped than a paraplegic child. Not only were the statutory categories of handicap illogical; they provided a strait-jacket which did not fit many of the pupils shown to have special educational needs.

The committee, therefore, recommended abolition of the statutory categories of handicap in favour of a broader, more comprehensive definition to encompass 'the whole range and variety of additional help, wherever it is provided and whether on a full or part-time basis, by which children may be helped to overcome educational difficulties, however they are caused'.

It is clear from this definition that children receiving help in the remedial department or adjustment unit of an ordinary school fall within the special education network envisaged by Warnock. The committee proposed the term 'children with learning difficulties' to include the ESN and pupils in remedial departments. The new term could be elaborated to distinguish between mild, moderate and severe learning difficulties.

Although rejecting the term ESN, the committee decided to retain the equally objectionable label of maladjusted, on the grounds that 'the implication of this term (namely that behaviour can sometimes be meaningfully considered only in relation to the circumstances in which it occurs) is an advantage rather than a disadvantage'. While this is certainly true it overlooks the fact that in practice the term is seldom used in this discriminating way; instead it has become a label useful only for the purpose of removing children to special schools. (Perhaps the Committee's difficulty lay in finding an alternative word to describe the kind of problem at present called maladjustment. An easy, and honest, solution would have been 'disturbing' children. By definition, children who are called maladjusted or disturbed attract these labels because they have disturbed adults. The adult's disturbance may be at the level of frustration or anxiety at not 'getting through to' the child, or it may be sheer physical fear of his violence. The term disturbing implies a recognition of the children's effect on adults, while the terms maladjusted and disturbed are too often taken to imply some para-medical state in the child. As we said in the Introduction, we reluctantly retained the term maladjusted in the title because of its greater familiarity.)

On a more favourable note, the committee recognised that abolition of the categories of handicap could lead to concern about how far to safeguard the interests of children with severe problems. They recommend that a formal system be established for local education authorities to record children who are recommended by a multi-professional team, broadly as recommended in the SE procedure described above, to need some form of special educational provision.

While the committee was deliberating, Parliament passed the 1976 Education Act. Section 10 of this required special education to be provided in ordinary schools unless this would be impractible, incompatible with the efficiency of the school, or would involve unreasonable public expenditure. Warnock takes these qualifications as indicating Parliament's concern about the quality of special education as well as its location.

The report points out that the qualifications are open to many interpretations, and advocates a generally cautious policy. Special schools would continue to be needed for three groups. In summary, these are:

1. Children with severe or complex physical, sensory or intellectual disabilities.
2. Children with severe emotional or behavioural disorders.
3. Children with less severe disabilities who do not perform well in an ordinary school.

This list is clearly open to as many interpretations as Section 10 itself. It is sadly clear that the ESN(M) and the maladjusted may have little to gain from Section 10 and the Committee's recommendations on children who will continue to need separate special schools. The qualifications in Section 10 can easily be taken to justify continued separate provision if that is the Local Authority's policy. On the other hand, Section 10 could prove a powerful instrument in the hands of people who want to cut public expenditure by closing expensive special schools without providing special help in ordinary schools. The 'medical' handicaps are likely to gain from Section 10, because they are supported by local pressure groups which will not only demand integration, but also the resources for it to succeed. For the non-medical handicaps the main pressure for integration may come from politicians seeking to cut public expenditure.

In spite of these criticisms, one hopes that Section 10 and the Warnock Report will accelerate the existing trend in public opinion and within the education system towards providing in ordinary schools the best aspects of special schools. We shall be discussing the facilities and resources needed for a successful policy of integration later in the book.

Chapter 2

The incidence of maladjustment and severe learning difficulties

A. What do the figures mean?

Problems in determining the numbers of ESN(M) and maladjusted children

The last chapter showed the enormous increase in provision for ESN(M) and maladjusted children since 1945. This increase in provision has been matched by a corresponding increase in concern for – or about – these children. It is important to be clear about this distinction. A secondary school head teacher may request a place in an ESN(M) school because his experienced staff have failed to produce any academic progress from a child who looks more and more miserable as the weeks go by and his failure becomes more and more transparent; the head may believe – and he will quite likely be right – that the child can only be helped over his social isolation and educational difficulties in a smaller, more protective school with more skilled teachers. Alternatively, the head may refer the child because he only feels able to allocate one part-time teacher to help the not insignificant minority of the 900 children on his roll who have learning difficulties; there does seem to be some inconsistency between demands on one hand that the top 5 per cent on the intellectual and behavioural continuum should no longer be creamed off into grammar schools, and requests on the other hand that the bottom 2 or 3 per cent should be separated into special schools. Increasingly, comprehensive schools are allocating the same proportion of resources to their dull and disturbing pupils as to their potential university candidates; nevertheless most educational psychologists have had to recommend children for special schools because their original school's remedial department and pastoral care organisation were run on a shoestring.

This all has to be seen in the context of increasing public (and hence political) concern both about educational standards and about the real or imagined increase in violence in schools and in society. The increase in violence is now an accepted piece of educational folklore, though no one wishes to specify the golden age when children were well behaved and quick to learn. Presumably it was before or after the Victorian era when Dickens described the educational standards at Dotheboys Hall, and the behaviour problems of (maladjusted?) pupils at our most famous public schools led to riots which could only be quelled by the army.

Almost invariably the 'discovery' of maladjusted children follows the opening of a school to cater for them. We are not, of course, arguing that opening a special school for maladjusted children creates 'unmanageable' behaviour problems which were previously contained satisfactorily in ordinary schools; there is, however, a very real sense in which the opening of a special school creates *maladjusted* children, namely that maladjustment is neither a clinical diagnosis nor even a descriptive term but an administrative category. As Graham and Rutter (1970) point out, the chief purpose of the term 'has been to provide a label under which special education may be provided according to the *Handicapped Pupils and School Health Service Regulations* (Ministry of Education, 1945 and 1959)'. The 1945 regulations define maladjusted pupils as those 'who show evidence of emotional instability or psychological disturbance and who require special educational treatment in order to effect their personal, social and educational readjustment'. The problem is not simply that the terms 'emotional instability' and 'psychological disturbance' stand as much in need of clarification as 'maladjusted'; the definition implies, illogically, that special *educational* treatment is needed for some (but not all) children with the quasi-*medical* symptoms of emotional instability and psychological disturbance. Further, all teachers in special schools for maladjusted know many children whose disturbing behaviour can reasonably be viewed as a normal, or even healthy, reaction to highly abnormal and stressful conditions in their families or even in their previous schools. Not surprisingly, maladjustment is not recognised as a clinical condition in the most widely used systems for categorising children's psychiatric disorders.

Thus Rutter (1965) classified psychiatric disorders as either neurotic disorders; antisocial or conduct disorders; a mixed group in which both neurotic and conduct disorders are present; developmental disorders (such as enuresis or speech problems); the 'hyperkinetic syndrome'; child psychosis; psychoses originating at or after puberty; mental subnormality; and educational retardation as a primary problem. Subsequently Rutter *et al.* (1969) proposed a three-part classification in which the first part related to the clinical psychiatric syndrome, such as 'specific developmental disorder', 'neurotic disorder' or 'conduct disorder'; the second related to the child's intellectual level (regardless of aetiology) and the third noted any associated or aetiological factors, such as contributory medical factors, and environmental factors such as parental friction or lack of warmth towards the child. The Underwood Report (Ministry of Education, 1955) could hardly avoid the issue by not using the term maladjustment (it was, after all, the Report of the Committee on Maladjusted Children); as we saw in Chapter 1 it anticipated Rutter's classification by grouping the 'symptoms' of maladjustment under six headings: nervous disorders; habit disorders; behaviour disorders; organic disorders; psychotic behaviour; educational and vocational difficulties. Stott (1971), too (from a psychologist's perspective), has sought to identify and describe types of maladjustment by means of teachers' or parents' completion of the Bristol Social Adjustment Guides. In the latest revision of the Bristol Guides behaviours are classified into two main groups: under-reactive behaviour, which includes problems such as depression, lack of energy, indifference to other people's opinions; and over-reactive behaviour, which includes hostility, 'showing off', distractibility.

The common point to emerge from medical and psychological attempts to classify behaviour disorders or describe types of 'maladjustment' is, as suggested in Chapter 1, that maladjustment is at best a ragbag term for describing *any* type of problem which does not slot neatly into one of the other nine DES categories. It would be logical, but not illuminating to accept as valid the definition of maladjustment as an administrative category. If we do so we find enormous variations in prevalence from region to region (DES, 1966). Thus in the northern regions a mere 186 children (3.4 per 10,000) were already being educated, or were awaiting placement, in special schools, special classes, hostels, or hospital schools. The comparable figure for the Metropolitan area was 2,010 (representing 28.3 per 10,000). With a range from 3.4 per 10,000 to 28.3 per 10,000, and an average for England and Wales of 11.0 per 10,000 there is obviously (*pace* northerners) good reason for believing that regional differences reflect differences in provision more than genuine differences in the incidence of maladjustment. It is clear from the Warnock Report (DES, 1978) that this situation has not changed. In January 1977 one London Borough ascertained as maladjusted ten times more children than another. An equally important point is that teachers and parents may be more likely to seek professional advice for aggressive, openly defiant behaviour than for inhibited, withdrawn behaviour; similarly some head teachers might be more likely to seek professional advice about a bright child who is failing in reading than about a generally backward child whose reading does *not* seem retarded relative to his overall level of development. For these reasons, referral rates cannot be taken as a valid index of the prevalence of different problems in the community as a whole.

Like maladjustment, educational subnormality is an administrative category as much as a descriptive term. As we saw in the last chapter, the 1944 Act empowered the Minister of Education to make regulations defining the *categories* of pupils for whom special educational treatment was needed. Regulation 14 of the School Health Service and Handicapped Pupils Regulations (1953) defined ESN pupils (the group we would call ESN(M) since the 1970 Education (Handicapped Children) Act) as those who 'by reason of limited ability or other conditions resulting in educational retardation, require some specialised form of education wholly or partly in substitution for the education normally given in ordinary schools'. Thus the term was explicitly intended to include children whose educational attainments were retarded for reasons *other* than lack of cognitive ability. With great optimism the Ministry had earlier suggested that special educational treatment would be appropriate for any child whose educational attainments lagged 20 per cent or more behind the average for his age.

One wonders whether the Minister and his advisers recognised the number of children for whom they were recommending a statutory form of special education. It would have taken (and in spite of the increase in provision would still take) a tiny proportion of the children covered by this definition to fill every recognised school or class for ESN(M) pupils. Hence, School Medical Officers (and later educational psychologists) resorted to the same principle of supply and demand which proved so convenient for maladjusted children. In other words, children were 'discovered' only when a supply of places became available (although 'discovery' could always be used as a political weapon to induce a reluctant authority to increase its provision). As with the maladjusted, this is seen most clearly in the regional variations in pupils in ESN schools (DES, 1966 and 1978). In Wales, 2,262 children (49.9 per 10,000) were being educated, or were awaiting places in special schools or classes, while the comparable figure for the South-East of England was 4,435 (92.1 per 10,000). The range was smaller than for maladjusted children. Only the North-West region joined the South-East in having more than 90 children per 10,000 in or awaiting places in ESN schools; in contrast the Eastern region of England had ascertained 5,056 pupils, representing a mere 59.9 per 10,000 children of school age. While not quoting regional rates for ESN(M) pupils specifically, the Warnock Report notes that ascertainment for special education – in which the ESN(M) is, of course, by far the largest single category – ranged from below 120 per 10,000 of the school population in a few rural areas to above 300 in a few large cities. The range is further shown from the fact that only 44 out of 105 authorities in England and Wales fell within a range 10 per cent above or below the average of 183. Somewhat dryly, the report comments: 'Some of the variations between authorities may reflect variations in local policy and the strength of assessment services, but they also suggest a relationship between the rate of ascertainment and the availability of special provision.'

Thus it is clear that the numbers of children labelled maladjusted or ESN(M) will give us no accurate picture of the total numbers of children with severe behavioural or educational difficulties. Further, we saw in the last chapter that intelligence, as measured by an IQ test, is not a valid way to estimate the numbers of children requiring ESN(M) type special education. It is here that the results of large scale surveys which include *all* children in a given population are so useful. The most detailed (and recent) studies to have been carried out in this country are the National Child Development Study (Kellmer Pringle *et al.*, 1966; Davie *et al.*, 1972; Fogelman, 1976) and the surveys carried out by Rutter and his colleagues on the Isle of Wight (Rutter, Tizard and Whitmore, 1970) and in an Inner London Borough (Rutter *et al.*, 1975a; Berger *et al.*, 1975; Rutter *et al.*, 1975b).

The National Child Development Study

The National Child Development Study investigated all children born between 3 and 9 March 1958. Each child's teacher was asked to complete an early verson of Stott's Bristol Social Adjustment Guide; in this the teacher is given a large number of statements about children's behaviour and asked to underline the ones which describe the child in question most accurately. When the Guide is scored the items which indicate some degree of deviance are given codes; coded items are then summed to obtain an overall total. Stott described children with scores from 0 to 9 as 'stable', those with scores from 10–19 as 'unstable', and those with scores above 19 as 'maladjusted'. On this basis teachers assessed 64 per cent of the children as stable; 22 per cent as unsettled and 14 per cent as maladjusted. Davie *et al.* (1972), emphasised that 'the terminology is not necessarily applicable in, say, a clinical context', since the assessment was carried out solely by the class teacher. In addition it is now known from other studies (Rutter *et al.*, 1970) that a majority of children with emotional or behavioural problems display them either at home or at school, but not both. Had it been possible to ask parents for similar information about their children's behaviour the results might have been quite different. In the same study teachers thought that 13 per cent of the children would benefit from special educational help, mainly on account of their educational attainments, but only 5 per cent were actually receiving it. However, the form of special educational help under consideration was in the ordinary school. When they were asked which children 'would benefit *now* from attendance at a special school', only 2 per cent fell into this category. Preliminary findings from the third follow-up of the National Child Development Study (Fogelman, 1976) showed that 17 per cent of sixteen-year-olds were thought by their teachers to have 'little, if any, ability' in mathematics. The corresponding figure for English was 11 per cent. Seven per cent were said to be receiving special help within the school on account of 'educational or mental backwardness'; this help was considered inadequate for 2 per cent, and teachers indicated that help was needed, but not being provided, for a further 2 per cent.

The National Child Development Study was a national survey, covering *all* children in the country born between 3 to 9 March 1958. This made broad regional comparison possible (for example, reading standards were rather higher in Scotland than in England while the reverse was the case with arithmetical ability: Davie *et al.*, 1972), but prevented a detailed study either of behavioural disorders or learning difficulties. With a sample of over 11,000 children, the project clearly had to rely heavily on screening techniques and questionnaires completed by (or under the supervision of) professional personnel on the spot. Problems over the definition of maladjustment have already been noted, and equally valid objections can be raised against the subjective manner in which both educational attainments and a need for special educational help were assessed. For the most detailed and scientifically most rigorous picture of the educational and behavioural problems of English children we must turn to the surveys conducted by Rutter on the Isle of Wight and an Inner London Borough.

Surveys in Inner London and the Isle of Wight

The Isle of Wight Survey included all ten-year-olds with homes on the island who attended local authority schools, or special schools whose fees were paid by the local authority. The Inner London Borough study included all children attending schools within the Borough. For the purpose of comparison with the Isle of Wight survey, all immigrant children and all children with immigrant parents were excluded from the Inner London Borough. This was to ensure that differences could not be attributed to the high number of immigrants in London; the immigrant children (mainly West Indian) were in fact covered by the survey, but the results were described separately (see below). Almost identical methods were used in each of the surveys. All children were screened in the summer term of their penultimate year at junior school by means of group tests of non-verbal intelligence and reading. In addition the teachers completed the Rutter Scale for Teachers (Rutter, 1967), a questionnaire in the form of twenty-six statements about behaviour in which the teacher is asked to state whether each behaviour occurs, sometimes occurs, or is absent. Children were selected for individual study on the basis of high scores on the Rutter Scale and low scores on the group reading test. They were compared with randomly selected control groups to allow comparisons within each area as well as between the two areas. The mothers of children selected for individual study on the basis of the Rutter Scale (or because they were in the random control group) were interviewed for two to three hours by a social scientist or psychiatrist. The reliability of this interview has been investigated in the Isle of Wight study (Graham and Rutter, 1968). This contained a series of set questionnaires about emotional or behavioural problems in the preceding year; family relationships and interactions were assessed in the same interview. A much shorter interview was carried out with the father, and both parents were asked to complete a health questionnaire which focused on symptoms associated with psychiatric illness or stress. In London, but not in the Isle of Wight, the Rutter Scale results were checked by means of an interview with the child's current teacher (not usually the one who completed the questionnaire), in which questions concentrated specifically on emotional disturbance, conduct disorder, and disturbances in relationships with peers and staff. Children selected for individual study on the basis of the group reading test scores were tested on the short form of the Wechsler Intelligence Scale for Children (Wechsler, 1949) and the Neale Analysis of Reading Ability (Neale, 1958) which measures children's comprehension and accuracy.

Psychiatric disorder

Psychiatric disorder was diagnosed from the information provided by teachers and parents as described above. There is a semantic problem here, and it is essential to be clear about the limitations of the term. Rutter and Graham (1968) are explicit on this point:

Psychiatric disorder ... refers to abnormalities of emotions, behaviour or relationships which are developmentally inappropriate and of sufficient duration and severity to cause persistent suffering or handicap to the child and/or distress or disturbance to the family or community. Our use of the term does not involve any concept of disease or illness, nor does it necessarily assume that psychiatrists are the right people to treat such disorders.

This definition clearly distinguishes psychiatric disorder from other medical conditions, yet discussion of diagnosis generally implies a medical condition. Some people might prefer another term, such as maladjustment, but this would suffer from similar objections with the additional one that it is primarily an administrative category.

That a child is said to have psychiatric disorder in this context implies that he has, or simply is, a problem; it does not imply that the problem lies primarily with the child, nor does it imply that his emotion or behaviour are necessarily in any way unreasonable, unpredictable or abnormal in the light of his current and past experiences. The results should be seen in the light of these comments.

Almost twice as many children were said to be 'deviant' on the basis of the Rutter Scale in London as on the Isle of Wight (19 per cent and 11 per cent respectively). The total number of children with psychiatric disorder in each area was estimated from the numbers diagnosed in the control group and in the group selected by screening; again the London rate was twice that of the Isle of Wight (25 per cent against 12 per cent). The higher London rate applied to both sexes, but was much more marked in girls (26 per cent against 8 per cent). This was largely due to the high number of London girls who were not selected by the teacher's questionnaire, mainly because their problems were confined to home. Turning to the study of West Indian immigrants and British born children of West Indian parents, (Rutter *et al.*, 1974; Yule *et al.*, 1975; Rutter *et al.*, 1975c) there are some interesting differences. The Rutter Scale distinguishes between 'conduct' disorder, 'emotional' or 'neurotic' disorder, and 'mixed' disorder. In both the mixed and emotional types of disorder no differences were found between the West Indian and non-immigrant groups. In contrast, conduct disorder as assessed by the teachers' questionnaire was a great deal more common among the West Indian groups. Interviews with the teachers subsequently confirmed these findings. Further, the pattern of deviance (as measured by a score of 9 + on the Rutter Scale) differed between West Indian and non-immigrant girls. In the latter 'emotional' problems were more common than 'conduct' or behaviour problems; in contrast, 'conduct' problems were many times more common in West Indian girls, as in West Indian boys. In this part of the research the total prevalence of psychiatric disorder was estimated first on the basis of interviews with the children's teachers and from interviews with their parents. From the teacher interview West Indians were found to have a slightly higher rate of disorder (38 per cent against 28 per cent) but the opposite applied from the parent interview (18 per cent against 25 per cent). Slightly more West Indians had problems which were confined to the home. Birthplace (Britain or the West Indies) did not appear relevant with the immigrant group; this was in contrast to the results of the research on intelligence and reading standards.

Specific reading retardation and reading backwardness

It is known that reading standards vary in different parts of the country. Scotland, for instance, has rather higher standards than England (Davie *et al.*, 1972) and an Inner London Education Authority report (1970) showed the average reading ability of London Primary school children to be below the national average. In Kent, Morris (1959 and 1966) demonstrated that ability varied according to the characteristics of the schools the children attended. Unfortunately none of these studies took intelligence into account. On common-sense grounds one might suppose that children whose reading is retarded relative to their general level of cognitive development (as measured by an individual IQ test) might have different characteristics and different remedial needs from children who are backward but not retarded relative to measured intelligence. The statistical technique of regression analysis was used in the surveys to identify severely retarded children whose scores on either the accuracy or comprehension scale of the Neale Test fell some thirty months or more below the score predicted from their age and IQ (Yule *et al.*, 1974).

On this basis (which excluded other data available from the original Isle of Wight survey), just under 3 per cent of Isle of Wight children were considered to suffer from specific reading retardation. In London the equivalent figure was just under 10 per cent. Backward readers (twenty-eight months or more backward on either accuracy or comprehension), accounted for 8 per cent of the Isle of Wight children (11 per cent of the boys and 6 per cent of the girls) but 19 per cent of the London children (22 per cent of the boys and 16 per cent of the girls). There was of course, very considerable overlap between the specific reading retardation and the general reading backwardness groups. (In the original Isle of Wight research, all but ten of the eighty-six children in the former were also in the latter.) Nevertheless, it is safe to assume that one ten-year-old in five, excluding immigrants, in the London Borough were reading below the seven-year-old level.

The results for immigrant children (Yule *et al.*, 1975) were not presented in the same way, since the main emphasis was on a comparison between children of West Indian parentage and non-immigrants. On the Neale Test the immigrant group as a whole scored about two years below age-level, or just over one year below the non-immigrant controls, who were themselves well below the national average. Similarly, the mean verbal and performance IQs for the West Indian immigrant group were 87 and 90 compared with 101 and 104 respectively for the non-immigrant controls. Taken in isolation these figures are misleading as the authors are at pains to point out. For example, the children who were born in the West Indies were considerably less successful on both intelligence and educational attainment tests than children born in the United Kingdom to West Indian parents. (This is, of course, scarcely surprising as the tests were standardised on a non-immigrant population.) However, there are many possible reasons for the children born in the United Kingdom having attainments below the indigenous population. There was a tendency for the West Indian children to attend less favourable schools (see below); they were more likely to live in overcrowded homes with poor facilities; their fathers were more likely to be semi-skilled or unskilled manual workers; they were more likely to have had child-minding by non-relatives in their early years; and other studies (Pollack, 1972) showed a tendency for them to have had fewer toys and less interaction with their parents. All these points question the suitability of IQ tests for predicting the educational attainments of West Indian children. Yule cites evidence (Watson, 1973) that West Indian children with WISC verbal scores below 80 increased their scores by an average of 8 points over a twenty-month period, compared with an average rise of 0.25 of a point in non-immigrant controls matched for age, sex and IQ. The authors warn that 'the lower mean IQ of West Indian children may result in their being more often classified ESN on the basis of their IQ scores alone, than would be warranted according to their reading attainment'; they acknowledge doubts (Coard, 1971) as to whether ESN schools provide the best help for immigrant children and suggest that educational decisions 'should be based primarily on levels of achieved competence in educational skills, taking into account the country of origin of the child'.

Conclusions from the major surveys

We have described the results of the most detailed and most recent surveys at some length as they were based on *all* children in a selected group or area, and not on the small minority who were referred to clinics or special schools. The results show beyond doubt that special schools can only cater for a very small minority of children who are seriously backward or retarded, or who show 'clinically significant' psychiatric disorder. It is easy to conclude that the surveys demonstrate a need for a massive increase in special educational provision, either within the ordinary school system or outside it. Indeed, as we said in Chapter 1 the Warnock Report recommended, on the basis of these surveys, that services should be planned on the assumption that one child in five may require some form of special educational provision in the course of his school career, and one in six at any one time.

The argument would go something like this: eminent psychologists and educationalists have claimed that academic attainments are falling, with an associated drop in standards of behaviour; we never had (or needed) special schools in the past, but the surveys now reveal an enormous number of children with learning and behaviour problems; therefore we need more special schools in order to allow teachers to get on with the job of teaching by removing problem children; (a more 'liberal' conclusion is to demand more special schools in order to help the unhappy and unsuccessful children in ordinary schools). This argument is as appealing as it is illogical; for it to have any validity at least two conditions need to be satisfied: (*a*) that standards in education and behaviour have in fact dropped; (*b*) that more children would benefit from attending special schools (as opposed to receiving special education in their ordinary schools). The second issue is discussed more fully in Chapter 3, but the first can to some extent be answered by comparing results from Rutter's surveys and the National Child Development Study with earlier, less detailed work.

We have already seen (Chapter 1) the limitations of IQ as a way of determining whether a child is ESN(M). If IQ were an appropriate measure we would not need to look at any survey results since we could estimate the prevalence of educational subnormality in purely statistical terms by calculating the predicted number of children who score below some arbitrary figure on some (often) equally arbitrarily selected intelligence test. (Of course, the cut off point – for instance, IQ 70, 75 or 80 – could be raised depending on the number of places available.) As we have seen, Rutter and his colleagues were the first people to relate reading standards to IQ in a systematic way (the implications of this for evaluating the results of special education provision are discussed in Chapter 3). Consequently we have to look to earlier surveys for some estimate of the prevalence of learning difficulties and behaviour problems early in this century. The Board of Education and Board of Control (1929) report on the incidence of mental deficiency concluded that 2.66 children per 1,000 were suitable for education in day or residential schools for the feeble-minded, but accepted that a very much higher proportion (up to 15 per cent) were educationally retarded. In the field of behaviour disorders, an early investigation by McFie (1934) suggested that as many as 46 per cent of children in the London elementary schools under investigation showed one or more of four problem categories, namely: 'behaviour deviations' such as timidity or lack of sociability; behaviour disorder such as truancy or stealing; habit disorders, such as nail biting or incontinence; and scholastic difficulties other than those due to mental defect. Four years later Milner (1938), reporting on a survey carried out for five schools in the Girls Public Day School Trust, found that 17 per cent were put forward for interview on account of their difficult behaviour.

What sort of child is being described in all these surveys? We have seen that the number regarded as having a conduct disorder, behaviour disorder, psychiatric disorder or simple maladjustment is remarkably stable from survey to survey. Similarly, there is no sound evidence that the number of children with severe learning difficulties has changed much since the early 1900s. Are we talking about the exceptional children who need treatment, ordinary children who live in exceptional circumstances, or about a group whose only sin is their failure (or refusal) to fit into the system as it is? One way of answering this question is to ask whether different rates of child psychiatric disorder and education problems in different areas can be attributed to regional differences in family and school conditions. In other words is the higher rate of problems in London due to a higher rate of problems in the London children themselves, or just to the fact that more London children live in circumstances which militate against high educational standards?

In fact, Rutter and Quinton (1977) have argued that different rates of psychiatric disorder are entirely due to regional differences in family and school conditions. Both in London and in the Isle of Wight the quality of the parents' marriage as assessed from the parent interviews was significantly worse in families where the child showed psychiatric disorder. The interviewer did not, of course, know whether he was visiting the parents of a child selected as part of the control group or selected as deviant from the screening. Similarly, children who had been in care were significantly more likely to have problems. The same applied to children whose fathers had a criminal record; like admission to care, this was much more common in London. Less predictably, perhaps, children from broken homes were considerably more likely to be diagnosed as showing psychiatric disorder in London. A closer look at the evidence showed that nearly half the Isle of Wight parents had married again, happily in most cases, while in London only a sixth of the parents had done so, and disharmony was more common. In other words, the term 'broken home' implied a more stressful set of experiences for London children than for those on the Isle of Wight. Another difference lay in the significance of the mother suffering from psychiatric disorder; on the Isle of Wight, but not in London, this was strongly associated with psychiatric disorder in the child. The reason seemed to be in the higher rate of psychiatric problems, mainly depression, in the mothers of 'normal' London children.

Turning to the influence of school on adjustment and attainment, schools with a high turnover of staff or pupils had high rates of behavioural deviance. The same applied to schools with high absentee rates or a high proportion of children receiving free school meals, though these were not necessarily the children who presented problems. London schools were more likely to have some or all of these characteristics, though it was found that the school itself exerted a considerable influence when the research looked at its effect on individual children. This point is discussed in more detail in Chapter 8, but what we need to consider here is how the influences and stresses on pupils and teachers alike create educational and behavioural problems. London children were shown in Rutter's surveys to experience more adverse conditions both at home and at school than their contemporaries on the Isle of Wight; predictably, these adverse circumstances were reflected in their educational attainments and psychiatric adjustment. In fact there is a philosophical problem of circularity here since a variable, such as high turnover of staff or pupils, can only be termed adverse if it is associated statistically with poor adjustment or attainments. This would lead us into the heated, but only occasionally illuminating, controversy between an empirical and a phenomenological approach to educational research (Hargreaves *et al.*, 1975); at the moment, though, we only need to note the *prima facie* (and unremarkable) evidence that greater problems in the families and schools of London children are reflected in their poorer attainments and adjustment. Thus, we can infer that the children with psychiatric disorder might in many, even most, cases not be abnormal children in any meaningful sense of the word, but essentially children who were responding to stressful circumstances. In other words they might form a group whose only common characteristic could be their failure or refusal to fit into the system as it is. At first sight the position is more complex in the case of children with specific reading retardation or reading backwardness since they were all identified on the same reading and intelligence tests; yet, in the case of children with specific reading retardation at least, the evidence suggests that the educational problems in London were associated with less satisfactory conditions at school and with one index of stress at home – psychiatric disturbance in the mother (Rutter *et al.*, 1975b). Thus problems originating within the child, such as low potential ability or some specific developmental problems like sensory defects or slowness in acquiring certain perceptual skills, may not always be the primary reason for the educational problem; rather, these will frequently be the result of unsatisfactory conditions at or outside school. On the other hand, the children with specific reading retardation did differ from the reading backwardness group, both in London and the Isle of Wight in terms of sex ratio (more boys than girls in the retarded group); neurological corrolates (more frequent signs of impairment in the backward group); developmental characteristics (again problems were more frequent in the backward group); and educational prognosis (better for the backward group) (Yule *et al.*, 1973).

B. The relationships and problem situations behind the statistics

Problem children or problem situations?

A recurring theme throughout this book is the essentially subjective process whereby children are identified as ESN(M) or maladjusted and referred to a special school. In the Introduction we saw how these two categories stand alone among the other categories of handicap recognised by the DES under the 1944 Education Act in describing psychological rather than medical limitations. In this chapter we have seen that special schools can never hope to cater for more than a tiny majority of pupils with severe behavioural or learning difficulties, and in Chapter 1 we reviewed the *administrative* processes whereby children are selected for special education. In the rest of this chapter we shall look at some of the *psychological* processes in the school, in the home, in the child himself which result in the labels (or 'discovery') of maladjustment and educational subnormality.

When making an assessment of a child's needs the teacher or psychologist has to understand not only the problems which originate within the child himself, but also how he interacts with the people with whom he lives, plays and works; he will affect them and be affected by them, for better or worse. This interaction can be expressed schematically and forms the basis for a comprehensive assessment of a child's needs (Fig. 2.1). For example, the school can affect the attitudes of the family or the community but can also be affected by them; there is a two-way process. How this process operates can be seen from a case study.

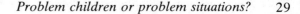

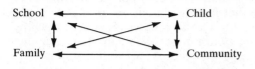

Fig. 2.1 A schematic background to assessment

Case study

Paul was a nervous, tense ten-year-old living in a middle-class area with ambitious but chronically ill parents. His teacher and his parents were equally dissatisfied with his progress in reading and in maths; his teacher was the school's elderly deputy head and was putting great pressure on the head to have Paul transferred to an ESN(M) school. After five years in school Paul was still mirror-writing, and his faltering attempts to decipher the improbable exclamations and adventures of the ladybird mother and her brood were full of reversals. In creative activities and practical subjects he was only slightly more confident than in reading and maths. An IQ test suggested that his reasoning ability was a long way below average, and a battery of diagnostic reading tests confirmed that he had severe difficulty with any visual sequencing work; at best his eye movements were jerky and erratic, but more often they seemed completely random. Temperamentally he seemed a tense, retiring, but sensitive boy, very easily upset by criticism from teachers, parents or other children; he was frequently in tears. It would be tempting to conclude that Paul's problems resulted from the fact that he was: (*a*) a dull boy with (*b*) a specific learning difficulty, aggravated by (*c*) a nervous, over-sensitive disposition. Although this conclusion would be a little more sophisticated than an assessment based solely on IQ, it ignores how Paul affected, and was affected by, the other people in his environment.

Turning to the family, Paul was the only child of parents who had both suffered chronic ill-health for most of his life. His father resented his enforced inactivity and concentrated much of his emotional energy on his ambition that Paul should have a more successful life than he had. Paul's increasingly obvious educational failure filled him with worry, and this the ten-year-old sensed unerringly whenever his father insisted on helping him with his reading. These sessions were painful for father and son alike, generally ending with Paul in tears and his father shouting that he wasn't trying. Paul's mother was an obese, stolid lady who waddled busily around the house seemingly oblivous to the tension between father and son. From this we can start to see how Paul and his parents affected each other; Paul's own difficulties created anxiety for his father and this anxiety was communicated to Paul to such an extent that he became unable to benefit from any of the help and attention his father wished to give him. Worse, the tension was focused on Paul's progress at school, so that the stress at home reduced still further his capacity for progress at school.

Paul lived in a middle-class area and was the only child in his avenue with problems at school; further, his father was the only father who was out of work. Paul knew this, so did his parents, so did his friends and their parents. He was not teased about his parents' health, the family's poverty or his own backwardness – at least not often – but the collective ethos of the local community was recognised by his parents and created, in his father in particular, a determination to prove that Paul was as clever as anyone else's son. Unfortunately, Paul was *not* as clever as anyone else's son, and as his educational failure became more transparent the gap between his achievements and the community norms widened. As a result his father felt under increasing pressure which was fully reflected in his attitude and behaviour towards his son. The community's expectations were also reflected in the attitudes and in the curriculum of Paul's school. Four or five years earlier, under a different head teacher, it had been common for parents to opt out of the state education system by sending their children to one of the three private preparatory schools in the area; they disliked the scruffy appearance of kids at the local school. The new head had countered by introducing uniform for everyone from the reception class upwards; he could not make this compulsory, but was able to exert a lot of pressure on parents and children who did not conform. Paul was an untidy child whose uniform was always getting dirty (at best), or torn, or lost. His parents could not afford constant replacements, so he started at a disadvantage at school by looking exceptional, much to his own embarrassment and that of his parents. Perhaps more importantly, the aspirations and anxieties of the influential parents were reflected in a formal curriculum and competitive classroom atmosphere. Most children thrived on this, and parents were happy to see the impressive displays of work on open evenings. Not surprisingly, Paul was one of the minority who did not fit into a system which contained insufficient flexibility to meet the needs of children with out-of-the-ordinary problems. The remedial classes, such as they were (three lessons a week, provided the part-time teacher who took them was not needed to fill in for a full-time colleague who was ill or on a course), sought to help children catch up with their ordinary classroom work. Remedial reading for Paul consisted of a dreary recapitulation of the last few pages in his current Ladybird book, part of a scheme with which he had already been failing to learn to read for the first five years of what his father with devastating pessimism assured him were 'the best years of your life'.

The formality, or rather the rigidity, of Paul's class at school suited the majority of children and their parents. It also suited the class teacher, a strong, kindly, elderly and (usually) benevolent despot of a lady who had been at the school for twenty years, the last ten of them as deputy head. Most children felt secure with her; she liked them and was liked by them. Alone among the school's teachers she never smacked a child and never had the slightest disciplinary problem. She worked in a Church school from genuine religious conviction, but did not like nonconformity in religion, appearance or behaviour. Part of her dislike of nonconformity was seen in her dislike of extremes; an outstandingly bright child was unlikely to excel in her class, and a child at the other end of the spectrum would either respond quickly to her methods and expectations or sink, just as quickly, to her stereotype of the ESN(M) pupil. Once her decision was made nothing could shake her from it, and the labelled pupil would drift until he either received the help he needed at a special school or moved into another class at the start of the next school year.

It should be clear from this brief description of Paul, his family, his school and his neighbourhood that his educational difficulties were the product of a complex set of interactions. Studying the individual child's behaviour is not so much pointless as impossible if it concentrates on the individual without due regard to the interrelationships within the family and to the social psychology of the school and the community. Whether a talented child develops his skills or a 'slow' child overcomes his learning difficulties depends at least as much on the encouragement he receives at school as on his own innate gifts or limitations. Paul was a dull child, but no duller than at least half a dozen other children in his school whose teachers never thought of requesting their transfer to an ESN school. He had a specific learning difficulty, but so did a similar number of other children in his school. More by good luck, helped by patience and sympathy from their parents and teachers, the rest overcame their difficulties; the process would have been faster and less painful for everyone concerned if their remedial classes had made a conscious effort to assess and then remediate the specific nature of their problems, but the end result was satisfactory. Paul did not fail because he was duller than the others or because his perceptual difficulty was intrinsically more intransigent. He did not even fail, as some labelling theorists might have us believe, because he found himself by an accident of fate in the deputy head's class rather than one of the two parallel classes, though this was probably a contributory factor. His failure to make educational progress resulted partly from his own relative dullness; partly from his perceptual difficulties; partly from the fact that he was temperamentally more vulnerable to pressure from his father than a less sensitive, more aggressive child; partly from the indirect pressure on his parents and his school from the local community's expectations; partly from his own sense of being different at school due both to pressure over uniform and to his slow progress; partly to the lack of adequate remedial classes at his school; and partly to his teacher's dislike of children who deviated from her own somewhat narrow conception of normality. Needless to say, none of these 'causes' can be viewed in isolation from all the others.

The argument is not that Paul should or should not have been considered for a special school (although in fact he did go to one where he made excellent educational progress and, as a result of the school working intensively on his parents, became a happier child at home). The argument is rather about the arbitrary process which results in a child being labelled a problem by his teachers or parents. If Paul had been brought up by different parents, or if he had attended a different school (or possibly even different classes in the same school) his end of term reports would in all probability have summarised him as 'a likeable boy; rather below average in most subjects, but tries hard'. (It is quite likely, incidentally, that he would still have fulfilled Rutter's criteria for backwardness in reading.) It was not problems in Paul himself, but his interaction with a complex variety of people and circumstances which resulted in him being labelled ESN.

Labelling theory: the sociology of selection processes

There is an even more important point at this stage: the report of the educational psychologist who supported the head teacher's request for special education constituted in practice a formal label of educational subnormality (see Ch. 1), yet this merely formalised a process which had started much earlier. By the time the educational psychologist saw him, Paul had been informally labelled 'slow' or 'dull' by his parents, his class teacher, and many other children in his class; of equal importance, he had labelled himself in the same way, thus legitimising the expectations of everyone else in his own eyes as well as theirs. No discussion of the needs of ESN(M) and maladjusted children can ignore labelling theory (Hargreaves *et al.*, 1975); the epidemiological and longitudinal surveys ascribed maladjustment, psychiatric disorder, reading backwardness or specific reading retardation to children who met certain highly specific criteria. Nevertheless these criteria were arbitrary to the extent that they constituted the research workers' opinion as to what constituted a clinically or educationally significant deviation from the norm. (Why, for example, select a reading age eighteen months below chronological age for inclusion in the reading backwardness group instead of a simple two years?) In practice, as opposed to research studies, children are not considered problems because they pass or fail some objective test of behavioural normality or educational attainment; they are considered problems because their teachers *feel* that they are, or have, problems. In their critical introduction of labelling theory, Hargreaves *et al.* (1975), rightly point out that it is an over-simplification to argue 'that labelling theory is merely asserting that people or acts are deviant when somebody defines them as deviant'. They distinguish between 'primary deviation' (Lemert, 1967) in which society (or teachers or parents) object to some action and create rules to curtail it, and 'secondary deviation' which is created by society's reaction to primary deviation. Rules are often broken *not* because of a desire to commit the action for its own sake, but because rule-breaking becomes an end in itself; in other words, the rule creates the deviance, either by creating resentment which requires an expression of hostility towards the people who enforce the rule or because the rules of the individual's own subgroup are more important than those of society. School uniform provides a good example. Some children find themselves in trouble for wearing incorrect uniform because their original uniform has been lost, stolen, grown out of or damaged, and their parents cannot afford replacements. Even though they are clean and tidily dressed they still attract punishment, if only in the form of public disapproval. More often refusal to wear correct uniform represents the child's or his parents' disagreement with the school and its regulations. Sometimes parents refuse to buy the necessary uniform, but sometimes the pupils themselves defy the united efforts of parents and teachers to persuade them to conform to the school's ideas of appropriate dress. In these cases the approval the pupil receives from his own peers is more important to him than that of his teachers or parents (Hargreaves, 1967). This can escalate in an amusing way. A number of pupils from a small comprehensive school in a town with three secondary schools were eligible for a grant towards the cost of school uniform as their parents' income fell below the accepted level; they collected the necessary form authorising the local shop to issue uniform without charge, and promptly exchanged it for the uniform of – the wrong school! These teenagers knew that wearing the wrong uniform was an offence resulting in immediate exclusion for the rest of the day. The following day they put their plan into action, and were gratified by prompt exclusion! Each of these pupils would probably have been included in the category of those suffering from psychiatric disorder or maladjustment in the major surveys described above, but one is entitled to ask whether the terms have any *educational* significance unless they are considered in the context of the child's interaction with other people in his environment.

Pupils are frequently labelled deviant (or maladjusted, or 'remedial') because they infringe some rule laid down by parents, teachers or society, yet the rule may have been broken *partly because* of this labelling process. Some labelling theorists would argue that the rule-breaking occurs *precisely* because of the adverse labelling, but this misses the point that self-labelling is often the immediate result of labelling by others. Thus, when a child is criticised in school assembly as 'antisocial' the effect may be to encourage his previous tendency to associate with other antisocial pupils who have rejected the school's mores. Since he is unlikely to succeed in any other group he identifies (labels) himself as a member of the anti-school group, and must continue to break the school's rules if he is to retain the approval of his peers in this group, or, more basically, to conform to his own self-image as someone who rejects the values of school or parents, or both.

This is the process which lies behind the phenomenon so often seen in special schools for ESN(M) and maladjusted pupils as well as in remedial departments and most ordinary classes of ordinary schools, namely the child who refuses to try because he cannot bear to fail. Sometimes this is seen in resistance to educational help; the child seems to be saying to himself: 'If I don't try to learn to read, I won't look stupid if I fail.' Sometimes it is seen in hostility or indifference to the teacher's approval or rejection of the school's values; the teacher frequently comments: 'He hates being praised in front of the others,' or 'He can't bear it if I display any of his work on the wall – he'll rip it down rather than leave it there.'

Summary

In this chapter we have reviewed the major surveys of prevalence of severe behavioural and educational problems. Quite consistently, the results show that the majority of these children concerned are being (and will remain) educated in their ordinary schools. We have also examined some of the ways in which children come to be regarded as problems, with a particular emphasis on the interactional nature of the process which results in the ascription of deviance or backwardness. In the next chapter we shall consider what is known about the progress of children in special schools for the maladjusted and ESN(M) and contrast this with what is known about the progress of other groups of children with similar problems.

Chapter 3

The results of special education

Maladjusted children

Introduction

It is sometimes said that special schools should be judged by the subsequent adjustment of children who have been through them. This is a high standard, though perhaps not as high as that of Shaw (1965): 'When asked (of our criteria for success) one day by a critic we replied: "Ah we can never say when we have succeeded with a boy. What we have to do is to wait until he has married, and after his children grow up and marry happily, then we know we have succeeded with him".' The trouble with this, as with most ideals, is not so much that it is unattainable as that we have to wait too long to know whether we have arrived.

Special education is no different from any other sort of activity in the sense that its success can only be measured against its aims, and if the aims of education are unclear, the aims of special education sometimes seem to be shrouded in fog. The stated aim is invariably to help the child, but how he is to be helped, by whom, to do what, and when, is often less clear. We can tackle the problem on two levels. First, we can look at the rather limited number of studies which have sought to assess the progress of children at special schools and after leaving them, and second we can look at the evidence on the progress of dull and disturbing children in ordinary schools. In an ideal world the same ethical and scientific standards would apply to the development of different forms of educational treatment as apply in theory to new drugs; for the latter, controlled trials are required in which patients are allocated at random to control and experimental groups, so that not even the prescribing doctor knows whether he is giving the patient the new treatment or a harmless placebo; moreover patients are continually examined for undesirable side effects. No such care has ever been taken in the development of separate special schools; administrators, teachers, doctors, psychologists and social workers all persuade each other that 'special' means 'better' – by definition. Their motivation is often admirable – a deeply felt sympathy with unhappy and unsuccessful children – but the lack of serious evaluation studies can only be described as regrettable.

As we shall see shortly, our knowledge about the effects of special schools is sadly limited, and in the absence of more substantial information exponents of special schools are forced back on hopeful optimism. Thus a group of head teachers in the London area produced a valuable report of local day schools for maladjusted children (Lansdown, 1970) but had to confine their remarks about the schools' results to a single study (ILEA, 1965) whose limitations were acknowledged by the author herself. Similarly, Laslett (1977) in the most detailed recent book about the education of maladjusted children summarises his chapter on evidence of achievement with the comment: 'That the schools have achieved something is certain. Many of the children admitted with very serious difficulties left them very much improved and successful beyond any reasonable expectation.' Yet Laslett does not justify his claim; teachers in ordinary schools can cite children who improved beyond any reasonable expectation, and special schools should surely seek to achieve something which an ordinary school cannot; more fundamentally he fails to consider the progress of psychiatrically disordered children who receive no form of treatment, let alone the administrative tag of maladjusted. A similarly hopeful but uncritical attitude is shown in an initial report by the Schools Council project on the education of disturbed pupils (Wilson *et al.*, 1977), in which the authors conclude that 'in view of their (teachers of maladjusted children) considerable experience (66 per cent of the schools had been open for more than eight years and 21 per cent for more than twenty-one years) their views cannot be disregarded even if there is at present no long-term evidence of their success'. The caring professions have never excelled in evaluating their own effectiveness, and those professions which specialise in interpersonal relationships and special education seem to have been the least conscientious in this respect.

Evaluation studies in residential schools

For reasons which were explained in Chapter 1, few of the pioneers in education of maladjusted children were teachers and none of them worked in the maintained sector. Shaw (1965) kept a record of the behaviour and adjustment of all pupils passing through Red Hill, his school for intelligent secondary age boys, since 1934. Apart from six pupils who had died since leaving the school and six more whom the school had failed to contact, he regarded 67 per cent as 'radically cured on a completely permanent and adjusted basis', with a further 21 per cent improved. Two per cent were not failures, but could not really qualify for description as improved, and the remaining 10 per cent were regarded as failures. Burn (1964), in his account of George Lyward's school Finchden Manor, reported that 290 boys had been through the school since 1930. Fifteen boys had attended for brief treatment in the early 1930s and had returned to the ordinary school system, though we have no information on whether or not they succeeded in their ordinary schools. Eighty-three boys were sent away as too difficult, went to mental hospitals, ran away, were withdrawn by their parents or guardians, or left on their own initiative against the school's advice. Of the remaining 192 (66 per cent) nearly all had settled down, often in distinguished careers. Both Shaw's and Burn's claims seem impressive (and many visitors to both schools were also favourably impressed), but neither give a detailed explanation of how they arrive at the figures; a further problem is that both schools were atypical in only taking boys of high intelligence and frequently keeping them until they were eighteen (at Red Hill) or later (at Finchden Manor). Nevertheless, each school claimed that around 66 per cent of its pupils achieved substantial and lasting improvement. As we shall shortly see, this figure recurs with almost monotonous consistency in studies evaluating the outcome of treatment, though it is more often reached by combining the 'greatly improved' and 'partly improved' groups.

Another study which investigated the subsequent adjustment of boys discharged from residential schools for maladjusted children was Balbernie's (1966). Unlike the bright pupils of Finchden Manor and Red Hill, the boys ranged from below average to above average in general intelligence, and only thirty-two were included in his study. When followed up at the ages of $17\frac{1}{2}$ to 22, only five had been able to settle successfully in their own homes and two of them were unable to hold a regular job. A further eight had achieved some degree of adjustment away from home and eleven were in Borstal, detention centre or mental hospital, or were seeking discharge from the Services after appearing in court. In other words, only 41 per cent of the sample could be rated a success, and this on rather generous criteria. Balbernie made the interesting observation that all the improved boys had made a good relationship with an adult at the school, usually someone outside the professional residential staff, such as a cook or gardener. An equally important point was that continued improvement seemed to be associated with continuance of this relationship, and that neither the boys' degree of disturbance when admitted to the schools nor their disturbance on discharge appeared as important in their subsequent adjustment as the amount of follow-up support they received. This observation held good irrespective of the boys' diagnosis; so-called psychotic or affectionless boys were as likely to continue to improve as ostensibly less disturbed boys, provided their support after leaving was adequate. From the depressing histories of the majority of the young men in Balbernie's survey, one can only conclude that adequate support was seldom forthcoming. A further and more fundamental point is whether residential placement was necessary in the first place if adjustment at follow-up depended not on the children's state on entering or leaving the school but on subsequent support in the community. This view is supported by Balbernie's observation that for the twenty boys whose families were very definitely rejecting before their admission to a residential school, the relationship problems deteriorated still further in the course of treatment.

All the studies mentioned so far are of independent schools which were among the pioneers of special education for maladjusted children in this country. Their books (Wills, 1945, 1960, 1971; Lennhoff, 1960; Shaw, 1965; Burn, 1964) have had a substantial impact on the training and subsequent thinking of teachers in state maintained schools for the maladjusted. Unfortunately, but perhaps inevitably, the enthusiasm of the innovators did not extend to carrying out a detailed investigation of their results in a way which would enable others to see whether similar methods could achieve the same results in different settings. This was particularly necessary as the most rapid expansion since 1964 in places for maladjusted children has been in day schools in the maintained sector. Apart from the question whether approaches which can be implemented successfully in a residential school are also appropriate in a day school, there is the more basic question about whether the bureaucracy of a local education authority could (or should) allow head teachers the degree of freedom enjoyed by the pioneers of independent boarding schools. Few people who had the privilege to meet such energetic, imaginative, sometimes eccentric and often caustically humorous men as Otto Shaw could imagine them working successfully within the restriction of a local education authority. Viewed in this light it is perhaps not surprising that the usefulness of ideas developed in the earliest schools has not received adequate scrutiny in the more numerous state maintained schools whose numbers have so dramatically increased (see Table 1.1). More disturbing is the fact that serious evaluation studies are still so thin on the ground. Apart from those already mentioned, there appear to be few worthy of mention and of these two are only accessible on short-term inter-library loan.

Shields (1962) described the work of a residential school at which psychoanalytical treatment was available to selected boys. In 1953 a consultant psychiatrist for the then London County Council compared present pupils who had received analytical treatment with those who had not. He based his comparison on ratings of the extent to which the children had improved on six factors, such as their relationship with parents and authorities and their capacity to learn; the ratings were from nought (no change), to three (marked or complete improvement). Shields reports that treated children obtained a mean score of 17.0, against a mean of 11.5 for the untreated children, the difference being statistically significant. Later he claims that of 216 boys discharged over an eleven-year period, 84 per cent had 'made a reasonably normal readjustment to life outside the school, at home or in work'. Unfortunately the difficulties in drawing any conclusion from these impressive claims are even greater than with most of the literature on maladjustment. Shields does not even tell us in his 'Progress Report' who did the rating nor whether the person or people concerned knew the purpose of the study; the research on the effects of teachers' expectations shows clearly that such information can have a crucial influence, particularly if the raters have a vested interest in showing whether treatment works. Similarly there is inadequate information about the ways in which children were selected for treatment; it may be that the ones selected for treatment were the ones who were most likely to improve without any form of treatment. As we shall see later in this chapter, children with some sorts of behaviour problem may be more likely to improve without treatment than others.

The subsequent employment history of maladjusted pupils is another subject on which we have insufficient information. The most detailed survey so far carried out is that of Tuckey *et al.* (1973), who followed up 788 leavers from special schools for all the main categories of handicap. Unfortunately this constituted only 58 per cent of their original sample – an unacceptably low proportion in view of what is known about the effect which lost cases (clients who refuse their cooperation) can have on the results (Rutter, 1977).

A more basic problem was that the study compared maladjusted school leavers with other categories of handicap; this was understandable, as it was a survey of all special school leavers irrespective of the category of their handicap. However, we have already seen that maladjusted children differ from many similar pupils who remain in ordinary schools only in receiving the administrative label which acts as passport to the special school.

A more useful comparison would have been with similarly disturbed adolescents leaving ordinary schools; the evidence reviewed in Chapter 3 suggests there is no shortage of these. This said, it is of interest that 50 per cent of the maladjusted pupils in Tuckey's survey left school at fifteen (when the statutory age for all special school leavers was sixteen), a feature which distinguished them from all other categories of handicap. All but one had worked since leaving school (97 per cent). Over three-quarters of the maladjusted pupils were considered suitable for further education or training, but of these less than a third actually received it. On a more optimistic note, although head teachers considered only 14 per cent suitable for employment without further education or training, 72 per cent in fact obtained jobs. (The comparable figures for ESN(M) pupils were 20 per cent and 73 per cent.) Head teachers were more pessimistic about employment potential than was justified by the outcome for all categories of handicap, but especially for the deaf and the maladjusted – a fact which may lend support to the view that special schools tend to over-protect their pupils. Less encouraging was the finding that the maladjusted group had a greater number of jobs per person since leaving school than any other category (an average of four jobs each, compared with just under two and a half for the ESN(M) group).

Cooling (1974) carried out a more broadly based but less detailed survey of boarding school provision for maladjusted children in England and Wales; he found that just under half the leavers from the sixty-eight schools in his sample (all but ten of which catered for secondary age pupils) left to start work. After this the commonest reason for leaving was transfer to an ordinary day school or a residential school for ordinary children (21 per cent). These figures appear quite encouraging at first sight, but unfortunately Cooling gave no details about the *reasons* for transfer, nor about the pupils' subsequent adjustment at ordinary school or in employment. It is possible, for example that some children left because no suitable secondary place could be found, rather than because of their improved adjustment.

A study in Inner London

The evidence for day schools is even more limited; the most detailed investigation is still the one carried out by M. C. Roe, one of the Inner London Education Authority's psychologists (ILEA, 1965). As well as children in ILEA residential schools, she studied the progress of maladjusted pupils in day special schools and tutorial classes. The children's age range was from five to fourteen, and the IQ range from 70–120. Their educational attainments and social behaviour were assessed at the beginning and end of a twelve-month observation period. The results were mixed. Assessing the children on the Neale Analysis of Reading Ability, a test which allows comparison of a child's accuracy with his comprehension of what he reads, Roe found that 17 per cent made encouraging gains of sixteen months or more in reading accuracy, and 50 per cent a similar gain in comprehension. On the other hand a considerably larger proportion of the children achieved ten months' gain or less in reading accuracy, though Roe cites various perceptual and developmental factors which might explain this. Gains in arithmetic were less satisfactory, with a majority of children in all three samples making gains of ten months or less; in the day school group, only six of the twenty children achieved a gain of eleven months or more in the course of the year. Again, Roe reasonably points out that mathematics can be a particularly disturbing subject to many maladjusted children, but her conclusion is perhaps rather optimistic in stating, 'the boarding school sample made a very satisfactory average gain', when thirty-seven of the fifty-nine children achieved gains of ten months or less, compared with the twelve months one might theoretically hope for. It is, of course, reasonable to assume that as the children were maladjusted they might be expected to make less progress than a 'normal' child in the course of the year; on the other hand, we could hope that the effect of smaller classes and, hopefully, more experienced teachers would compensate for their emotional and behavioural problems on admission.

When she studied leavers from five day special schools for maladjusted pupils (in the ILEA, 1965 study) over a two-year period, Roe found that 16 per cent had returned to normal school; she comments that 'the proportion of pupils transferred to normal schools is not high but it is most encouraging'. However, it is not clear whether this optimism is justified. It is important to be clear that 16 per cent *of leavers* returned to normal school, and *not* 16 per cent of the schools' populations. We do not know what proportion of the children who had spent over (for instance) two years in special education returned to normal school, but it must have been greatly less than 16 per cent. On the basis of the most pessimistic figures about 'the spontaneous remission' of behaviour problems (the tendency to clear up without any formal treatment) we should expect a much higher proportion to return to ordinary school. This point is discussed in more detail later in the chapter. Of the twenty-four children who returned to ordinary schools, ten had made a very good adjustment and a further eight passable adjustment. Four had broken down, and questionnaires about two children were not returned.

Changes in the children's personal attitudes and feelings were rated by means of:

1. A Sentence Completion Test devised by the educational psychologist.
2. The stories children made up about a number of pictures.
3. An Anxiety Scale.

Roe rightly points out that the material from the first two techniques has low reliability, and that this problem was aggravated not only by her own knowledge of the children but also by the fact that she alone was responsible for rating the responses. In view of these admitted flaws in research design it is doubtful whether one can accept the judgement that the Sentence Completion test indicated that 74 per cent of the children had improved, while their stories about pictures indicated that 57 per cent had made progress. Even if one accepts these results, it is scarcely impressive that one test indicated that the attitudes and feelings of 43 per cent of the children had deteriorated after a year at special school. Roe also found that the children tended to be less anxious and more extroverted on an Anxiety Scale (the reference of which is not given), but here too there are methodological problems which prevent any firm conclusions from being drawn.

In addition to rating the children's own attitudes and feelings the ILEA study obtained head teachers' and educational psychologists' assessments of improvement. Unfortunately their criteria for rating improvement are not clear. The heads tended to be more impressed by the children's progress than the psychologists, but both professions agreed that the great majority of children in boarding and day special schools and in tutorial groups had improved.

Their optimism was not altogether supported by the results of a Bristol Social Adjustment Guide (Stott, 1963), completed half a term after admission to the school and again a year later. Both the validity and the reliability of Stott's guides have been challenged (Yule, 1976) though they are widely used in educational research. In the boarding school sample Roe found that original very high scorers tended to have reduced scores, while original low scorers tended to have somewhat increased scores. The same trend was evident in the day school sample, though there was actually an increased number of maladjustment pointers. This trend was explained on the grounds that experienced workers with maladjusted children often expect rapid improvement in the more extreme cases of acting out children, while the more inhibited, withdrawn pupils need to go through a more difficult stage before their behaviour eventually stabilises. The picture is further complicated by evidence from one school whose head teacher completed Bristol Guides on 103 children at six-month intervals throughout a two-year period. He found a decrease in the group's mean scores and in their range over this period, though progress of individuals was frequently erratic. More important for the present discussion, he also found that scores tended to drop three to six months after admission (the time at which class teachers completed the Guides for the first time in the ILEA study), but at the third assessment (one year after admission), nearly 80 per cent showed deterioration compared with their scores six months earlier. No explanation is offered, but if this phenomenon is a general one in special schools for maladjusted children it throws some doubt on the validity of the ILEA results.

The inconsistency in the ILEA study between head teachers' estimates of improvement and the (possibly more objective) estimates obtained from the Bristol Guides was confirmed in a smaller study by Critchley (1969). He reported on the progress of thirty-two boys of low average intelligence aged from six to twelve in a day special school. Using the Bristol Guides he found that just under two-thirds of the boys had improved, and that the ten boys who did not improve were perceived as hostile to adults by the teachers completing the guides. As in the ILEA study the head teachers thought the majority (twenty-seven of the thirty-two) had improved, but this optimism was not altogether supported by the Bristol Guides. Critchley's findings were also consistent with the ILEA results in that the boys in his sample made more progress in reading than in arithmetic.

Conclusions from studies in special schools for maladjusted children

The best one can say of this brief review of the progress of pupils in day and residential schools for maladjusted children is that it fails to justify the schools' existence on the basis of their results. None of the surveys provides a comparison with control groups of difficult children who remain in ordinary schools, yet they even fail to demonstrate convincing evidence of progress or deterioration when using the less rigorous criterion of the children's attainments and behaviour on entry. That this criterion is a less rigorous one than comparison with a control group should be clear from the fact that many disturbed children improve spontaneously without any formal kind of treatment. It is, of course, possible that only the most severely disturbed children (or perhaps those who are most severely disturbing to adults), are selected for special schools but this is a point on which there is not as yet adequate evidence. The subjective impression of some head teachers and educational psychologists is that a child's need for special education depends as much on his class teacher's experience and the stability of other children in his class as on the child himself; teachers differ in their interests and skills just like any other groups of people so it is not surprising that some unsettled children appear relatively well-behaved, happy and confident with some teachers but desperately anxious, unhappy and badly behaved with others. The argument that maladjustment results from the interaction between a number of individuals and circumstances is developed elsewhere in this book. Meanwhile we need to see if there is any other evidence about maladjusted children (extending the term beyond its strictly administrative meaning to include the much larger groups described in the last chapter), which could justify their placement in special schools. As the evidence about the schools themselves is so slight, we have to look elsewhere.

Spontaneous improvement without treatment, and the effects of psychotherapy

One approach is to ask whether children who receive (*a*) other forms of treatment, or (*b*) no treatment at all, tend to improve more than those who are placed in special schools. The effect of one form of treatment, psychotherapy, has attracted extensive research. This research has been motivated largely by controversy within the medical and psychology professions regarding the relative success of psychotherapy and behaviour therapy. Psychotherapists tend to assume that the presenting problem is symptomatic of hidden, underlying problems which the patient can be helped to resolve as he develops 'insight'; in contrast behaviour therapists regard the presenting problem as their starting point and often work directly towards treatment of the child's symptoms. This distinction is discussed in more detail in Chapters 7 and 8. It could, of course, be argued that some of the children receiving psychotherapy are also in schools for maladjusted. This is certainly true, but probably applies to a relatively small minority, and does not invalidate the case for examining the effectiveness of this form of treatment for difficult children.

In fact, although the results of psychotherapy with children are unimpressive they are not quite as unimpressive as was originally claimed by its early critics. In an early article Levitt (1957) reviewed articles which described the results of psychotherapy with children in the period 1929–55. Of nearly 8,000 children treated, two-thirds were rated improved at the end of treatment, and three-quarters at follow-up. Levitt compared these cases with those of children who were accepted for treatment but never began it (defectors), and found similar percentages. He concluded that the results lent no support to belief in the usefulness of psychotherapy, but was promptly criticised on the grounds that defectors were an inappropriate group with which to compare children who received treatment (Hodd-Williams, 1960). The argument was that defectors might be less disturbed children, who could respond favourably to a diagnostic interview alone. This is certainly a possibility, but different studies have resulted in conflicting findings, and Levitt (1963) suggested that a more useful approach is to examine the outcome following psychotherapy for children with different groups of symptoms. Reviewing twenty-two evaluation studies, he found that children with 'acting-out' problems such as delinquency were significantly less likely to improve following psychotherapy than children with identifiable behavioural symptoms like enuresis or school phobia. However, Levitt did not have information about the diagnostic categories of children in the defector groups; hence it was possible that children with some symptoms might be more likely to improve without any treatment than children with others. Unfortunately, there is little information on this point, but other studies have confirmed the relatively poor outlook for aggressive and antisocial children, while most neurotic children grow up into normal adults (Robins, 1966). Further modest support for the usefulness of psychotherapy with some children was provided by Eisenberg *et al.* (1965), and by Wright *et al.* (1976), who re-examined some of the studies in Levitt's (1957) review. He confirmed that children who received treatment were no more likely than untreated controls to show improvement by the close of treatment; nevertheless, they did seem to have improved by the time they were followed up, although they had received no further treatment.

Similarly inconclusive results were obtained in the Buckinghamshire study of 6,000 children attending the county's schools in 1961 (Shepherd *et al.*, 1971). From their study of children attending child guidance clinics, the authors concluded that the severity of disturbance was not the main criterion in determining which children were referred for specialist advice; many children with equally severe problems were never considered for psychiatric assistance. Further, the Buckinghamshire survey supported Levitt's conclusions, since child guidance clinic attendance made no appreciable difference to whether or not the child got better; both groups tended to improve spontaneously as they grew older. Shepherd's conclusions were criticised by Rutter (1972) on the grounds that the sample of clinic children was unrepresentative of the children attending child guidance clinics at the time; moreover they differed from the untreated control group on a number of potentially important factors such as separation experiences and parental attitudes.

Another way of looking at the outlook for disturbed children is to ask how many of those who present problems in childhood will continue to have difficulties in adolescence, and *vice versa*. A frequent argument at teachers' conferences is that if problems are detected early, subsequent difficulties will be reduced. Will they? Rutter *et al.* (1976), found a slight rise in the rate of psychiatric disorder during early adolescence, but the increase was only moderate. More important, just over half the children with psychiatric disorder in early adolescence developed these disorders in adolescence; just under half persisted from early childhood. This hardly supports the view that specialist services (including special schools) should concentrate on the younger age group in order to prevent more intransigent problems from developing later. However many of the younger children are treated, and however successfully, there will continue to be many problems which arise for the first time in older age groups.

It would be nice to be able to compare the evidence on the 'spontaneous remission' of disturbed behaviour among the general population of children attending ordinary schools with the progress of children attending special schools for the maladjusted; unfortunately we are not yet able to make this vital comparison. Nevertheless, it is fairly clear: (*a*) that a majority of disturbed children remain in ordinary schools, and it seems likely that for every one child selected for special education, other equally disturbed pupils are not selected; (*b*) that a majority of children with 'clinically significant psychiatric disorder' improve spontaneously within two or three years, though the proportion is probably higher for neurotic and single symptom problems than for delinquent, or antisocial forms of behaviour.

The question is further confused by the lack of information about the problems of children on admission to schools for the maladjusted, as the type of problem effects the prognosis. The ILEA report (1965) already mentioned found that just over half the children admitted to day schools were considered too timid or withdrawn to cope with the demands of ordinary school; in contrast, this applied to only 8 out of 34 children referred to residential schools. Similarly, only 2 out of 28 day school referrals were thought to be becoming delinquent or to be at risk in other ways in the community, whereas 25 out of 42 boarding school referrals fell into this category. From the evidence presented earlier that 'acting out' problems have a worse prognosis than 'neurotic' conditions (Levitt, 1963; Robins, 1966), we would expect maladjusted children from the day special schools to improve more rapidly than those from the residential schools.

As we saw earlier, only 16 per cent of the leavers from five day special schools returned to an ordinary school. The ILEA study does not report what percentage of the total number on roll was discharged, improved, to ordinary schools, nor do we have adequate information about children attending the residential schools. Cooling's (1974) figure of 21 per cent of leavers returning to the ordinary system is somewhat higher, though he gives little or no information about the children's condition on discharge nor about their subsequent adjustment. To summarise, the only reported instances in which children attending schools for the maladjusted make as much progress as one should expect from the evidence on the spontaneous remission of behaviour problems appear to be those of Shaw (1965) and Burn (1964), though even here the evidence is rather incomplete. Because so little is known about how, or even whether, children selected for special schools differ from severely disturbed pupils who remain in ordinary schools, the evidence does not justify a conclusion that special school placement may be positively harmful to the children concerned, even though on the basis of around 66 per cent of problem children improving within two years it is tempting to expect a much higher rate of return to ordinary school than seems to be the case. On the other hand, nor does the limited evidence so far available lend much support to the belief that referral to special schools for maladjusted pupils is likely to benefit the children concerned.

B.   ESN(M) children

ESN(M) children in special schools

As with maladjusted children, provision for ESN(M) children has expanded enormously since the 1944 Act; indeed almost the first practical effect of the Act, apart from the abolition of fees in secondary schools, was the expansion of facilities for these two groups. Yet ESN(M) schools have increased with as little serious evaluation of their effect on the children who attend them (and the classes from which these children were removed) as has been the case with maladjusted children. It is a sad reflection on the uncritical attitude of educationalists and administrators in this country towards children with special needs that almost all the most relevant research has been carried out in the United States and Sweden. Whether findings about special classes or schools for the North American or Scandinavian equivalent of ESN(M) pupils can generalise to this country is a matter for debate. What is not a matter for debate is that in the absence of serious attempts to compare the progress and adjustment of pupils at special schools for ESN(M) children in the United Kingdom with that of similar pupils attending ordinary schools, we have to look elsewhere. Extensive research has been carried out in America on the efficacy of ESN(M) schools (generally known as schools for the educable mentally retarded: 'EMR'), and the results are quite well known (Osterling, 1967; Johnson, 1962). Nevertheless there are two moderately consistent trends: first that children tend to make better educational progress in ordinary classes, and second that they tend to be socially better adjusted in special classes or schools.

As early as the 1930s Bennett (1932) found that ESN(M) children in ordinary classes obtained higher scores on reading and spelling and arithmetic tests than other children, matched for age and IQ in special schools. As with almost all the research, however, there were questions as to whether the two groups were really comparable. Thus in Bennett's survey, there were more boys in the ordinary class group and there were further differences in the prevalence of physical factors such as defective hearing and eyesight. Perhaps more important, there was no attempt to control for emotional stability and general motivation towards school when selecting the groups. Thurstone (1959) obtained similar results when she compared children with IQ scores in the 50–79 range. She suggested four possible explanations for the superior educational attainments of the ordinary class children; first it was possible that ESN(M) pupils were stimulated by being in an ordinary class; second it was possible that their motivation decreased in a special class; third, dull children selected for special schools differ from those who are not; finally, teachers in special schools might place less emphasis on improving educational attainments than their colleagues in ordinary schools. All these possibilities merit consideration, but no real conclusions can be drawn without more evidence about the possibility that dull children selected for special education are selected because they have *additional* problems.

Other projects have investigated the children's social adjustment as well as their educational attainments. Ellenbogen (1957) compiled two groups on the basis of age, sex and school district; all the special school children had already received special education for at least two years. The educational attainments of children in ordinary classes were consistently higher than those of special class pupils, but the latter were regarded by their teachers as socially more active and better emotionally adjusted with regard to school and the future. Ann Jordan (1959) also found better general adjustment in special class children, emphasising the social isolation of ESN(M) children in ordinary classes. Cassidy and Stanton (1959 and 1961), Wrightstone et al. (1959) and Johnson (1961) all conclude that special classes promote social adjustment, while ordinary classes promote educational attainments. On the other hand not all studies have found consistent differences between special classes and ordinary classes. Blatt (1958) tried to eliminate selection errors by comparing dull children in a district with special schools with dull children in a district which had no such provision. In other words, he compared a group of children who had been selected for special education with a group consisting not only of children who *would* have been selected if facilities had existed, but also of children who would have been overlooked even if facilities had existed. He found no important differences between the two groups in the results of achievement tests. Similarly, Ainsworth (1959) found no important differences in educational progress or social adjustment, while Mullen and Itkin (1961) came to a similar conclusion about educational attainment.

In one of the few British studies Maurice Ascher (1970) compared children aged eleven to thirteen in ESN(M) schools with children of similar age and IQ in the remedial departments of ordinary schools. Only children with an IQ in the range 60–90 were selected for inclusion (in either group); in addition they were regarded by their teachers as having 'normal' behaviour, health, physique and attendance for that particular type of school. (Whether special school teachers regard 'normality' in these respects in a different way to ordinary school teachers is not known.) As would be expected from other research, most of the parents were in Social Classes IV and V and lived in council property, mainly flats. The children were tested individually in their first or second year of secondary education, and again a year later. Results showed that the remedial department group had significantly higher scores on vocabulary and reading tests, both on initial testing and re-testing. The number of children improving over the year was also greater in the remedial group. To a lesser extent the same applied to scores in an arithmetic test. Children with the lowest initial scores tended to make the most improvement – an encouraging finding, but disconcerting if there is an inclination to concentrate on practical activities for slow-learners.

A battery of tests investigating the children's preferred social contacts out of school and their preferred leisure occupations suggested greater maturity in the children from remedial departments. Unfortunately this aspect of the survey was not discussed in detail. Concluding, Ascher remarks that 'stated in very conservative terms, the special school children showed no particular advantage by their educational placement and also possibly suffered some segregation from children in ordinary schools'.

Ascher's study suffers the same problems concerning selection of children for each group as the American literature; to put it very simply, we should expect the differences if the ESN(M) children had been placed in special schools for reasons other than intellectual dullness and educational backwardness, for instance maladjustment or family problems.

Another English study (Shearer, 1977) investigated the way in which ESN(M) provision was perceived by children, teachers and the parents themselves. Over three-quarters of the parents and children said they were happy with their classes or schools, and satisfied with their educational progress. Unfortunately, no conclusions can be drawn from these superficially encouraging results as there was no comparison group of children who remained in ordinary schools. Might parents who were not offered special education (or who refused to accept it) have been equally happy about their children's progress in the local secondary schools? Might the children themselves have told the researchers they were glad they had not been sent to special schools? Equally unsatisfactory is Shearer's evidence on the children's improvement in behaviour, since this was based on informal opinions as to whether the children had improved, remained the same or deteriorated. We have already seen (in relation to maladjusted children) the wide disparity between informal opinions about improvement and slightly more objective assessments with techniques such as the Bristol Guides.

It will be clear from the review so far that a cardinal weakness in all the quoted studies has been the difficulty in comparing two groups. None of the studies was based on a *random* allocation of pupils to special schools or ordinary classes. The idea of allocating children at random to special schools or ordinary schools would cause many teachers and educationalists to throw up their hands in horror. Nevertheless, we have already seen evidence that 'special' may not necessarily mean 'better'. In spite of the horror of thalidomide, it is doubtful whether the medical profession has ever allowed new drugs on to the market with the same haphazard, random enthusiasm which has characterised the development of special education.

In one of the few controlled studies of the effects of special education, Osterling (1967) was able to allocate children in Swedish primary schools to slow-learner classes or to ordinary classes. However, no child was selected with an IQ below 70, so his research is less of a comparison between ESN(M) classes and ordinary classes than between remedial classes and ordinary classes. The children were tested at regular intervals in Swedish and arithmetic; the ordinary class group showed a gradual improvement relative to the slow-learner classes, especially in arithmetic. When Osterling investigated the pupils' social adjustment, he found that both groups experienced a good deal of frustration, mainly due to their sensing the negative expectations of the people around them. Nevertheless, there was an important difference between the two groups. With the ordinary class children, frustration was focused mainly on school, perhaps reflecting their relative failure compared with their peers; in contrast, children in the slow-learner classes tended to experience greater frustration outside school, at home and in the community. Osterling does not comment on which group is likely to have better social adjustment in the long run, but his investigation does place a large questionmark on the American studies which found better social adjustment among children in ordinary classes than in special schools or classes. Might the special school children have appeared more disturbed if the inquiry had focused on their behaviour out of school, and might the ordinary class pupils then have appeared less disturbed? Osterling himself points out (in his review on the American literature) that 'since the regular class may be more analogous to post-school life than the artificial environment of the special class, it is conceivable that optimal accommodation for mentally retarded children in school could result in post-school problems of adjustment'.

One point which does emerge from the research on special provision for ESN(M) children is that disagreement does not focus on whether children benefit in terms of educational attainments. None of the studies so far reported has shown this; instead, the conflicting evidence has been about whether or not the children benefit educationally from staying in ordinary classes. Johnson (1962) has argued that criticism of the research on the grounds of methodology is not valid as several different experimental designs have yielded consistent results. More challengingly, Dunn (1968) says that:

If I were a Negro from the slums or a disadvantaged parent . . . and knew what I now know about special classes for the educable mentally retarded, other things being equal I would then go to court before allowing the schools to label my child as 'mentally retarded' and place him in a 'self-contained special school or class'.

What then is special about special education? More basically the question is whether certain special needs can be met more adequately in special classes or schools than in ordinary schools. One American study which attempted to answer this question had the additional advantage that children with IQs between 60 and 85 were allocated randomly to ESN(M) classes. However, the curriculum for the special class was based on a specific educational programme designed as a long-term experiment with the emphasis on understanding rather than acquiring mechanical skills. Results (Goldstein *et al.,* 1962) suggested that teachers in the special classes were more successful in adjusting to the needs of the duller half of the class, since these were the ones who showed the greatest increase in IQ. Over two years the special class group obtained better results in a maths test, though not in vocabulary. Investigating creative thinking as part of Goldstein's project, Tisdall (1962) found the special class children significantly superior in their command of language and in their flexibility in solving problems. In spite of the possibility that the special class children's superiority could be due to a Hawthorne effect (in which an experiment seems to work precisely because of the enthusiasm generated by the experiment), Tisdall's study is of interest in showing that special classes can obtain superior results when they set themselves specific goals within the framework of a clear philosophy and well-defined methods.

Effects of remedial teaching

We have already argued that the process of selection for special education in ESN(M) schools is more than a little haphazard. For example, we saw in Chapter 2 that a very small minority of children who could be regarded as ESN(M) according to the broad criteria which were issued after the 1944 Act are actually placed in special schools; even if a narrower criterion based on an IQ of less than 75 is adopted, a substantial majority of the children concerned will remain in ordinary schools (due to lack of special school places, if not for other reasons).

As the majority of dull children remain in ordinary schools, evaluation of special educational treatment should also consider the progress of these children in the remedial departments of ordinary schools. However, this raises a number of practical difficulties. By no means all the children selected for remedial education are dull – indeed the term implies the possibility of 'remedying' or 'remediating' problems which can presumably occur in any child irrespective of intelligence. Most of the research describes the progress of children who received specified amounts of remedial teaching, yet in practice the remedial departments in a secondary school and the remedial class in a primary school are sometimes a cosy euphemism for the 'D' stream, except that all the other classes are often run on a mixed ability basis. Full time remedial classes are generally smaller than other classes, but as few of them contain less than twenty children the possibility of individualised learning programmes to remediate specific problems is strictly limited. Whether or not this actually happened in the remedial work which has been investigated in research studies is by no means certain. Nevertheless it is as well to be clear about the hazy nature of a concept which can mean almost anything to anyone.

Cyril Burt's early optimism (1937) has not altogether been justified. He hoped that special attention would so greatly accelerate the progress of retarded children that they would be able to return to ordinary classes within one or two terms. Birch (1950) and Valentine (1951) reported striking improvements, but their methodology was criticised by Curr and Gourlay (1953) whose own study suggested that the children selected for remedial teaching hardly made any more progress than matched controls who received no special help. Nevertheless, other studies subsequently demonstrated impressive short-term gains.

Yet although short-term gains from remedial reading have been reported quite consistently (Samson, 1975) there has been less agreement about whether this improvement is maintained over the next few years. Lovell, Johnson and Platts (1962) and Lovell, Byrne and Richardson (1963) carried out a large-scale investigation of the long-term effects of remedial education on children who were taught individually in child guidance clinics or in small groups at their own schools. Both groups improved initially, but neither group maintained the improvements. Lovell's rather gloomy conclusion was that the results seemed to be more or less the same whether the children were dull or of average intelligence, and whether they were taught singly or in groups.

More optimistically Kellmer Pringle (1960) found that most parents of children who had received remedial teaching at least eighteen months earlier were satisfied with their children's educational progress and social adjustment. Shearer (1967) obtained similarly encouraging results with a smaller group who were taught in a primary school adjustment class; he showed that the loss of progress achieved during remedial teaching could be reduced if the children received adequate follow up in their ordinary classes. This point was made more clearly by Tobin and Pumfrey (1976) who followed up primary school children who had received remedial education. As usual, the 'tested' children were found to make better progress in the short term, but a disturbing pattern emerged when they entered their secondary schools. The 'untreated' children continued to make progress after leaving their primary schools, while the 'treated' pupils actually regressed, though only marginally in the case of children at Roman Catholic schools; although the 'treated' groups were still showing some benefit, the gap was narrowing. Reinforcing an earlier suggestion (Cashdan and Pumfrey, 1969) the authors comment on this rather widespread tendency:

It has been argued that this is hardly surprising. If a pupil is returned to a situation which initially contributed to his need for remedial help and the situation is essentially the same, then regression seems extremely likely. A strong case can be made for continuing the help that appears to have been effective in the short term.

Epidemiological studies

The large-scale studies relevant to educational standards and social adjustment were reviewed in the last chapter. Their value here lies in providing an overview of the progress of a total population of children (or of randomly selected samples within a total population). The Isle of Wight study (Rutter *et al.*, 1970) distinguished between backward readers whose reading level was twenty-eight months or more below their chronological age and children with specific reading retardation; these children were at least twenty-eight months retarded in reading when compared with a prediction based on their age and intelligence. The two groups differed consistently in other ways as well. The backward readers had higher rates of neurological abnormality, speech or language handicap, and (to a somewhat smaller degree) clumsiness. Conversely, there were more boys in the group with specific reading retardation. This group also obtained higher scores on an individual IQ test; an average of over twelve points separated the two groups. On these grounds one might perhaps have predicted that they would make better progress. In fact, a five-year follow-up (Yule, 1973) showed the reverse. Although they appeared duller in IQ terms, and although they suffered from more neurological, speech and motor problems, Neale's test (1958) showed that they made significantly *more* progress than the children whose retardation was more specifically related to reading. Of equal importance was the fact that the children with specific reading retardation made more progress in arithmetic over the five-year period, thus providing further evidence that their difficulties were specifically connected with reading.

This has interesting implications for the selection of children for special education. In the first place it confirms some of the research on remedial reading that IQ does not have a crucial influence on the chances of a backward or retarded reader making progress, at least in the ranges encountered in ordinary schools and the upper half of ESN(M) schools. Unfortunately it is still not unknown for psychologists to use IQ tests as the basis for selection for ESN(M) schools; the use of group intelligence tests for selection purposes within ordinary schools is even more widespread. A more fundamental point is the possible inference that resources for special education should be aimed at the group with the worst prognosis, namely children with specific reading difficulties, rather than at more globally retarded children who may have a better outlook in respect of educational progress.

A valid objection to this argument would be that many, if not most, of the children selected for ESN(M) schools are in fact retarded in reading, even when retardation is assessed in relation to age and intelligence level. On the other hand children in ESN(M) schools form a very small proportion of the children with specific reading retardation, and one wonders whether resources might more profitably be directed at reducing this problem than at providing a total educational environment for a minority. There is firm evidence from research on remedial reading that short-term improvement is possible, and several indications that these improvements can be maintained if adequate follow-up support is provided.

Conclusions

This review of work on the progress of slow-learning and disturbing children makes uncomfortable reading, not only for the caring professions of psychology and psychiatry, but also for teachers, both in special and in ordinary schools. The progress of ESN(M) pupils selected for special education has been studied in somewhat more detail than that of the maladjusted, though with results that are no more encouraging. Significantly the Warnock Report is almost totally silent about results of special education.

The fact that so many studies indicate that the better social adjustment at school of ESN(M) pupils is associated with lower educational standards, when compared with their peers of similar intelligence who remain in ordinary schools, is scarcely a matter for congratulation when the handicap is defined as *educational* backwardness. Admittedly, most of the research was carried out in the USA or Scandinavia, yet Ascher's (1970) study shows the same trend in the UK. Osterling's (1967) disturbing suggestion that better social adjustment at school may be the price of poorer social adjustment at home is one which requires more detailed examination. If confirmed, it would provide a powerful argument against the separate special school system. The Warnock Report (DES, 1978) called for further research in special education; this is an area which could usefully be investigated.

The main conclusions to emerge from studies of remedial reading are that short-term progress is quite possible, but is only likely to be maintained if adequate follow-up is provided. Combining these conclusions with those on the progress of pupils in ESN(M) schools, there is clearly a case for concentrating resources on providing better facilities within the ordinary school.

In the case of maladjusted children, rather more research has been carried out in this country. The suggestion that spontaneous remission is less likely from special schools than from ordinary schools requires more detailed study. It may be that the pupils selected for special schools are the ones with the worst prognosis, though this is not obviously the case from the available evidence. In Chapters 7 and 8 we review some of the recent attempts to cater for maladjusted pupils in ordinary schools. The point which emerges here, however, is that the prognosis for a pupil admitted to a special school for the maladjusted seems to be poor. It may well be the case that placement benefits the children and teachers in the child's original school by removing a major source of disturbance. This area too might usefully be investigated if the Warnock Report's recommendation for further research is implemented, since a major gap in the literature both on ESN(M) and maladjusted children is the progress of their previous classes following their removal.

Chapter 4

The practice and theory of integration

Introduction

Special education has probably attracted more attention and controversy in the 1970s than at any time in the past. Certainly there was sharp disagreement both about aims and about methods among the pioneers in the education of mentally handicapped children, as we saw in Chapter 1. However, this disagreement took place against a background of public apathy; the argument was not so much whether they should be educated in ordinary schools or special schools but whether they merited special educational attention in the first place. This principle was not fully accepted for maladjusted children until the 1944 Act.

The major legal development since 1944 has been the transfer of responsibility for the education of severely mentally handicapped – ESN(S) – children from the health services to local education authorities in 1970. ESN(S) children differ from most of their contemporaries who find their way to ESN(M) schools in a number of ways apart from degree of mental handicap (Burden, 1977), of which the most important here are:

1. The higher prevalence of congenital or constitutional defects.
2. A more even social class distribution, indicating that the handicap is not nearly so much determined by cultural factors as is the case with ESN(M) and maladjusted children.

The 1970 Act reflected increasing public irritation at the scandal whereby the only group of children to be denied any form of education were the most handicapped. Yet the Act also reflected an awakening of public conscience about all groups of handicapped children, not just the severely mentally handicapped. This led to the appointment of the Committee of Enquiry into Special Education in 1973 under the chairmanship of Mary Warnock. The Committee's terms of reference were 'to review educational provision in England, Scotland and Wales for children and young people handicapped by disabilities of body or mind . . . to consider the most effective use of resources . . . and to make recommendations'. The Warnock Committee published its findings in the summer of 1978. They were discussed in more detail at the end of Chapter 1.

An important side-effect of the Warnock Committee's investigations has been the publicity it has drawn to special education. Much of this publicity has focused on the question whether handicapped children should continue to be educated in special schools separated physically from the mainstream of the education system. The debate sometimes seems to have attracted more heat than light. Some teachers in both special schools and ordinary schools have strenuously resisted calls for greater integration; it is argued that schools are already labouring under enough difficulties, particularly in inner city areas, without having to accommodate handicapped children as well for the sake of some egalitarian theory. At the other end of the political spectrum, at least one local education authority made inquiries before the Warnock Committee reported about the possibility of saving money by closing some of its special schools if the Committee were to make recommendations in favour of integration (Britton, 1977).

More sober and less politically motivated opinion has accepted integration as a long-term goal, while emphasising the need to ensure appropriate educational and social opportunities for the children concerned (British Psychological Society, 1976; Department of Education and Science, 1974a; Scottish Education Department, 1975). Implicit in this argument is the recognition that integration is not a cheap alternative to traditional special schools; on the contrary, it might be cheaper to concentrate scarce resources of specialised educational materials and equipment, as well as medical and ancillary resources, in one special school. Nevertheless, some groups have called unequivocally for a rapid move towards full integration for the majority of children. Thus, a report commissioned by the National Fund for Research into Crippling Diseases (1976) under Lord Snowdon's chairmanship concluded that policy for special education over the next decade should aim explicitly at 'the planned introduction of a system of integrated education for the handicapped'.

The strongest demands for a move towards more integration have come from associations of parents of handicapped children and from the handicapped themselves. It is hardly surprising in consequence that more discussion has centred on appropriate provision for physically handicapped children than for the larger groups of ESN(M) and maladjusted pupils, neither of whom can call on powerful pressure groups to support them. The reason is not that parents of children in ESN(M) and maladjusted schools are indifferent – though, sadly, this is occasionally the case – but that they lack the knowledge and the administrative skills to form self-help groups at a national level.

Recent research findings, too, have directed attention at the needs of physically handicapped children. Elizabeth Anderson's (1973) study of nearly one hundred disabled children in ordinary infant and junior school classes suggested that the majority of parents had wanted ordinary school placement and that class teachers agreed with parents that most of the children were happy at school. Apart from a group with neurological abnormalities, the physically handicapped children did not display more behaviour problems than their able-bodied peers, and were also making satisfactory educational progress. A more recent study (Cope and Anderson, 1977) of special units for physically handicapped children in ordinary schools came to similarly encouraging conclusions and recommended the establishment of more such units as an alternative to the traditional special school provision.

These results have important implications for physically handicapped children but there are obvious objections to extending the conclusions to cover ESN(M) and maladjusted pupils. Research suggests that physically handicapped children can make satisfactory educational progress and achieve good social adjustment in ordinary schools; ESN(M) children are usually removed precisely *because* they have failed to make satisfactory educational progress, and the maladjusted because they have failed to achieve an adequate level of social adjustment. This, at least, is the theory and there is no doubt that it motivates recommendations for special education. Whether or not the theory is correct – in other words whether the children concerned benefit educationally or socially from transfer to a separate special school – remains an open question, as we saw in the last chapter.

An unfortunate side effect of the 1944 Act arose from the requirement that local authorities 'discover' handicapped children in their areas and allocate them to one of the statutory categories of handicap. This policy had implications at the level of programmes for building schools to cater for the children concerned. As more schools were built it was naturally assumed that they should be filled, and the fact that most of them were built on their own sites rather than as an extension of an ordinary school, led to an 'all or nothing' attitude in which special education could only be provided at the appropriate special school. A similar attitude is sometimes evident in the current controversy about integration. The Joint Council for the Education of Handicapped Children has argued that it is a false alternative to demand integration *or* segregation. Thus, a child can be physically integrated into an ordinary school yet feel socially isolated; the same can be true of special units in ordinary schools, and even of remedial classes which have no pretensions to providing special education in the administrative sense. Conversely, residential special schools may achieve a high level of social integration in their own districts and the quality of education and of personal relationships may provide the basis for highly successful integration when the child leaves.

A continuum of special educational provision

Cope and Anderson (1977) have described the alternative forms of special education which might, in theory, be available to a physically handicapped child (Fig. 4.1). With minor modifications this range of provision might also apply to ESN(M) and maladjusted children. The research surveys described in Chapter 2 suggest that there are many dull or difficult children who remain in their ordinary class with no special help. This must to some extent be due to the still widespread failure to provide maladjusted – and to a lesser extent ESN(M) – children with anything between full-time placement in a special school with no ordinary school link, and remaining in their ordinary classes.

ESN(M) and maladjusted pupils are much more numerous than other categories of handicap (over 68,000 and 14,500 respectively receiving special education or awaiting places in 1970, compared with 12,000 physically handicapped children); consequently it is doubtful whether there should be so much emphasis on catering for them in groups in specially adapted ordinary schools as suggested in Cope and Anderson's continuum. Nevertheless with this proviso their continuum is basically as valid for ESN(M) and maladjusted children as for the physically handicapped. Ancillary help on the care side will be needed less often with the ESN(M) and maladjusted, but its value should not be underestimated. Most infant schools now appoint at least one child care assistant (sometimes called welfare assistant) whose role is to assist class teachers in activities which do not require formal teacher training. In addition

Range of educational provision available to physically handicapped pupils

Suitable for individual PH children placed in their *local* school.

   1 Ordinary class, no special help.
   2 Ordinary class + ancillary help on the care side.

Suitable for *groups* of PH children placed in a *selected* (adapted or purpose built) ordinary school in which extra ancillary help, and speech and physiotherapy is provided.

   3 Ordinary class as base + 'resource room' part-time.
   4 Special class (base) part-time, ordinary class part-time.
   5 Special class full-time.

   6 Day special school formally linked (e.g. same campus) to ordinary school.
   7 Day special school, no such link.
   8 Residential special school.

Fig. 4.1 A continuum of special educational provision (*reprinted from* Cope and Anderson, 1977)

to general supervisory work they often help with teaching activities under the class teacher's supervision. In practice this is similar to the situation in nursery schools, where teachers and nursery nurses work alongside each other. With physically handicapped children a child care assistant can be responsible for routine physical aspects of the child's care, but as this is unlikely to occupy her full-time, she will be able to help the class teacher in other ways as well.

The physical problems involved in retaining ESN(M) and maladjusted children in ordinary schools are obviously less severe, though by no means non-existent – for example, a significant minority of ESN(M) children suffer from mild forms of epilepsy. Class teachers often complain that they know what sort of help a child needs; as they cannot provide it in a large class the child must go to a special school. In such cases a child care assistant might be able to help by carrying out a remedial programme under the class teacher's supervision. This obviously imposes additional responsibility on the class teacher, which should be recognised in her salary. (The administrative implications of integration as regards salary and in-service education are dealt with more fully in Chapter 9.)

In the case of exceptionally difficult children, child care assistants can help simply by providing close supervision. More constructively, they can play an important part in the development of 'nurture groups' (Chapter 7) for seriously deprived and disturbed children in infant schools, and may even be able to assist in implementing a behaviour modification programme (Chapter 8) worked out in discussion with an educational psychologist or advisory teacher.

As the criteria for selection for special education are so vague, there would be obvious difficulties in deciding which schools merited an additional child care assistant to help with their ESN(M) and maladjusted children. We have already seen that the majority remain in ordinary schools, and whether a special school is recommended can depend on such arbitrary criteria as who the child's class teacher happens to be, or which educational psychologist happens to see him. If DES and local education authority policy were to favour the appointment of child care assistants to facilitate the integration of dull or difficult children, the same sort of selection procedures would presumably be needed as at present govern the admission of children to special schools. To cope with problems arising from children leaving their current school, it might be necessary for the CCAs to have a central base similar to that of supply teachers. More important, it would be essential to review their activities in order to ensure that they were capable of supporting the class teacher in a way that could benefit the children concerned without reducing her commitment to the rest of the children in the class. There would be perfectly understandable fears, not only of 'integration on the cheap', but also that the scheme might be used as an argument against reducing class size.

The appointment of additional child care assistants to help class teachers retain ESN(M) or maladjusted children in their classes is probably most appropriate in infant schools, though it may also be helpful in junior schools. Although a number of authorities make this kind of provision for physically handicapped youngsters, few if any have extended the scheme to cover dull and behaviourally disturbed children. This is unfortunate as many infant school head teachers will admit that they could not retain a child in his ordinary class without support from the school's regular CCA.

Type 3 provision in Cope and Anderson's continuum is already available, at least in theory for children receiving remedial teaching in most ordinary schools. Both the organisation and the amount of remedial teaching vary widely from school to school. Generally children are withdrawn from the ordinary lessons for special help with the subject they find difficult, though they are sometimes placed more or less full-time in a class for children with learning difficulties.

Following publication of the Bullock Report (DES, 1976) on reading, many schools have set aside rooms specially equipped for intensive remedial work in reading and writing. Unfortunately the same amount of energy and thought has not concentrated on improving facilities for children with arithmetic difficulties. Anderson (1973) found that few of the physically handicapped children in ordinary schools who needed extra help in this subject were actually receiving it. (The same may, of course, also be true in special schools; the welcome attention to reading and literacy of the last few years should have benefited them as much as ordinary schools, but there has been a corresponding lack of attention to the needs of children with maths difficulties.)

Organising a school's remedial provision on the basis of one or two more or less full-time classes for children with learning difficulties (Type 4 and 5 in Fig. 4.1) suffers from a number of practical and psychological objections. To start with class size is seldom less than fifteen or twenty, so that much of the teaching has to be done in groups, with a consequent reduction in the chances of 'remedying' specific problems. More important, this form of organisation does not differentiate between children who are slow in most areas of development (and certainly in all academic subjects) and children whose difficulty is with one particular subject. For example, Yule *et al.* (1974), have shown that an unexpectedly high number of children of average intelligence have serious reading difficulties, and that they differ in a number of ways from children whose reading backwardness is more predictable on the basis of their intelligence. Socially, too, there are potential difficulties in the full-time remedial class, as children can easily come to regard themselves – and be regarded by their peers – as members of the 'nutters' class'. A frequent, and often justified, comment in special school staffrooms is that special schools can help a child achieve success and acceptance; children can be physically integrated in an ordinary school, yet feel isolated socially. The research evidence reported in the last chapter seems to support this possibility, though it is not clear whether social confidence in a special school may not be bought at the expense of reduced social confidence outside school (Osterling, 1967).

Special classes within ordinary schools for the behaviourally disturbed have developed in the last decade, though to nothing like the same extent as provision for children with learning difficulties. They are described in more detail in Chapter 7. Here we only need to note that they are undoubtedly expanding, though perhaps not in the direction which would be approved by their early advocates; this is because the primary aim is sometimes to control or even deter the children selected to attend them, with less emphasis on their potential therapeutic function. It is possible nevertheless that such classes may achieve as much therapeutically as those claiming an explicitly therapeutic orientation, and also that they may achieve as much in terms of supporting and integrating difficult pupils. That, though, remains a matter for future research.

There are few examples in the UK of day special schools formally linked to ordinary schools (Type 6 provision); the majority of special schools for all categories of handicap fall into Types 7 or 8. This does not necessarily mean that they have no informal links with ordinary schools in their neighbourhood, though it appears rare for these links to extend far beyond arrangements for a successful special school pupil to make a phased return to the ordinary system by means of part-time attendance at the neighbourhood school.

Unfortunately the extent of provision of Types 2 to 5 is not as impressive as may at first sight appear. Although an increasing number of secondary schools are opening so-called 'disruptives units', they are still in a small minority while special groups or classes for the withdrawn child are even less common. In practice, the alternative for 'disturbing' children lies between survival under the pastoral care and disciplinary systems of their ordinary schools (perhaps with psychological or psychiatric support), and a full-time special school which has no regular links with ordinary schools. For dull children the choice is not always a lot better; either they cope in their ordinary class (which may or may not be organised on a mixed ability basis with whatever additional help the school or the authority can offer in terms of withdrawal for remedial teaching) or they must transfer to a full-time special school.

It is true that some authorities have peripatetic remedial teachers, but this sort of service is often provided as an alternative to remedial departments within ordinary schools rather than as an additional form of support. A peripatetic remedial service can have the advantage that the teachers are all experienced and trained in remedial education, in striking contrast to the part-time staff who too often find themselves taking remedial classes in ordinary schools. On the other hand, it is difficult for a peripatetic teacher to be aware of the teaching methods (or personal bias) of all the teachers in the school she visits. Without such knowledge she cannot easily relate her own work to the work the children are doing in their regular classes. An additional difficulty lies in providing follow-up support, while yet a further danger is that the remedial teacher may come to be regarded as the 'expert', so that class teachers feel they no longer have an active responsibility for this side of the child's education.

The last problem can also apply both to attendance at a special class once or twice a week in some centre away from the school, and to full-time (but short-term) centres in schools which admit children for a period of intensive remedial education, in the hope of returning them to their original schools after a short period ranging between two terms and two years at the most. It is a difficulty which can be overcome if the special centre teachers are able and willing to devote enough time to establishing close and informal links with their feeding schools. This could constitute an additional point on the continuum in Fig. 4.1, between Types 5 and 6. However, it is a form of provision which is still not widely available.

Limitations of existing policy and provision

Two trends emerge from this summary of existing facilities for ESN(M) and maladjusted children. First, if *all* the available facilities are considered, we do have the makings of a well-phased continuum of special educational facilities in this country, ranging from survival with no special help in an ordinary class to permanent placement in residential special schools.

Secondly, and less satisfactory, is that the various points on this continuum have developed in an apparently arbitrary, haphazard way with little obvious indication of a coherent philosophy for meeting the needs of exceptionally dull or difficult children. Few authorities can claim that their facilities include every point on the continuum, and fewer still can claim that the continuum operates in a flexible way to enable children to move smoothly from one point to the next as they make progress or their circumstances change. This is not to deny that individual special schools may achieve outstanding results, nor that individual ordinary schools do not achieve a high degree of social integration with some very difficult children (some notable examples are given later in this book). Nevertheless, it remains true that transfer from an ordinary school to a special school is generally a one-way process.

The divide between special schools and extra help in remedial classes (or special groups for problem children) in ordinary schools is further accentuated by an administrative policy which often appears unwilling or unable to offer the same support to handicapped children in ordinary schools as to similar children in special schools. This was one of the more depressing findings in Anderson's (1973) inquiry into physically handicapped children in ordinary classes and also applies in the case of the ESN(M) and maladjusted. Head teachers who are willing and able to retain such children in their schools have to do so without additional resources from the LEA, except what is available in the normal way from the advisory services. Some authorities have given secondary school heads an extra member of staff above their normal establishment in order to start a special group for problem children; this is potentially a welcome move, but may be as much a reaction to political pressure (allied to lack of special school places) as part of an overall strategy for meeting the needs of such pupils without removing them to special schools.

At present handicapped children are retained in ordinary school by virtue of the goodwill and professional expertise of their teachers. Good will is clearly necessary, but is not sufficient without additional facilities of the sort available in the best special schools. The ideal of a continuum of special educational provision for ESN(M) and maladjusted children will not get off the ground until there is greater opportunity for extending the best aspects of special schools (such as smaller classes, more ancillary help, higher capitation allowance for teaching materials and equipment, as well as more experienced and more skilled teachers) into ordinary schools. Ironically, the reluctance of some local education authorities to implement the recommendations in the latest circular from the DES on staffing ratios in special schools (DES, 1975) has meant that some children are in smaller classes in the remedial department of their local comprehensive school than would be the case if they transferred to a special school for ESN(M) children. Admittedly, this can only happen when:

(a) the head of the comprehensive school attaches the same priority to the needs of his dullest and most difficult pupils as to the needs of his sixth-form university candidates (and both the existing capitation allowance and the points system for allocating posts of special responsibility to schools make this extremely difficult) and
(b) the special school's staffing ratio has not progressed far beyond the pre-1975 stage.

It should be clear that we regard existing policy and provision for dull or difficult children as both arbitrary and inflexible. It is arbitrary, as the heads of ordinary schools receive little guidance about the resources of staff and equipment which are needed to cater adequately for these children, and the little guidance they do receive is seldom backed by practical support in terms of additional staff or money. It is inflexible because the movement to special schools for the ESN(M) and maladjusted tends to operate on a one-way system. Tutorial classes and schools for children with learning difficulties go some way towards meeting this objection in some areas, but do not overcome the basic point about the long-term, segregated provision which is still all that is offered by a majority of ESN(M) and maladjusted schools.

Existing policy is also unsatisfactory for parents. Even the most articulate and best informed parents may have considerable difficulty in finding the answers to questions about the quantity and quality of support for their dull or disturbed child in his local school. This is not due to a conspiracy among head teachers or administrators to 'cover-up' what is happening, but to a quite understandable and reasonable reluctance to make value judgements about individual teachers or schools. (Heads also have a responsibility to their colleagues and sometimes have to defend actions in public which they subsequently criticise in the privacy of a meeting with the teacher concerned.) When a parent does feel that his child is being catered for inadequately in his local school he may have difficulty in securing a transfer to another school as head teachers are reluctant – again quite reasonably – to accept problems from outside their own catchment area.

In theory an LEA has powers under the 1944 Education Act to enforce a child's attendance at a special school against the parents' wishes. In practice this seldom happens, and a parent has to choose between accepting the offer of a special school place and insisting that his child remains in a situation in which he has already been failing for some time. Parents are not always made aware, however, that acceptance of a special school place is generally an irrevocable step, since many ordinary schools are unwilling to admit a child from a special ESN(M) or maladjusted school unless he has made unusual progress.

Levels of integration

Discussion so far in this chapter has concentrated on problems arising from the present policy (or lack of one) on provision for ESN(M) and maladjusted children. We now need to look more critically at what we mean by integration, and how far it is a practical possibility for these pupils.

The Warnock Report (DES, 1978) distinguishes between locational integration, social integration and functional integration. Taking these in order, locational integration refers to self-contained special units in ordinary schools, or situations where ordinary and special schools share the same site. It does not necessarily imply sharing of facilities, even at different times, nor does it imply any social mixing between the pupils. Although this is perhaps the first step on the ladder towards a fuller, more genuine form of integration its significance for parents – and indeed the children themselves – should not be underestimated.

Social integration refers to examples of handicapped and ordinary children sharing the school's facilities. Obvious examples are the dining room, playground and assembly hall, though in larger schools other facilities, such as those for PE and swimming may also be shared. The Warnock Report notes that 'even for children with profound learning difficulties, the friendship and society of other children can effectively stimulate personal development'.

Finally, the fullest form of integration, functional integration, occurs when handicapped children share educational programmes with ordinary pupils. This can only occur when locational and social integration have already been achieved. Naturally, it makes more demands on school staff.

Although formulated primarily with children suffering from the medical handicaps in mind, this three-part distinction also applies to the ESN(M) and maladjusted. As we have seen, the majority of pupils who might legitimately be described with either of these labels remain in ordinary schools, where they provide examples of functional integration at work. How successful this is clearly varies from school to school, depending on the quality of teaching for duller and more difficult pupils. As we shall see in Chapter 7, some secondary schools have set up special groups for troublesome pupils, in some of which the children are consciously kept separate from their peers in the rest of the school. It is ironic that the only examples of locational integration for 'maladjusted' children appear to be where: (*a*) the pupils have never formally been labelled maladjusted, and (*b*) the facility is intended to separate them from their peers, albeit temporarily, rather than to integrate them.

As described above, locational integration, social integration and functional integration are primarily administrative terms. We have already noted that a handicapped child may on the surface be fully integrated within an ordinary class in an ordinary school, yet feel socially isolated because he is not accepted by other children. It might be worth distinguishing here between educational integration, in which the child is taught in an ordinary class, and the level of functional integration. The first level, as described above, is achieved by means of an administrative decision that handicapped children share work or play facilities with, and at the same time as, ordinary children. The second level is one which cannot be achieved by administrative decision alone, and relates to whether they actually work and mix with their non-handicapped peers in a cooperative way. To some extent this must depend on the social relationship within the school, but whether or not social integration takes place at the level of friendship between the handicapped is a matter for research. The available evidence (Anderson, 1973; Cope and Anderson, 1977) suggests that genuine social mixing does occur.

It is possible that here, as in so many other ways, ESN(M) and maladjusted children differ from the other categories of handicap. A characteristic of the maladjusted is that they do not easily form consistent friendships, while the ESN(M) are often thought to need removal as much because of their unhappiness and embarrassment at their lack of progress, as because of their lack of progress on its own. It can be argued just as validly though that the social isolation experienced by many dull and disturbing children in ordinary schools results from the schools' inability in the present circumstances to adjust to their pupils' needs. With additional facilities they might be able to do so.

Normalisation

The principle

Development of services for the handicapped within a country can be thought of as passing through four main stages, aiming towards 'normalisation'. First, there is the diagnostic stage in which specific handicaps are diagnosed and treatment plans formulated to meet them. Historically this started more or less simultaneously with the introduction of free and compulsory education in the UK. However, it is possible that the progress of industrialisation and urbanisation in the nineteenth century, with the concomitant reduction of small caring communities providing for their own handicapped people, contributed to the second stage. This is specialisation, in which particular needs are met with specific solutions. Thus certain forms of care and (possibly) education were thought to be appropriate for the mentally handicapped, while special teaching methods were needed to educate deaf children. The process of specialisation led to many services becoming centralised in large, purpose-built institutions, often in the middle of the countryside. As more institutions were built, so the number of professional bodies responsible for them proliferated. It is interesting to note that the same process has happened in the field of special education since 1944 as had happened in the health services in the previous seventy-five years (and has continued since). Just as medical and para-medical specialisation led to vastly increased and more complex services for the mentally ill and mentally or physically handicapped, each with its own professional training, professional association and restrictive practices, so the increase in special schools since 1944 has been matched by a similar increase in the number of professional associations looking after the interests of handicapped children. Teachers of maladjusted children, for example, have to decide whether to join the Association for Therapeutic Education or the Association for Workers with Maladjusted Children (or both) in addition to one of the recognised teachers' unions.

An argument in favour of separate special schools, as of the large purpose-built hospitals of the last century, is that they allegedly offer a specialised service and protect handicapped children from the embarrassment and failure involved in attending an ordinary school. Less often voiced, but often suspected, is the feeling that this protective function can operate two ways; not only do the handicapped get support and protection from society, but society is shielded and protected from the handicapped. The presence of handicapped people is a threat to our own ideas about normality, arousing in all of us feelings of guilt and insecurity which we would often prefer not to face. If handicapped children are educated separately, it is easy for teachers, children and ultimately the wider community to rest content in the belief that 'they' are doing whatever is needed; as *they* have accepted responsibility *we* need not worry ourselves about them. A penetratingly honest example of this attitude was given by an ordinary school teacher describing his anxiety before taking his class on a visit to the local blind school: What would the blind children be like? How should he talk to them? How would his own pupils get on with them?

Recognition of this and other problems associated with separate provision for the handicapped led to the third stage in the development of services for the handicapped, namely differentiation. As the handicapped do not slot neatly into administrative categories, it follows that they differ in their needs, so that services must be based on needs instead of being standardised on the basis of a particular service for all clients in a given category. A range of services is required, each one accessible to all clients who need it. Thus children with learning difficulties are found in all the recognised categories of handicap; placing an asthmatic child of average intelligence in a school for the delicate can only be appropriate if the school is able to provide a curriculum which is sensitive to his educational retardation.

How is the principle of differentiation equated with a policy of integration? At some stage in our lives all of us will need specialised help, if only at the level of seeking medical advice when we are ill with 'flu or have a minor accident. The principle of differentiation merely implies that different children have different needs, and that services should be adapted to cater for them. However, there is an essential distinction between catering for an individual's special educational needs and providing him with a special environment which seeks to cater for all his educational needs. The former discriminates between ordinary needs and special needs, while the latter focuses exclusively on special needs and deprives the child of a normal existence in those aspects of his life which do not require special attention.

The principle of differentiation leads logically to the most recent stage in the development of services for the handicapped. This is the principle of normalisation which occurs when medical, educational and support services are decentralised and integrated with those similar services which non-handicapped people receive from the community. In other words the handicapped no longer have to travel – often considerable distances – to receive special care, education or training away from home: the services are brought into the community. In an educational context this clearly makes major demands on the various support services which have hitherto been concentrated in special schools, but has the potential advantage of making the skills of personnel in these services available to more teachers and children than is possible when they concentrate on the (elitist?) minority in special schools.

Implications of the principle

It is worth comparing the principle of normalisation described here with the 'normal child model' set out by Luke Watson (1973), one of the leading American exponents of behaviour modification principles with mentally handicapped children. Watson's work is based on the assumption that educational and therapeutic programmes should aim at a gradual approximation to what a normal child of the same age would be able to do. By definition, mentally handicapped children of school age will require special educational help, yet it does not necessarily follow that they will also need specific training in the basic self-help skills such as toileting or dressing themselves. Similarly, by no means *all* display behaviour problems which create embarrassment to adults or other children in the family, and many have valued social relationships with other children in their neighbourhood; their play is less creative and less varied, yet they can still play happily with other children. If a handicapped child is deficient in any of the skills required by a normal child, Watson's team produces a detailed programme designed to help his parents or nurses teach him this skill. The programme starts at the level of development at which the child is now, and gradually becomes more complex as it works towards 'a normal child model'. Just as a legless child becomes more competent with his artificial limbs, though he can never become as competent as an ordinary child, so the mentally handicapped can acquire the basic social skills expected of ordinary children even though they will never master tasks which require more complex reasoning skills. To take a simple example, a mentally handicapped ten-year-old is handicapped by his lack of reading ability, but not nearly so handicapped as he would be if he was not toilet-trained and showed the bizarre, self-mutilating, stereotyped behaviours so often seen in the unstimulated back wards of the worst mental subnormality hospitals.

Watson's work was mainly with children whom we would regard as ESN(S) and maladjusted. Some of this work is described in Chapter 8. More important for this chapter are the implications for the supply of special educational treatment. If the aims of education and of intervention by doctors or psychologists are to help the child become as 'normal' as possible, it can easily be argued that he may need some sheltered provision in order to achieve his full potential. In other words, separate special schools may be necessary *as a means to an end,* even though they can never (under the normalisation principle) provide a satisfactory long-term educational alternative to an ordinary school. Unfortunately, the principle could be used as a loop-hole to secure long-term segregation through the back door. Recognising the danger is perhaps the best way to prevent it.

That a few separate special schools may be needed for intensive short-term investigation and treatment can be seen, ironically, from an analogy with the model of medical illness which we have been criticising elsewhere in the book. Most patients are treated at home; some enter hospital and some require an Intensive Care Unit in which there is a high concentration of medical skill and technical facilities. Similarly, most handicapped children can – and should – be educated in their ordinary schools, some will require special units or special classes, and some will require the more intensive treatment, combined with greater expertise, at a separate special school. However, there should no more be an expectation that children will remain long-term in a special class or special school than that they will remain indefinitely in an ordinary hospital bed or in intensive care.

This medical analogy is in fact unduly generous to the medical profession which has itself been accused of misusing resources by keeping patients in hospital unnecessarily. All the same, it holds good in the sense that some children may require a higher concentration of resources than is likely to be possible in most units attached to ordinary schools, or even, if it comes to the point, in most special schools at the moment. Educational psychologists, for example, are still scattered so thinly between special and ordinary schools that it is difficult to see how they can make the central contribution to assessment and intensive educational treatment which their training and salaries suggest they should be making. One wonders whether intensive work in one or two special schools, working with teachers to develop programmes to enable the child to progress from the special school to the next stage on the special education continuum, might be a better use of their skills than their present diffuse coverage.

This argument in support of separate special schools contrasts starkly with the commoner ones about their protective function for handicapped children. It envisages them as having an important place in a special education system, but insists that their function is remedial, rather than custodial in the sense of providing a long-term alternative education. They would be remedial in the sense that they would exist to teach children the necessary social and (in the broadest sense) educational skills which are needed to function successfully at a less specialised, less intensive, and physically more integrated point on a continuum of special educational provision. If valid, it implies that educationalists should regard integration as a desirable outcome rather than as an alternative way of educating handicapped children. To put the argument on a more concrete level, teachers who believe that integrated education *per se* constitutes the best provision, might wish to place a withdrawn girl with a severe facial deformity and speech defect following an accident in an ordinary class and ensure that she receives appropriate encouragement and support within this setting. In contrast, those who believe (equally passionately) that integration is a desirable and necessary outcome might wish to use a short spell in a separate, protective special school to build up her confidence and improve her speech prior to return to the ordinary class.

The distinction presented here has policy implications which go beyond a decision on whether:

(a) special schools, classes or units are desirable as a means to an end (rather than as an end in themselves, as implied by arguments stressing their protective nature),
(b) they should be phased out as far as possible in favour of a policy for supporting all children with special needs in ordinary classes.

Concentrating the controversy on schools and education (in other words the suggestion that integration is a more satisfactory way of educating handicapped children, rather than a desirable outcome) has the unfortunate effect of diverting attention from the medical and social services. Since these services are just as involved in the welfare of the handicapped as the education service, this can only be unfortunate.

The philosophy and practice of special education should itself be integrated into a broader philosophy for the care of the handicapped or less fortunate members of society. The principles of differentiation and normalisation described above have obvious implications both for educational policy and also for that of the medical and social services. This is particularly evident in the case of the ESN(M) and maladjusted who seldom show the acute medical symptoms which can only be treated in a highly specialised setting. As we shall argue later (Chapters 7–8) the traditional child guidance and psychiatric services are seldom appropriate for children whose problems result from an interaction between family and environmental stresses. The development of community based social services and health centres is more consistent with the principle of normalisation than the traditionally more remote services. As social workers have discovered throughout the years since the Seebohm Report (Department of Health and Social Security, 1968) recommended a generic service, there is a world of difference between a generic social worker and a generic *team* containing specialists in different fields. Applying the normalisation principle successfully requires that teachers, medical personnel and social workers cooperate in formulating a programme to meet special needs which arise at school, at home or in the community.

Chapter 5

Innovations in Scandinavia

Introduction

In the last chapter we looked at some of the thinking behind the move towards integrating handicapped children in ordinary schools. Work carried out in the Scandinavian countries of Denmark, Norway and Sweden has had an important influence in this. As we saw, there is some disagreement as to whether integration is desirable in its own right, or whether it should be regarded as secondary to the primary aim of 'normalisation' (Wessman, 1976). Discussion and controversy about special education has undoubtedly been more lively in Scandinavia than elsewhere in Europe. These are still the countries which educationalists are most likely to visit when they wish to see integration in practice (Haskell and Paull, 1975; Anderson, 1971). They were also visited by members of the Warnock Committee (DES, 1978).

How far it is in fact possible to see integration in practice in the Scandinavian countries is of considerable interest to a country such as the United Kingdom which has recently passed legislation which may accelerate the movement away from traditional separate special schools. This chapter will examine some of the recent developments in the education of handicapped children in the Scandinavian countries. These countries share many of the educational issues that we face. For example, they have had to review the established secondary school system, to expand nursery education as the number of working mothers increases; to consider the effect of large-scale unemployment of school leavers on their needs and attitudes in the final compulsory school years; and to adapt special educational facilities as the political and social climate of opinion moves in favour of integrating handicapped children. The solutions which are being discussed or adopted in Denmark, Sweden and Norway may influence the way similar problems are tackled in Great Britain. It is important first to examine the general education system in Scandinavia.

The Nordic Council was created in 1972 to foster cultural cooperation between its five members countries: Denmark, Finland, Sweden, Norway and Iceland. It has done a good deal to spread information about, and to harmonise, their educational systems.

The compulsory schools in Scandinavia are administered by local authorities which have much less power than English LEAs, and are also much smaller – generally catering for a population of 10,000 to 30,000 people. In Norway, Sweden and Denmark, compulsory schooling begins at seven and ends at sixteen. Scandinavian schools are usually small by our standards – Norwegian law restricts new schools to a maximum of 450 pupils; Danish to around 800.

Denmark's schools are generally all-through from seven to sixteen, whereas Swedish and Norwegian children usually change school at the age of thirteen (Brickman, 1967). In Denmark and Norway the prevailing belief is that small schools are better at pastoral care and social education, and foster better personal relations. The comprehensive school system in the Scandinavian countries is considerably older than that in England. Sweden introduced comprehensive schooling in 1950, Denmark in 1958 and Norway in 1959. Classes are mainly unstreamed, although option choices in the later years lead to some selective groupings; the authorities appear keen to avoid early specialisation because of restriction on later career choice. At the age of sixteen a high percentage of pupils go on to upper secondary schools where they can choose to follow more specialised courses of study. In 1975 80 per cent of children in Oslo stayed on beyond compulsory school age, 40 per cent in Sweden.

Organisation within comprehensive schools differs in several respects from that of Great Britain. Class sizes are smaller than those in England; the maximum size in Denmark is twenty-eight; in Norway, thirty. The teacher–pupil ratio is lower during the early years in contrast to our own system. For example, Swedish classes have a maximum size of twenty pupils at Grade 1 (7 years) increasing to thirty pupils in Grades 4–9 (11–16 years). In Sweden strict curriculum guidelines are laid down by the Board of Education, which detail subjects to be taught, time allocation per subject, and syllabi covered. Denmark and Norway have curriculum 'guidelines' which are less detailed than those in Sweden (National Swedish Board of Education, 1975). Nonetheless, all pupils in the ordinary comprehensive system are expected to fit into the model laid down by central government.

Schools in the Scandinavian countries place a more explicit emphasis on social education and pastoral care than is often the case in England. Class teachers in Denmark generally continue with their class from Grade 1 to Grade 6 (7–13 years), during which time they may teach that class for most of their weekly timetable. Swedish schools have social care committees. Psychological support services tend to be better staffed than in England; the psychologist–pupil ratio in Sweden varies from 1:6,000 down to 1:1,500, compared with an average ratio of 1:10,000 in England.

Most teachers working in comprehensive schools have taken a four-year teacher training course. Those working in upper secondary schools must have a university degree and a post-graduate teaching certificate. Most teachers in the early grades (1–6) are trained to be generalists (that is, to teach most subjects in the curriculum, rather than become subject specialists).

The organisation of special education in Scandinavia varies from country to country, the Swedish and Danish systems being the most similar (Jorgensen, 1973). In Sweden and Denmark the mentally handicapped are divided into two groups. The more severely mentally and physically handicapped, roughly equivalent to our ESN(S) children, are catered for by the Ministry of Social Welfare in Denmark. At present the Ministry of Education caters for children with milder handicaps – for example ESN(M) children. Sweden has a similar pattern, but the Board for Provision and Services for the Mentally Retarded usually caters for *all* mentally retarded children, who in England would normally be within the special school system (Grunewald, 1974). This division of responsibility between two ministries is similar to that which existed in

England until the 1970 Education Act when the severely mentally handicapped were still the responsibility of the health authorities. Both countries are hoping to end this division in the near future.

In Norway, the church appears to retain a great deal of influence over the provision of special and ordinary education. The responsible government Ministry is that of Church and Education, and compulsory religious instruction is strictly observed as part of the school curriculum.

It is interesting to look at the thinking behind the recent government policies towards integration in Scandinavia. In Norway, integration appears to be regarded as a good aim *per se,* whereas in Sweden, and lately in Denmark (see Chapter 4) normalisation is regarded as the aim in the provision of educational and social facilities for the handicapped person, and integration is merely one means of achieving that aim.

Norway

Norwegian legislation in January 1976 required that handicapped children should, as far as possible, be sent to a school within their local area, taking into account the sparse population and large area of the country. This may mean that many handicapped children outside Oslo should attend their local comprehensive schools. A great deal of discussion is taking place about the precise interpretation and implications of this Act, both in the authorities themselves and in the teachers' unions.

In Norway, possibly because the overall ideal of integration is seen as a good thing in itself, the main emphasis recently has been on the individual integration of a handicapped pupil within an ordinary class of his local school. Financial provision is naturally likely to influence the extent to which the 1976 Act is implemented. As we shall see in Chapter 9 this will also apply in England, with respect to the implementation of Section 10 of the 1976 Education Act.

The Norwegian authorities are attempting to modify policy within their special schools in line with new government thinking on this issue; for example, as a preliminary measure, some special schools are beginning to appoint teachers for liaison work between the special school and the ordinary school to which a pupil returns. Hang School, near Oslo, has a special teacher whose brief includes supporting pupils returning to the ordinary school system. In the last two years, however, only eleven pupils have transferred from this ESN(M) school back to their local school but none had needed to return to Hang because of difficulties encountered. The aim is to increase the number of children attending Hang for a shorter period of time, and smooth the passage back into ordinary school with the aid of the liaison teacher. She may offer regular sessions working with the class teacher in the ordinary school for a few weeks, then gradually decrease her involvement over a period of perhaps two years. It is likely that the number of appointments to specific posts of this kind within special schools will increase in Norway over the next few years.

At present the annual sum of money given to any school for the allocation of staffing and expenditure (called the capitation allowance) includes a percentage specifically provided for pupils who have special needs. In the first six years of school this sum is calculated by adding around 20 per cent teaching hours per week to the basic allowance in order to provide facilities for teaching in small groups for pupils who may be slow learners, have difficulties with reading or writing or number, or who show emotional or behavioural problems. These teaching hours are specifically allotted to schools for this purpose, and so may not be given over to other teaching needs in that school. This allowance is provided routinely, though the exact amount is up to the local school board, which takes account of factors such as the catchment area.

In addition, individual handicapped pupils may have extra hours of teaching allocated for their own needs. If a comprehensive school has a mentally retarded child who is taxing the school's usual teaching resources, then the head can claim extra teaching hours for that one child. This must be claimed annually from the local director of education, and be supported by the school psychologist. The teachers' unions are negotiating to increase this national fund, arguing that the total sum at present available is inadequate to meet the increasing number of claims being lodged. Some teachers complain about their claim being rejected, with the explanation that a particular child's need should be met out of the school's normal capitation money. Many teachers feel that having to make an annual claim adds an element of insecurity to the school placement of a child, and that, once allocated, the allowance should continue automatically until the child leaves school. These points are naturally arousing controversy, as local administrators and teachers begin to discuss the New Education Act and its financial implications.

Sweden

In contrast, Sweden has more special classes within ordinary schools (Stenholm, 1975). This may well be due to the compulsory curriculum guidelines which make it difficult for a pupil to fit into one of the ordinary classes; teachers in special classes usually follow a special curriculum model (National Board of Education, 1975). Another factor may be that social integration of individual pupils with their non-handicapped peers is not so highly valued as an end in itself (Wessman, 1976). In Sweden and Denmark it would be fair to say that if, in certain circumstances, a segregated form of education could in the long run lead to a greater degree of normalisation, then this might well be a necessary interim step (Bank-Mikkelson, 1974). In Sweden the Board for Provision and Services to the Mentally Retarded often provides special classes by negotiating the use of rooms within a local school. Sometimes this means renting classrooms in Ministry of Education schools with declining pupil numbers. New buildings are now being planned jointly between the two authorities responsibile for education, each contributing a proportion of the capital cost. Running costs for such a unit are paid by the local authority, but the Board for the Mentally Retarded pay for extra resources such as equipment and teaching over and above those given to an ordinary child.

Arrangements about the daily administration of the unit, are usually made with the head of the comprehensive school, who is responsible for the care of the buildings, for caretaking and school meals. Extra space can be negotiated in the school hall, gymnasium and craft rooms, which can be used by handicapped as well as non-handicapped pupils. In addition, some allowance is made for teaching time given to the unit from the staff of the comprehensives; some craft and music teachers for instance, may teach small groups of the mentally retarded as part of their normal timetable.

The teaching staff in these units are employed directly by the Board for the Mentally Retarded. There may be a teacher in charge of the unit, with several assistants working with him. He will be responsible to an administrative headmaster employed by the Board, who is in charge of a wide variety of 'units' and special schools within one geographical area. This headmaster has a psychologist and social worker who advise him on the admission and discharge of mentally retarded children to the units and schools in his area. He may also run in-service training courses for teachers and advise on the policy towards the mentally retarded.

This type of organisation also allows a flexible career structure for teachers working within the field of mental retardation, though it does not facilitate transfer between the 'special' branch of the teaching profession and the mainstream. In Sweden a newly trained teacher takes up employment as an assistant teacher in a unit or special school, and may, after a few years' experience apply for promotion to a variety of deputy headship and headship jobs within units and special schools. The top post within an area is that of the headmaster responsible for all types of provision.

This system does, however, have several disadvantages. The administrative division of responsibility for education between the local school board and the regional Board for the Mentally Retarded is generally agreed to be less satisfactory than the single administrative body we have in England. It is also easier for the Board to rent classrooms in comprehensive schools in areas where the school population is declining than where it is increasing. Thus, the siting of provision may be less dependent on the needs of the children in that area than on where classrooms become vacant in schools. Similarly the appointment of teaching staff by the Board often seems to lead to a 'staff-within-a-staff' being created in the comprehensive school, each with its own separate responsibilities, group support system and sometimes staffroom. There often seems to be little functional integration in classroom work; the amount of social integration varies from school to school and from child to child.

The problem of providing equipment for the rarer, more severe handicaps, has been facilitated by setting up resource centres which are sometimes attached to special schools. These are staffed by resident teachers who will demonstrate the aids and equipment to teachers on in-service training courses; they also have peripatetic staff who are able to loan this equipment to the ordinary school. In a country as large as Sweden, however, there are great problems of distribution of this specialised equipment, problems which resource centres can only go some way towards meeting.

It may be helpful at this point to give a detailed account of one Swedish school where this type of integration operates. Maltesholmsskolan in Vallingby is an ordinary comprehensive school of 350 children aged from seven to sixteen years. In 1975 it had six special classes for 35 ESN(M) children and one class for ESN(S) children attached to it. These classes were financed separately by the Board for Provision and Services to the Mentally Retarded; the five teaching staff and one speech therapist were employed directly by this Board.

The ESN(M) children were divided into six classes according to age. All ESN(S) children were aged fourteen and above, as this class was being phased out of the school as a matter of policy. In future, it will be rare for ESN(M) and ESN(S) classes or units in Sweden to be attached to the same school. This change of policy appeared to be because of the identification of ESN(M) children with their more handicapped contemporaries by ordinary children in the school. The Swedish authorities believe that the stigma attached to being mentally retarded is increased where the two groups are brought together, a point which has also been noted in a different context in England (Burden, 1977).

All special-class children remained in their own class for lessons, as there was no functional or work integration with the non-handicapped. Woodwork, metalwork, PT and music lessons were taught by a teacher from the ordinary school staff. Some social occasions involved special and ordinary class children joining together – for example, film shows and assemblies, though these are comparatively rare events in daily school life. The children shared the same playground at breaks and the amount of social mixing varied greatly from child to child. Staff were of the opinion that most special class children stayed within their own groups for friendship, and this is hardly surprising in view of the lack of daily contact between handicapped and non-handicapped.

Children in the special classes followed the 1975 curriculum for the Mentally Retarded, with some modification to fit the needs of the individual child. Few children transferred from the special class to ordinary class, mainly, it appeared, due to the difficulties of having to follow the ordinary curriculum when they left the special class.

Staff employed by the Board for Provision and Services to the Mentally Retarded saw themselves as a special school sharing the same building as a comprehensive school. Thus, there was a separate staffroom for special class teachers and appeared to be little mixing between ordinary and special class staff. Nor were there links with the remedial staff in the ordinary school. The impression was of a special school sharing the same facilities as an ordinary school.

This type of provision for the mentally retarded also applies at the pre-school level (i.e. before the age of seven). In Vattmyra pre-school and day-care centre in the suburbs of Stockholm the Board for Provision and Services to the Mentally Retarded rented a classroom for handicapped children. Here again, special class staff were employed by the Board, whereas other child care staff were employed by the Ministry responsible for pre-school provision in Sweden, the Ministry of Social Welfare. Vattmyra was a nursery and day care centre catering for eighty children from one and a half to seven years of age, between the hours of 6.30 a.m. and 6.30 p.m. The accent throughout the Centre was on play, rather than formal activities, such as early reading and number activities. This division of role is general policy in Sweden. The mentally handicapped children attended three hours a day in a special class attached to the ordinary centre. Four children in the morning and four in the afternoon were taught by one teacher and one nursery nurse. The teacher was not specially trained for this work, but had previous experience and intended to take a further specialised course in the near future. More social and functional integration appeared to take place here than in the comprehensive school, and the staff were discussing ways of extending this further by handicapped children joining ordinary groups at certain times during the day, or vice versa.

From the administrative point of view the facilities were financed separately and it was extremely difficult to move a child from a special into an ordinary group. This was because a mentally handicapped child was classed as two ordinary children for nursery numbers, and as the system operates at present this change would cause administrative and financial difficulties. Hence, integration within the Centre depended largely on staff initiative.

Denmark

In Denmark, there are many special classes attached to ordinary schools, although present policy of the Board of Education appears to move away from this form of integration, towards withdrawal group work (Jorgensen, 1976). Thus, in 1972, 3,501 pupils were in special classes for reading (0.5 per cent of school population). In 1975 this had decreased to 2,416 (0.35 per cent). Similarly in full-time classes for retarded pupils, numbers dropped slightly from 1.5 per cent in 1972 to 1.4 per cent in 1975. This move has been encouraged, particularly for children with emotional or behaviour problems, as the Danish inspectorate were concerned at the growth in numbers of 'sin-bin' units for these children in the ordinary schools (Jorgensen, 1975).

This has resulted in an increase in different forms of special help in the comprehensive school. Between 1969 and 1972 the number of teacher hours for handicapped children other than those in special classes increased by over 50 per cent to more than 61,000. One form of additional help which avoids the use of special units is auxiliary teaching, in which the child's ordinary class teacher is released to teach him individually for up to two hours a week. A second is that of 'clinic teaching', in which a group of up to six pupils is withdrawn from ordinary lessons to be given special tuition, usually by the school's remedial teacher. Auxiliary, clinic and special class teaching are funded in a similar way to comparable provision in Norway. The Danish Ministry of Education has laid down a formula for assessing the number of teaching hours to be allocated for providing children with special help. One extra lesson per week is allowed for every ten pupils in Grades 1–3; and one extra lesson per week for every twenty pupils in Grades 4–9 of the school. The school psychologist in consultation with the headmaster may supervise the actual allocation of this money to specific types of help in any school.

The role of the school psychologist in Denmark is interesting. A local authority with about 5,000 children may have a principal and two assistant psychologists, a social worker, a clinical psychologist and various part-time advisers for special education; thus one psychologist may work in only two schools, and he can therefore be intimately involved in planning suitable work for children with special needs in the schools he covers. Many psychologists see their main role as working with the child's class or remedial teacher. As children from special schools are increasingly transferring to the ordinary comprehensive school system, the psychologist is becoming a necessary link between the school and outside services.

Danish educational psychologists are certificated teachers who later go on to take a further qualification in psychology. Thus the Danish educational psychology service differs markedly from its English equivalent, both in training of staff and number of children covered by each psychologist.

Turning to the more severely handicapped, Denmark has developed a system of regional special education centres, attached to one or more ordinary schools in any one area. These cater for children with more severe vision and hearing deficiencies, the speech impaired, and those requiring intensive psychiatric treatment. Some centres have a Monday to Friday boarding hostel near them for children who live too far away to travel daily by taxi. Thirteen such special education centres have opened in Denmark, each with slightly different policies and teaching methods. Some cater for only two or three of the more severe forms of handicap, and have part- and full-time classes attached to several comprehensive schools. Children who attend the centre may go into a special class full-time at first, in order to settle in, or to receive intensive help in some particular skill. Gradually the child may begin to spend time in ordinary classes, with the aim of increasing to full-time ordinary class attendance, by which point he is transferred back to his local comprehensive school. This flexibility has the advantage of allowing the needs of the child to determine the amount of segregated teaching he receives, yet preserves some centralisation of the specialised resources and teachers for the more severely handicapped.

The Ringsted Special Education Centre is one of thirteen such centres under the Ministry of Education. It is based in two comprehensive schools, Valdemarskolan and Parkskolan. The former has twelve classes with twenty-two speech handicapped children distributed between five classes, and thirty-four physically handicapped children between seven classes. It also has nine pupils individually integrated into the comprehensive school. By contrast, Parkskolan caters mainly for the hearing handicapped, with eight classes of five children, plus twelve children individually integrated (Chisholm, 1977b).

Pupils are grouped in special classes primarily according to their medical label, but this policy has not been followed strictly, as other factors often appear to be more important from the teaching standpoint. In the main though, Valdemarskolan offers therapy for the physically handicapped, while Parkskolan offers technical aids for hearing-impaired children.

The special classes in Parkskolan were placed alongside ordinary classes as this was a new school. Valdemarskolan, on the other hand, had older buildings, so the special classes were housed in an annexe behind the school. This physical separation of classes at Valdemarskolan limits contact between children in special classes and those in ordinary classes. In contrast, at Parkskolan, contact is facilitated because the special classes are part of a partitioned open area. These facilities appeared to affect, to some extent, the degreee to which children could be individually integrated into ordinary classes in each school.

The aim in all the centres is to move children gradually from the special classes into ordinary lessons, and then transfer them back to their local school. About half of the pupils are sent back to their local school after two years in the centre, and only a small minority are said to go through their whole educational career in the centre. Children who return to their local school are supported there by peripatetic staff attached to the centre.

Implications of developments in Scandinavia

We can see from this summary of certain trends in special education in Scandinavia that the popular myth of full integration of handicapped children into the ordinary class is far from being achieved. Special schools exist in

Norway, Sweden and Denmark, and the numbers of pupils within them are only declining gradually. In Denmark special classes or units for mentally retarded or emotionally disturbed children are being phased out, but again as a result of a gradual change over a period of years. In contrast, Sweden encourages special classes for the mentally retarded attached to ordinary schools, and this frequently leads to little social, or functional integration of the retarded with their non-handicapped peers.

A number of problems remain to be tackled in each of the three countries. Norway, for example, must work out with the local education authorities and the teachers' unions the judicial implications of the 1976 Act. At present many teachers feel that money allocated to individually integrated handicapped children is not large enough. In addition, the local education authorities are faced with a curious anomaly. If a child attends a special school or full-time special class, then the cost of his education is supported directly by the state; the local authority pays only the cost of educating an ordinary child, the remainder being make up by the Department of Education in Oslo. In contrast, when a child is individually integrated into an ordinary class, or given withdrawal group help, then the local authority will at present shoulder the full cost. Thus it would appear to be in the local authority's interest at present to encourage the setting up of special classes for handicapped children or to send a child to a full-time special school, rather than attempt to meet his needs by providing extra support within an ordinary class. Local authorities themselves appear to be increasingly aware of this danger, which in fact militates against the implementation of the 1976 Act, and are hoping to negotiate with the Ministry of Education to solve this financial dilemma (Goodwin, 1977).

Similarly teachers' unions are well aware of the danger of implementing the spirit of the 1976 Act without providing adequate financial resources to back it up. Thus it seems likely that the special funds will be increased several-fold over the next few years to cater for the increased demand. One interesting point worth noting is that the existence of this sum of money, despite its many drawbacks, does have one major advantage, namely that the school and psychologist normally apply for it and are thus highly motivated towards making the arrangements work for the child.

Sweden's educators must face the dilemma of how far their centralised school organisation, teaching arrangements and curriculum guidelines are in fact discouraging a trend towards integration which they are hoping to encourage. As described above, the classes for mentally retarded pupils attached to Maltesholmsskolan in Vallingby faced precisely this problem. A child who moved from a special class to an ordinary class, from which he was given remedial help in small groups, had to follow the ordinary school curriculum. Thus there was little evidence of such moves, and little discussion either within the Board for the Mentally Retarded or the Ministry of Education to see whether such movement could be increased.

Other factors within the Swedish education system are more likely to favour successful integration of individual pupils. Examples are the attention given to pastoral care and social education in the comprehensive school, and the class teacher system which aims for one teacher to take his class of children for a large part of each week over a period of some years. Another example of special relevance to ESN(M) and maladjusted children is the emphasis placed on preventative work in the earliest school years, when the pupil–teacher ratio is at its lowest, and in some schools two teachers are attached to the reception class. All these factors would be expected to facilitate a retarded child's integration into the school.

The Scandinavian countries' geography is another factor needing to be considered. The mass of the country, and the ensuing difficulty in communications means that some children in the north of Norway and Sweden may have to travel several hundreds of miles to reach a special school. These travelling distances have led parents into considering other forms of education for their handicapped children, and parents' organisations in their turn have placed pressure on the governments.

In the last few years parents of handicapped children in Scandinavia, even more than in the United Kingdom, have been starting to recognise and exploit their potential influence on government policy. The Parents' Association in Denmark, formed as a charity organisation in the 1960s, has begun to turn into a pressure group attempting to exert political influence on government policies. Many of its members at present are professional people, some of whom have access to the media which they appear to use to the full.

In Sweden, one parents' organisation has sponsored a research centre in Stockholm to look into the problems of the mentally retarded. One aim of this body is to promote action research, and it is at present attempting an evaluation of various types of integrated living arrangements for retarded people. This organisation has outlined the problems of the mentally handicapped to the general public on TV and radio. One aspect they have particularly emphasised is the need to promote integration in home, work and school, and to advertise the problems created by institutionalised forms of care. Some of the professional parents have links with members of the Rikstag, the Swedish parliament, and are attempting to influence the major political parties towards a policy of normalisation for the handicapped.

Many major parties in all three countries support normalisation as an aim; little dissent on the philosophical level is apparent, perhaps testifying to the success of the parents' pressure groups. This policy also appears to be widely accepted in the higher levels of administration in the Departments of Education and Social Services. In Sweden and Denmark, it was the Directors of Social Services who initially started the thinking on normalisation, and these ideas gradually spread to the Education Services. The pressure for change in policy therefore appears to be largely political, stemming from parents of the handicapped. After gaining political credibility, the ideas on normalisation have become translated practically into normalising the home and living conditions of the handicapped, and have recently begun to extend into thinking about their educational needs.

Chapter 6

Innovations for ESN(M) children in the English education system

Introduction

A number of experiments have taken place in the British state education system over the last few years which aim to provide a more 'normal' form of education for ESN children. Within the current special school framework, it is possible to aim at 'normalisation' (Chapter 5) in a number of different ways. One is to accept children on a short-term basis for intensive help in certain skills; another is to offer an advisory or resources service to local schools; yet another is to accept children part-time, and to work with their ordinary school's teachers towards a full-time return to ordinary classes. Similarly, a variety of approaches is possible within the ordinary school. One school, for instance, may set up a special unit for ESN(M) children; another may operate a withdrawal group system for children with learning difficulties, while another may concentrate on giving class teachers additional facilities and practical support to cater more adequately for slow-learning children in their own classes. This chapter will describe some of these innovations. We should say at the outset that they are merely examples, and should not be regarded as the only projects of this sort in England.

Integration from an ESN(M) school

It may seem odd to begin an account of innovations in the integrated education of ESN pupils by describing a special school. The logic is apparent, however, when we view the provision of special education in the light of a continuum, from wholly integrated to wholly segregated as suggested in Chapter 4.

Special schools of all types have a place at the 'segregated' end of this continuum and they can also make a contribution by publicising special education within the ordinary system through their use as resource centres, or through short-term placements for children with specific difficulties.

Park school, Blackpool

Park School in Blackpool is an ESN(M) school covering both primary and secondary age groups which aims to return selected children to their local primary or comprehensive school (Thompson and Jones, 1974). In the five years up to 1974 around 40 per cent of the children passing through the ten-year age group (forty-one children) transferred back to ordinary schools. Hence, in a typical class of about twenty, eight pupils might be expected to return, though not all in the same year. In practice the number varied from year to year. Preparation for return naturally involved detailed discussion with the receiving schools, who for their part knew that return to Park was possible if problems arose. As might be expected from the research described in Chapter 3, the principal difficulty facing pupils returning to the ordinary system lay in social relationships with other children. Nevertheless, only two of the forty-one pupils mentioned above had to return to Park School.

The school also has a diagnostic and assessment unit for the youngest children, aged four to six years. This unit has up to eight children at any one time (Thompson and Jones, 1974). As the difficulties of many of the children make the use of formal intelligence and attainment tests inappropriate, the staff have developed their own assessment battery based on detailed but wide ranging observations of the children in addition to more traditional techniques. Over a five-year period, forty-one children were reported to have passed through the unit. Of these, seven went on to an ESN(S) school, seven to a normal infant school, two to a school for physically handicapped children, one to a deaf unit and one to a psychiatric unit. The remaining twenty-three remained at Park, forming the nucleus of a reception class for pupils aged five to seven years. As in the diagnostic unit, selection of teaching materials for each individual in the reception class was based largely on a continuous assessment of his social, educational and emotional development.

Children are referred to Park School through the usual administrative channels. Until recently the psychologists' reports indicated that the majority had an IQ in the 50–75 range, but there is now a greater emphasis on specified educational needs, with correspondingly less on fitting children into discrete diagnostic categories (C. Jones, 1978). There is no reason to suppose that they are specially selected as likely to make rapid progress, nor that the basic curriculum is orientated to 'cram' them with the basic subjects in order to hasten their return. The fact that so few of the leavers needed to return suggests that they were well prepared for the ordinary school system. One point which might well be crucial to the success of Park's policy was that most children entered the school before the age of eight. Another might be that the number of pupils returning each year was relatively small, even though around 40 per cent eventually returned to ordinary school; the annual loss therefore had little effect on the stability of the total school community.

Looking towards the future, Thompson and Jones envisaged the use of special schools as resource centres for ordinary schools in the area, a possibility also envisaged by the Warnock Report (DES, 1978), which is discussed further in Chapter 9. If this were to happen, special school staff might be released to work with colleagues in ordinary schools on a regular basis, helping groups of children with specific difficulties: 'Why not begin to integrate school staffs as well as children?'

The success of Park School raises several important points about the aims of special education for ESN(M) pupils. It suggests how *existing* special school buildings and staff may be used to offer help to more children each year. Thus, if children were more often admitted to special schools with specific goals, these goals would form the basis of individual teaching programmes. Progress in these areas could be monitored continuously as part of the programme. Once these had been achieved, the child would be expected to return to his local primary or secondary school. This system would naturally need to be sufficiently flexible to cater for those children who showed secondary difficulties during their attendance at special school, perhaps resulting from problems which were not recognised at the time of initial assessment. In addition, return to the scene of failure at a child's local primary school would often be inappropriate, necessitating consideration of another ordinary school. The length of time needed to reach the agreed objectives of special school placement would naturally vary from one child to another. Even accepting the flexibility needed to cater for such variations, this model would give parents and children specific reasons for attendance at a special school, in the knowledge that this would, in many cases, occupy only a comparatively short period of the child's school career. It should offer the head and staff of the special school definable goals towards which to work, and help from outside agencies, such as educational psychologists and advisory teachers in setting up a programme and providing continuous monitoring of each child's progress. One further implication would be that the child would be expected to leave his ordinary school for a certain period of time and the ordinary school would keep in contact with the child's progress throughout this period. These possibilities will be discussed further in Chapter 9.

Integration of young ESN(S) children

The principal emphasis in this book is on the mildly and moderately handicapped, the ESN(M) group. There are several reasons for the division of children variously described as mentally handicapped into ESN (moderate) and ESN (severe) categories in the diagnostic process. First, there is evidence to suggest a qualitative, as well as a quantitative, difference between moderately and severely handicapped persons (Burden, 1977). Most severely subnormal people are unlikely to lead an independent life in the community. More form part of a distinct clinical entity, such as Down's Syndrome which affects around 25 per cent of the severely subnormal group. The incidence of severe mental handicap across the social classes is known to be even, and there is a more explicit educational emphasis on social skills before progress is possible in reading, number and so on.

In contrast the ESN(M) group has a high proportion of children from social classes IV and V. Their special needs are generally viewed as primarily educational rather than medical and most are likely to lead independent lives after compulsory school age. Indeed, as has been argued previously, the ESN(M) group is an administrative category, rather than a homogeneous grouping of children with certain easily-defined characteristics.

Nevertheless, while accepting those differences between children at present labelled ESN(S) and (M), it is instructive to look at projects in educating severely mentally handicapped in ordinary primary and comprehensive schools. If some success appears possible with the severely handicapped, how much more ambitious ought we to be with the ESN(M) group?

Infant schools in Bromley

On 1 April 1971 the Education (Handicapped Child) Act 1970 became law, requiring that local authorities should now provide for the education of those children over the age of three who had been deemed 'ineducable'. Bromley had set up classes in 1963 within its infants' schools, for retarded ESN(M), hyperkinetic and disturbed children. As this type of provision had been successful, the LEA began to look in the same direction when considering the needs of the ESN(S) child. Previously Bromley had only provided eighty places for such children in the old training centres, so expansion of provision was necessary. Members of Bromley Society for Mentally Handicapped Children began to press for the education of their children within the ordinary school system. Together these factors led the Education Department to consider opening up special classes for the ESN(S) child attached to some infant schools. The first one opened at St Paul Woods School in 1973, and others followed later at Alexandra, Crofton and Poverest schools (Chamberlain, 1973). In each of these classes the aim is to provide for the total educational needs of ten ESN(S) children between the ages of three and eight years.

The schools prefer to admit the children as early as possible; children are referred to them by a local playgroup for mentally handicapped children, and the schools' psychological service. There is no selective intake of children, all the children being placed in the class nearest to their home although some ESN(S) children needing special care are sent outside the borough. The children themselves have a variety of problems; for example, of the twenty children in the Poverest School in 1975, six had Down's Syndrome, one Hurler's Syndrome, one Cris du Chat, two epilepsy, one heart murmur, one a severe speech disorder, and the others unknown brain damage in the prenatal or antenatal period.

The classes are staffed with one qualified infant teacher and two welfare assistants to ten children. An additional part-time teacher is appointed for one day a week to enable the class teacher to do home visits and to teach in the main school; two dinner supervisors take charge of the children during the lunch break (Tuckwell, 1976).

The physical siting of the classes within the school building appears to vary from school to school. In Crofton, a new school, the room is centrally situated near to the school entrance, whereas in the older building at Poverest two rooms have been adapted in an annexe close to the school nursery. Each room has a large space for group activities, such as Wendy house, painting, books, and water and sand play. In many there are quiet rooms off this larger area. In Poverest additional facilities included a kitchen, sluice room, toilet room and staff toilet room, necessary because of the somewhat remote siting of the two classes.

Taxi transport was provided daily for the children, who naturally came from a wider 'catchment area' than did the other children within the same school. Parental involvement has been harnessed by close liaison with parents both before and during entry, the provision of monthly mothers' meetings in some schools, and the inclusion of two members of the Bromley Society for Mentally Handicapped Children on the governing bodies of primary schools with special classes attached.

Initial assessments of the children on entry are done by the Schools Psychological Service. Psychologists are also involved in an in-service training programme for the teachers of such classes, who themselves have often little previous experience in teaching handicapped children. This service also attempts to monitor the progress of the children during their stay in the infant schools (Preston, 1975).

The amount of social or work integration of the ESN(S) children with their non-handicapped peers seemed to vary from school to school, and from child to child. In the Poverest School some classes join the reception class for music, movement and singing. The accent is on the teacher's wish to institute such sessions rather than it being formal school or LEA policy. In June 1976 seven of the children joined the reception classes for a short time each day, and another child spent the major part of the day in one class. A welfare assistant accompanied the children to these ordinary classes, which allowed the staff to be seen as more accessible to children in the whole school. The ESN(S) children appeared to take part in special school occasions, such as parties, assemblies, films, etc (Lyons, 1976). The extent of integration in the school yard at break or in the dining-room at lunchtime varied from school to school. In Poverest School most of the children ate in their own classrooms, and played in their own small playground. In Crofton four children in 1976 went to eat in the main dining room, and three regularly played within the main playground. The children were always supervised by a welfare assistant on such occasions.

It is interesting that neither of the two headmistresses felt that there had been difficulties with the parents of ordinary children. Before the first class opened the head teacher at Poverest wrote a letter to all parents of infant children, telling them about the new entrants, saying that she hoped this group would join in with other children whenever possible, and offering to answer any queries about the new class. She notes that there were no such queries, and the general response from parents was favourable. The parents of the handicapped children also appeared to find the local infants schools acceptable.

Three problems have been thrown up by these classes in Bromley. The first is that the financial cutbacks have meant that there are no equivalent junior school classes for the children to attend from the age of eight. Children must then go to a variety of different special schools, ESN(M) and (S). The second and third problems concern the administration and the teaching careers of staff working in these classes. The assistant education officer in Bromley, John Chamberlain, points out that all the rules about the education of handicapped children and the regulations about salaries and the qualifications of teachers were drafted with special schools in mind (Chamberlain, 1973). There may at present be a dead end, in career terms, for teachers working in such classes. Bromley is keen to avoid this wherever possible, by encouraging secondment to courses such as the Child Development Course at London University. One teacher who had previously taught a class at Crofton Infants School has moved to a deputy headship at a local hospital school, perhaps giving some indication of the current difficulties. This question will be discussed further in Chapter 9.

Despite these difficulties, there appears to be a positive commitment to the provision of this form of integration and a belief in its success both among the teaching staff and head teachers of the infant schools themselves, and among advisory and administrative staff in the Local Education Authority.

Integration in ordinary secondary schools

The Pingle School, Derbyshire

Sceptics may argue at this point, that the social and local integration of even severely mentally handicapped children is feasible only while the children are very young; and that the larger size and older children in comprehensive schools would make this impossible. However, this problem has been faced with twelve- to sixteen-year-old moderately and severely handicapped children at the Pingle Comprehensive School at Swadlincote in Derbyshire. The Pingle school is one of the very few examples of the attachment of an ESN(S) unit to a secondary school in Britain. It provides an example of provision across the whole range of mental retardation (with the exception of children needing special physical care), from remedial provision in withdrawal groups, to classes for the ESN(S) group in a unit adjacent to the school.

The Pingle School is a comprehensive school for eleven- to eighteen-year-olds (with an annual pupil intake of around 185; the number on roll including the sixth form is over 1,000). It also serves as the South Derbyshire secondary school for ESN(M) and (S) children, taking the children falling into these categories from units attached to local primary schools. The head of the Remedial Department is responsible for both curriculum and pastoral needs of pupils who are offered additional 'remedial' help, who are assigned to the special class of ESN(M) children, or who work primarily in the ESN(S) unit (Fisher, 1977).

Remedial provision at the Pingle School is organised so that low ability children, or those needing extra help in the basic subjects are placed in mixed ability classes, but formed into small groups for specialist remedial teaching in English and mathematics. These groups have between ten and fifteen children, and are staffed by a teacher attached to the remedial department. In the first year, the 'lowest' and smallest of each group is formed immediately on the basis of junior school reports, and the larger second group is formed at half-term on the experience of subject teachers, and after the application of group tests in reading and maths. Some children move in and out of these groups each year.

The special class of ESN(M) children has around fifteen children, and is composed primarily from the children who had attended the junior school class in Swadlincote, with perhaps a few other children added, after consultation with the Junior School head teachers. These children spend about half their time on lessons within their own special class, with staff from the remedial department. The other half is spent with specialist subject teachers, in some cases integrated with children from other bands in the school, for example in craft, metalwork, woodwork, domestic science, etc. These classes are placed physically within the main school building, in adjacent rooms. The children join in social activities with other pupils in the school.

The ESN(S) unit is sited at the entrance to the school, and is joined to the main building by a covered walkway. There are about twenty children who have been diagnosed as severely subnormal, mostly coming from the ESN(S) unit attached to the local junior school. Some children can use this unit as a self-contained school; others may join lessons with specialist teachers. Some of the ESN(M) special class children use the unit during the day at some time, and children from the older classes in the school are encouraged to help with play activities. Generally the unit children remain there during the lunch hour. There is a small play area outside the unit, but sometimes children join others in the main school yard.

The slow-learner department has four full-time remedial teachers, and two ESN(S) teachers, who spend some time teaching the ESN(M) or remedial groups, together with two full-time and one part-time welfare assistants.

The aim within the department is for the social integration of handicapped and non-handicapped children. This is achieved by providing a continuum, by which a child can be moved around for part of his week, or at different times in his school career. Both the headmaster of the Pingle School, and the head of the slow-learner department were initially somewhat anxious when the ESN(S) unit was proposed by the Derbyshire authority. The head of department had no previous experience with severely handicapped children. Parents' evenings were held to provide information for the parents of non-handicapped children about the new unit. The head reports that he has no difficulties with parents nor, it appears, with other children showing hostility towards the handicapped children.

The role of the head of department appears to be crucial within the school; he has to keep the main school staff informed about the pupils and the work within his department, and to liaise with the parents of the children in his care. Despite the age of the children with whom the Pingle School is concerned, and its size, the headmaster and head of department believe that this sort of provision needs to be developed in the future. In the head of department's words: 'Generations of "normal" schoolchildren will accept these mentally handicapped youngsters as an integral part of the school, and of their own society instead of being in ignorance of them' (Fisher, 1977).

A description follows of two schools where more mildly handicapped, ESN(M) children are being educated in ordinary comprehensive schools, the first in the Cooper School, in a unit attached to the comprehensive school, the second in Countesthorpe College, by the use of withdrawal groups for basic skills work.

The Cooper School, Oxfordshire

Bicester School was initially a comprehensive school of some 1,800 pupils, which serves a mixed urban and rural community in Oxfordshire. In 1969 a unit of fifteen ESN(M) children aged eleven to twelve opened on premises in its grounds. The unit comprised three classrooms, which were essentially separate from the main school. The unit shared the main school building for administration, registration, assemblies, dinners, and some craft and practical lessons, but the unit children were taught separately from others within the school. It was basically a separate special school, sharing the same campus as the comprehensive.

Three main problems appeared. These were teasing and rejection of the children in the unit by the others in the main school; the unit staff feeling increasingly isolated by themselves; and some practical difficulties in arrangements for subjects such as PE and games (Garnett, 1976).

The second year led some of the main school staff to accept the need for greater integration. This interchange took place principally between the main school remedial staff and the teachers in the unit, but even heads of department in games and English began to discuss the possibilities of integrating the ESN(M) children into mixed ability classes. Gradually some of the unit children began to attend these classes, their special teachers going with them, wherever possible. This move appeared to be reasonably successful, and the experience gained was used in planning the new High School in Bicester, the Cooper School.

This High School opened in 1971 and catered for eleven- to thirteen-year-old children in the town. A base similar to the one in the upper school was incorporated into the design, the unit being more centrally situated within the main school building. The aim here was to move towards a continuum of provision for the slow-learner, by having the unit staff work closely with the remedial staff, and enabling the child's individual timetable to be varied according to his emerging academic and social competence. The staff in the remedial department operated a policy of withdrawing groups from mixed ability classes. The group size varied from two to ten with one group catering for poor readers with a reading age within the approximate limits of a seven- to nine-year-old. The second group was larger, and catered primarily for children with a reading age of nine to ten years who needed extra reading practice.

The 'Progress Unit', as the new special unit came to be called, caters for some children in the first year, most of whom could be described as falling within the ESN(M) range; occasionally the unit is used for ESN(S) children, thus recognising that there is no clear dividing line between the two groups. Jean Garnett, the head of the progress unit describes the placement of Carol, an ESN(S) child whose parents would not accept special school placement for her. She had previously attended a local primary school and received extra help from a visiting teacher. In the secondary unit staff have primarily concentrated on the development of her social competence by teaching her to read essential notices and to cope with basic money, and by encouraging the development of peer group friendships.

The progress unit in the Cooper School was specifically designed to be more open and less separate than that in the old upper school. Children were individually timetabled into the two rooms of the unit, and spent varying amounts of their weekly timetable in the mixed ability classes.

Here the role of the progress unit staff was to support the children, particularly in science and maths, by working alongside subject teachers and providing modified materials for children with reading problems. The main subjects covered in withdrawal lessons in the unit rooms were reading and basic number. French was said to be one of the favourite lessons during which children were withdrawn for extra help, but the exact lessons missed varied from child to child.

There are two remedial staff employed at present, and two teachers attached to the progress unit with one qualified helper. The school receives the capitation allowance equivalent to that for an ESN(M) child in respect of children in the unit. The number of children receiving extra help in the unit decreases as the child progresses up the school. Thus in the first year around fifteen children receive help in the progress unit, and sixty from the remedial department. In the second year this decreases to fifteen children in the progress unit and six in the remedial department. By the fourth year it is extremely rare for children to be attached to the unit but some are asked to come and 'help' the younger children for certain lessons in the week.

Using this model Jean Garnett notes that there seemed to be a decrease in the teasing and bullying which had been a problem in the upper school (Garnett, 1975). She reported that the integration of ESN(M) children was aided by developing positive attitudes among the comprehensive school staff and head. The unit also received support from outside the school from the

Oxfordshire Vulnerable Child Scheme. This scheme comprises all those teachers working in special and remedial education across both primary and secondary schools, together with members of other agencies. The aim of the scheme is to give a supportive structure to staff working in the units, and to identify the needs of all school children who are at risk.

In many ways it appeared somewhat of a historical legacy that the remedial department and progress unit had not been merged in the Cooper School, particularly as one of the expressed aims was to lessen the labelled identity of the ESN(M) pupil. One reason why this may not have happened could be the labelling applied to the unit staff by support services outside the school, who would thus be unwittingly reinforcing the division.

The head of the unit, Jean Garnett, has attempted to make some evaluation of the success of the units attached to both the Bicester and the Cooper Schools. She admits that this is extremely difficult (as we have seen, former research in this area has tended to be inconclusive), but she is currently trying to develop a social competence profile, against which to assess the child's progress. In 1974 she carried out a comparative study of school leavers in the upper school in Bicester, with those in a segregated unit, and others in a special school, matching all the leavers for age and IQ. She found the attainment levels of children in the units to be slightly higher than those in the special school. Using Rutter's Behaviour Questionnaire she found the levels of 'maladjusted' behaviour to be similar in all three establishments (Garnett, 1975). This, of course, is in keeping with the research results described in Chapter 4.

The experience of staff in the Cooper and Bicester schools led them to move gradually away from segregating children on a full- or part-time basis in a separate unit for slow-learning children. As described above, the emphasis is now on timetabling children individually to come to the unit for help in the basic skills, the children being in ordinary class groups for most of their time.

Countesthorpe College, Leicestershire

The experience of Bicester and of schools in other parts of the country was considered by the head and senior staff when setting up a new comprehensive school in Leicestershire. Countesthorpe College is now a Leicestershire Upper School, a comprehensive of some 750 pupils aged fourteen to eighteen in a small village about eight miles south of Leicester city. It takes children from two villages, Countesthorpe and Blaby, and from a large urban council estate on the outskirts of Leicester. Children come to the college from one of the three main feeder high schools (eleven to fourteen age group), which themselves have great variations in school organisation, teaching styles and curricula. One of these high schools, Leysland, shares a campus with the college. When the college was opened in 1970, the high school staff and pupils were housed in the main building, but in 1973 they moved out to their own purpose-built accommodation.

When the college opened, the staff began by examining many previous assumptions about, and practices in, education of secondary age children. Tim McMullan, the first head commented:

We have a chance to rethink the total process of learning within a school, subject only to the demands made by outside institutions — i.e. universities and parents —

and the personal and material resources available to us. This does not mean that everything we do will be different from what has been done before, but it should mean that we do not automatically repeat an established practice without considering why (McMullan, 1969).

One of the areas in which this happened was in the education of children who may be labelled 'slow-learners', 'ESN(M)' or 'maladjusted'. Rather than beginning by seeing these groups as reasonably homogeneous and making provision for them within the school accordingly, the head and senior staff at Countesthorpe began by placing the emphasis on looking at the needs of *all* children within the school, on an individual basis. Children fitting into the ESN(M) category, therefore, had their needs considered alongside those of other children, and these needs in turn influenced the school organisation, timetabling, pastoral care system and curriculum design. Any structures were intended to be flexible, and responsive to change, so we need to see how the teaching organisation developed over the few years since Countesthorpe's forming.

The College is a Leicestershire Upper School, taking children aged fourteen to eighteen years. In accordance with Leicestershire policy only a few separate special schools exist in the county, so children with special needs are catered for primarily within the comprehensive schools. Countesthorpe College in a similar way to most of the upper schools in Leicestershire, has some physically handicapped children, some partial hearing, some partially sighted, together with other children who may be termed ESN(M) or maladjusted. There are difficulties over defining the problems with children falling into these last two categories, as we have already noted. The need to label children as maladjusted or ESN(M) arises because of the need to gain entry to specialised facilities such as a special school place. Where few such special schools are provided, and children are catered for by remedial specialists in the ordinary school, then the labelling process is not necessary. All that can be emphasised in support of the claim that such children were indeed catered for in the school is that all three remedial staff in the early years had previous training in child psychology, and were of the opinion that about three or four children a year out of some 200, would normally be catered for in an ESN(M) school. It is more difficult to estimate the number of children per year who may have been labelled as maladjusted, but it could be estimated that some two or three children could be said to fit into that category.

A description of provision for ESN(M) and slow-learning children is only possible within the context of the overall organisation of teaching. This is because the teaching by staff within the remedial department is not isolated, but depends on the philosophy and organisation on the school as a whole.

In the early years of the school (1970–71) each child was placed in a mixed ability tutor group, based on friendship groups. Students followed a basic 'core' curriculum, for about half of each week. This core would tend to comprise English, social studies and maths. Very often a class might be taught by different teachers for each of these subjects. For the other half of the week the pupils could choose from a wide variety of options, some of which would tend to be self-selecting on the basis of the child's own ability to cope with and be interested in that particular subject. The options were chosen by the students themselves, after consultation with form teacher and parents. Work at Countesthorpe College has always tended to be individualised as far as possible. This means that the student will work at his or her own pace, and class teaching is generally avoided. This principle tends to operate across the whole curriculum, although it is naturally more difficult to achieve in subjects which involve cumulative learning and oral communication, such as modern languages. This individualisation of work is basic to how how ability and slow learning children fit into the school as a whole. It is much easier to accept that the child will work at his own pace if this is the general norm within the class, and a wide variety of materials and books are in use at any one time. In most subjects the staff produced worksheets to facilitate this individualised approach.

Mixed ability teaching needed to be supported by a remedial department in the school. Three teachers, each given a free timetable, worked with the High School students in the first three years, and two teachers, one per year, worked with the fourth and fifth years. The main aims of the department at its formation were:

1. To withdraw some children for extra help in basic reading, writing and spelling.
2. To support slow-learning students and their class and subject teachers in the mixed ability classes.
3. To provide suitable and modified materials for children with reading problems in subjects across the curriculum (Goodwin, 1974).

The remedial staff use two withdrawal rooms in the college, one primarily for the fourth and fifth years, the second for the first three years. The remedial staff were all free-timetabled, and organised their commitments depending on the time allocation which they wished to give to each of the three areas outlined above. The size of the withdrawal groups for the basic skills work also varied greatly, dependent on the task being tackled, the level of competence of the students, and so on.

The worksheet based approach in the mixed ability classes posed several problems for the remedial department staff, the children with reading problems, and subject teachers. For the staff of the remedial department it meant a great deal of work, modifying materials in humanities, science, maths and other subjects which subject teachers often tended to produce only a few days before the work was needed. Even children with reading problems tend to cover a wide range of difficulties, in both type and severity, so it was almost impossible to pitch the reading level of the modified materials so that it was suitable for the whole range of children with reading problems. Also much of the material produced could not be simplified linguistically and conceptually with ease. Too often, when a piece of work was modified it lost its conceptual structure or proved to be either linguistically too complex or too simple for many students. The problem raised for subject teachers was that they were given material with which to work, but which they did not themselves design. This led to problems in the daily use of the worksheet.

As the difficulties arising when some slow-learning children were faced with a large number of teachers throughout their working week were recognised, it became clear that the system needed modification. In many secondary and primary schools it is a widely held opinion that less able students perform better from the security of a small number of teacher relationships. The organisation of one teacher to each subject naturally limits the teacher/pupil contact time, and therefore the danger is that the teacher will not have sufficient time to get to know the individual needs of pupils. It is important to emphasise here that the sort of problems outlined were in no way confined to those pupils who may fit into the categories of ESN(M) and slow-learning. The difficulties of these pupils tended to be only highlighting problems which students across the whole ability range were finding, a point which is discussed more fully in Chapter 10.

The second aim of providing support for pupils and teachers within class also proved to be difficult to arrange in practice, as students would often be spread across twelve different classes in any one lesson. In such a situation, the children would tend to be grouped together physically by the remedial teacher within, say the science area, thus forming a remedial class within the overall group. Withdrawal lesson organisation was somewhat easier, but still posed its own problems. It was frequently difficult to get together the same group of children several times in the week to tackle a particular piece of work. These sessions tended to be seen as separate from work going on in other sections of the school. Certainly the withdrawal of pupils for remediation in the basic skills could in no way be said to increase the class teacher's knowledge about the difficulties a child was having in these skills, nor about how he himself might cater more effectively for the child. There was thus little integration in working relationships between the remedial staff and subject teachers in other parts of the school, nor between the child's work on reading and his practice of this in other lessons.

After a long series of discussions an alternative model of organisation for the whole school was reached (Chisholm, 1977a). The needs of the slow learning and ESN(M) child were seen within this overall system. This model was to divide each year of pupils up into two teams, each team having their own group of staff. For about 130 children there would be around six teachers who would work with that team for the majority of their teaching time. Work was largely on a primary model of tutor-to-group, but some specialisation did take place, depending on the interests of the teaching staff within each team. The basic team work covered RE, maths, social studies and English, and was as far as possible integrated with other areas of the curriculum. There have been suggestions to bring science staff into the team areas for some time during the week. The work tended to be project based, and was still individualised, but there was far less emphasis on the worksheet, and more on the team teacher aiding the pupil in planning projects, and directing him to resources in the School's Resources Centre, or to resources available from the child's family, friends, or the wider community.

The other half of the week most students spent in options with specialist teachers. These options were intended to be mixed ability, but the guided choice system naturally needed a degree of selectivity. Some slow-learning students in particular opted for withdrawal lessons in basic skills at this time, and might also return to their team for extra 'team time', under the supervision of one team teacher. In this way the general school organisation allowed a good deal of flexibility for the slow learning child. One teacher would be responsible for at least 50 per cent of his weekly work, and in this way the curriculum and pastoral responsibility for any child rested with the person most immediate to him – his class teacher. The two elements in the child's school life were therefore brought together instead of being organised separately as they are in many secondary schools.

The main difficulties in this model were those facing the class or team teacher rather than the child. He might not feel competent at first to teach his group all the team subjects, so there was a move towards subject specialists working alongside team teachers, in order to pass on their own skills. This was emphasised particularly in remedial work, where the staff moved away from a centralised department approach, towards being part of the teams themselves.

The aim was to attach one half-time remedial specialist to each team, the specialist spending time in other types of teaching for the remainder of the week. They would be based in a small room in each of the team areas, and could choose to work either with a withdrawal group or by supporting other staff in the ordinary class. It was hoped that this would aid the integration of the remedial staff within each team, and help other team members to consider the needs of the child with reading problems, when planning programmes of work. It would also allow for a more genuine and informal support network to build up between remedial and team staff, in which the emphasis could be on 'giving away' the skills of the remedial teacher to other members of staff. This was to some extent formalised by remedial teachers running in-service courses on the teaching of reading, spelling etc for staff in other parts of the school. These groups were well attended and were useful in allowing an interchange of problems and ideas between teachers in different subject areas.

Conclusions

The emphasis on the integration of ESN(M) and maladjusted children at Countesthorpe is on looking at their needs as children in the process of learning and attempting to see how far the overall organisations of the school can be altered to meet those needs more exactly. Repeatedly, the difficulties shown by such 'special' children have only been magnified versions of problems which other children have experienced, while nevertheless appearing to 'cope' somewhat better (or at least, less obviously failing to adjust to the system as imposed from above).

It is this aspect of provision for 'special' children which is so important. The units for ESN children attached to ordinary schools in Bromley and Derbyshire seem to have had considerable successes. However, their presence seems to have had limited impact on the thinking and organisation of the main school. In this respect the units acted as special schools on the campus of ordinary ones, albeit at times within the same school building. In this sense, they were good examples of locational and social integration (DES, 1978).

At the Cooper School in Bicester the limitations of this form of local integration were recognised, with a consequent attempt to move towards greater social and work integration of ESN(M) pupils. This does not yet seem to have been fully achieved, however, as indicated by the division between progress unit and remedial department pupils and staff, and by the need to label certain pupils as ESN(M) on entry to the school.

Countesthorpe, and some other Leicestershire schools, have gone further than this. Far from seeing the need to divide pupils into categories and then offer teaching arrangements on that basis they have attempted to tackle the problem from the other end. Concentrating on the needs of all children, and seeing children previously labelled 'special' as having perhaps differing, but by no means exclusive needs with regard to teaching and pastoral care, the emphasis has been on creating a system which can respond to changing conditions within the school. Thus, change is expected to occur if pupils or staff are seen to be failing to cope adequately with certain aspects of school life. Also, the accent here is on how the system can change to *allow* the child and teacher to learn, rather than viewing the child's failure as evidence of some cognitive defect or psychiatric state, or the teacher's failure as evidence of poor performance.

We are moving in this discussion towards seeing provision for 'special pupils' within a school simply as good school organisation, responsive to the needs of the pupils. Similarly, we are moving towards the view of special education and teaching arrangements for such children as examples of good teaching practice, in which the school's curriculum is child-centred and involves an explanatory approach to apparent failure to learn (Watts, 1976).

These points will be examined in greater detail in the concluding chapters. But first we must look at parallel developments in the education of 'maladjusted' children in special units and ordinary schools in Britain.

Chapter 7

Innovations in the education
of maladjusted children: I

A. Extending special facilities

The background to recent developments

Any review of innovation in the education of maladjusted children is bedevilled by the semantic problems which this book has already raised a number of times. We have argued that maladjustment is a ragbag term for describing any towards-the-end-of-spectrum cases who cause concern to ordinary class teachers either because they are so withdrawn or so erratic or aggressive in their behaviour; we have also argued that no logical and coherent view of maladjustment can focus solely on the problems which the child presents, but must rather seek to understand a problem situation in which the child, his family, his teachers and his peers are interacting with and influencing each other. If this view of maladjustment has any validity, it follows that no account of innovations in the education of maladjusted children can be complete without reference to the contribution of school organisation and attitudes in reducing its prevalence; taking the argument a step further, we must look at the growing body of evidence that the classroom teacher and the school as an institution have a critical influence on children's behaviour and examine this evidence in relation to the ways in which the ordinary school's curriculum and pastoral care structure can meet the needs of pupils who might otherwise be labelled maladjusted.

First, though, we must look critically at some of the growing number of initiatives of the last ten years in the education of maladjusted children outside the full-time special school system. Probably the one point of agreement which unites the widely differing projects is dissatisfaction with the service provided to children by traditional child guidance clinics with their long waiting lists, their remoteness from the day-to-day problems facing schools, their helplessness with families who won't keep appointments (how many problem families will?), and their emphasis on the internal problems of the child and his family with a corresponding disregard for the influence of unsatisfactory living conditions and learning experiences. In an influential and much quoted article Professor Tizard (1973) described them as wasteful in their use of resources and inefficient in their results. This dissatisfaction, however, was found within some of the clinics as well as in the schools of the children they served; many of the early projects started as cooperative ventures between schools and a clinic team. The intention was to utilise the knowledge and skills of members of the clinic team to greater effect by offering a support service to the teachers who would be running the project. In other words the clinics, or at least a few of them, were acknowledging their limitations as a treatment agency and recognising the important role of schools in promoting children's social and emotional adjustment. A move from the cloistered security of a traditional clinic to a wider advisory role in which teachers are seen as equal partners responsible for providing help which might in theory formerly have been provided in a specialist clinic is a challenging one, as it allows teachers to see (often for the first time) the limits of the 'specialist's' knowledge and competence. Fortunately it also allowed the clinic's educational psychologist, social worker, and psychiatrist to demonstrate their usefulness; hopefully the growing demand for school psychological services should be seen in this context.

Nurture groups

Among the earlier initiatives to help deprived and disturbed infant school children was the Inner London Education Authority's decision in 1970 to establish two 'nurture groups'. The problems which these groups sought to counteract were graphically described in an article by Marjorie Boxall (1973), an educational psychologist based at the Woodberry Down Child Guidance Clinic which was associated with these groups:

The children in the nurture groups show serious problems in school. They range from 'those described as destructive, dangerously aggressive and difficult to contain in a group, to those who are resistive and hostile, or inert, unresponsive and unable to make relationships. Their histories demonstrate the many faceted problem of deprivation and disadvantage, and their symptoms reflect impoverished, impaired or ruptured early nurture. All live under stress, often in overburdened, fragmented families, in overcrowded circumstances; early experience is limited and disorganised, but overstimulating at an instinctual level, and control is frequently rigid and punitive. The subtle and joyous interaction between parent and child through which he is helped to play imaginatively, use his experiences constructively and develop inner controls, is eroded or lost. School, into which these children are flung without relevant preparation, demands a level of personal organisation which they are not able to meet. The problems they then present are essentially a product of deprivation, aggravated by the sophisticated expectations of schools.

The schools were based in problem areas and one can safely presume that all but a minority of the children for the groups would have been expected to sink or swim in their ordinary classes if the nurture groups had not existed. On the other hand, it may be equally safe to assume that the majority might have been put forward for special education had they, by some quirk of fate, found themselves attending a school in a middle-class district with high standards of social behaviour and educational attainment. From the descriptions of their behaviour it is fairly clear that the children would have been considered maladjusted on the basis of screening with the Bristol Social Adjustment Guide, or to suffer from psychiatric disorder on the criteria used in Rutter's studies.

The nurture groups aimed to give children the social, emotional and play experiences which they had missed before starting school. Children were selected by the teachers concerned and not by the clinic personnel – an important feature which is also emphasised in other school-based projects described below. The average group size was twelve, but sometimes increased to as much as eighteen, in the charge of a teacher and a helper. Furniture and equipment emphasised the group's function as a home–school unit, with comfortable chairs and cooking equipment in addition to plenty of play space. Although the teacher–child ratio was less favourable than that now recommended in schools for maladjusted children, there was a conscious effort to provide a closer, warmer relationship between adult and child than was possible in the ordinary class. This did not, however, imply unconditional acceptance; Marjorie Boxall emphasised that the children were not allowed to choose at random from the available activities, but that the teacher would select and supervise things for the children to do, with specific instructions and frequent repetition. Social training was equally explicit: 'I see, I grab . . . I don't get.' In the same way, children were consciously trained to carry on with their own activities when a fight started, and the child in a temper would either be held by an adult or 'left on the bed to pummel the cushions and fights are as far as possible ignored'.

The children could form close, dependent and accepting relationships with teacher and helper, but these relationships were formed as the basis for future development rather than as an end in themselves. Thus, food became an important group experience and importance was attached to special occasions that might frequently be ignored or forgotten in their own home. The ILEA's nurture groups sought to give children some of the learning experiences which are taken for granted in a caring, stimulating home and without which any child is likely to start school at a serious disadvantage. In many ways the atmosphere and activities are reminiscent of those in a good nursery school, but as all infant teachers are painfully aware, the children who most need nursery school experience are all too often the ones who are least likely to receive it. The nurture group concept was, and is, 'remedial' in the literal sense of the word, though not in the traditional educational sense; the difference lay in the 'remediation' focusing on earlier and more basic learning experiences such as those inherent in acceptance from a caring and consistent adult and cooperative play with other children.

The Woodberry Down Clinic's involvement in the early nurture groups did not stop at encouraging and facilitating the activities of the groups themselves. Recognition of the stresses facing the children led to a similar awareness of the stresses experienced by their parents – in many cases West Indian in this area – and recognition that a clinic-orientated service would fail precisely because of the children's or parents' sense of failure and personal worthlessness. 'The clinical interview, far from being seen as a help was seen as acknowledgement of failure and in such a situation, little could be done to improve things' (Gorrell-Barnes, 1973). In contrast, 'school was viewed differently, for as long as the child stayed in school and was seen to thrive, there was hope'. The clinic social workers visited the children's homes as school social workers, seeking to link the world of school with that of home. Many of the parents felt socially isolated and lacked the confidence to visit their children's school; they were frequently depressed, and so disillusioned with life in London that they had little emotional or physical energy left for their children, whom they needed largely in order to confirm their own sense of identity. The welcome which the clinic's social workers received on their home visits led them to start groups for the parents at the children's school. The groups were held in the classroom (in the children's absence) with emphasis on 'shared participation with one another and with the professional people'. Seeing that the teachers and other professionals valued their children, helped the parents to revalue their own worth and to discover that in a group they could not only share but start to cope with their loneliness, fears and anxieties. This concentration on work with parents anticipated the Warnock Report's emphasis that parents should be recognised as partners, and involved at all stages in planning their child's future.

The ILEA's nurture groups raise a number of issues about the development of services for 'deprived' or retarded children. In the first place, one might ask whether the same learning experiences could be provided for more children by running the groups on a part-time basis, with each child attending, perhaps, for a maximum of half his school day; similarly one might ask whether the ordinary infant class might not be expected to provide these experiences, particularly if the teacher has the assistance of a stable, motherly welfare assistant. Indeed, if the group's aim is primarily to help the child acquire greater confidence, a greater sense of personal worth and more acceptable social behaviour, such a welfare assistant could have an advantage over a teacher by virtue of a greater understanding of the children's backgrounds; in one authority nurture groups are supervised by the children's class teachers, but much of the hour-to-hour organisation is in the hands of specially selected welfare assistants. Another issue is that child guidance clinic and school psychological service social workers do not exist in sufficient numbers to make any impact on more than a tiny minority of receptive schools. In contrast, every school or group of schools has its own educational welfare officer; one wonders how long it will be before more local education authorities wake up to the possibilities of this service as a way of developing an effective and accessible educational social work service, with all its implications for home–school understanding and cooperation. This, however, will depend not only on more authorities implementing the recommendations of the Local Government Training Board's Report (1972) which recommended that social work training should form the accepted qualification for education welfare officers, but also on a willingness among head teachers and administrators to accept that the service should have a wider role in promoting the welfare of children and their families than its traditional one of enforcing school attendance.

Primary and secondary school adjustment groups

Although children in inner city areas are known to have higher rates of disturbed behaviour (Rutter *et al.*, 1975a) not all the initiatives in the treatment of maladjusted children took place in such districts. Special 'adjustment groups' were established by West Sussex local education authority in an attempt to cater for disturbed children in primary schools. Formed in 1971, the groups were based in a limited number of primary schools, and staffed, as with the ILEA nurture groups, by teachers appointed by the head of the school. The majority were married women returning to teaching when their children reached school age, and many had previously been responsible for remedial work in the same school (Labon, 1973). Head teachers emphasised the need for personal maturity rather than expertise in the more mechanical aspects of teaching. Children were selected for the groups by the head and adjustment group teachers after consultation with the children's class teachers. Groups were small – up to six – and children attended for around two half-hour sessions weekly. In addition, the adjustment group teachers were expected to set time aside for record-keeping, discussing the children's progress with their ordinary class teachers, and meeting parents. This last assignment was given some priority as it was felt that the adjustment group teacher might often be the most appropriate link between school and parents.

Two-thirds of the children selected were boys – on the face of it a higher proportion than might be expected from the epidemiological research described in Chapter 2, though not higher than one would expect from the number at special schools for maladjusted children. Four-fifths of the selected children had reading difficulties (rather more than one would have expected from the epidemiological research on the connection between reading attainment and emotional adjustment), but this may simply have reflected the skills of the adjustment group teacher, since the principal criterion in selection was whether a child would benefit rather than whether his problems were more acute than those of another child. Assessed on the Bristol Social Adjustment Guide (Stott, 1963) the selected children were more often restless and aggressive than anxious or withdrawn, though the latter constituted a sizeable minority. Sociometric assessment suggested a strong tendency for the adjustment group children to be social isolates, though not all of the social isolates were regarded as suitable for this form of help.

Whereas the ILEA nurture groups set out to recapture, or rather to capture, some of the atmosphere of a caring, accepting, stimulating home, the West Sussex adjustment groups aimed at something between normal home and school atmosphere. The orientation was explicitly towards therapy rather than remedial education, but the choice of activity lay with the teachers concerned. In general they aimed at things which could be done either at school or at home, so that creative activities such as model making, painting and role-play were frequent. It was felt that such activities formed the most appropriate way to help the children overcome their difficulty in forming relationships with other children and with adults. The small size enabled teachers to talk with each child individually and in the informal atmosphere they could more easily encourage children to talk about themselves.

The West Sussex adjustment groups operated on a part-time basis. On one hand this could attract the emotive cry of 'integration on the cheap', while on the other hand we might question whether the children would have benefited to a greater extent if they had been able to attend more often. Certainly, head teachers reported that a small minority of children appeared not to benefit at all from the group, and it was never suggested that they should replace either the existing child guidance and educational psychology support services or the full-time special schools for maladjusted children. At a different level it would be difficult on strictly educational grounds to justify such a heavy emphasis on 'therapeutic' activities for a major portion of the week; maladjusted children have as much need for a varied curriculum as any other children, and it can be argued that they are as likely to experience success through the more formal subjects in the curriculum as from the 'therapeutic' creative activities practised in the West Sussex groups, though the choice of activity may in some cases have been determined by a wish not to overlap or conflict with work which class teachers or remedial teachers were already doing with the child.

Recognising the possibility of such conflict is, of course, one way to avoid it but there are the related dangers of the adjustment group teacher becoming isolated within her own school as well as isolated from other teachers doing similar work in special schools and in other ordinary schools. The first can be overcome by close informal cooperation between class teachers and adjustment group teachers, so that the child's treatment is viewed as a cooperative venture by both, and the second requires in-service education and support for the teachers concerned. In West Sussex teachers attended regular meetings at local teachers' centres to examine their ideas and methods, discuss problems they were experiencing and take part in seminars run by the educational psychologists who had initiated the groups on topics such as group management principles and the observation and interpretation of behaviour.

The background thinking at one of the earlier secondary projects (at Brislington comprehensive school in Bristol) was similar to that already described for nurture groups and adjustment groups. The Brislington project was started by the school's headmaster in 1967 as a way of improving the quality of the education available to the school's disturbed pupils and reducing or removing the necessity to refer them to special schools. The project was also seen as a way of utilising the skills of child guidance staff in the school, and as an opportunity to develop treatment programmes which could be adopted elsewhere. Initially the unit was based in a classroom in the main school building, but this was found to be unsatisfactory due to the immature and aggressive behaviour of some of the children interfering with normal lessons; the unit was therefore transferred to a special building adjacent to the main school block. It was staffed by two teachers who worked together with the same group of children. The majority of children attended full time for an average of nine months, though it was possible for some to attend part-time; return to ordinary classes was generally a gradual process. As in the West Sussex adjustment groups, some children attended the unit for shorter periods to tide them over a difficult time caused by such family stresses as death of a relative or break up of the home. An important point emphasised by the educational psychologist originally associated with the project (N. Jones, 1973, 1974) was the need for the children to be able to adapt from the requirements and expectations of the unit to those of the school as a whole:

The extent of the children's flexibility is a guide in deciding which of them can be helped in units that are attached to normal schools. Every child has a daily opportunity to live as a member of the normal school community — he can test this experience out at his own pace — and a time comes when the child asks to spend more and more time attending normal lessons and less and less time in the unit. There never comes a day when he is discharged and is abruptly expected to give up one way of living and to take on another.

B. The concept of maladjustment: implications of interaction analysis

What is being treated?

Implicit in the last remark about the need for a gradual return to 'normal' lessons is the assumption that the needs of maladjusted children differ in some rather fundamental way from those of ordinary children, so that 'treatment' provided in a special unit must logically differ in a similarly fundamental way from the 'education' provided in the rest of the school. This assumption arose from the understandable influence of the pioneers in the education of maladjusted children in this country who in their turn were heavily influenced by a medical model which viewed maladjustment as abnormal, 'pathological' behaviour arising from some quasi-medical state in the child or his family. It could be argued that this model was the only credible one in the social and educational climate in the first half of the century – neurotic children attract more sympathy than delinquent children; sick children attract more than bad ones. Chief education officers and chairmen of education committees may have private views about the competence of medical experts, but private views do not always justify public refutation of expert advice.

This is not the place for a historical review of the theory of maladjustment; suffice it to say that opinions of psychiatrists and educationalists working with maladjusted children (Wills, 1941; Lane, 1928) contributed to official recognition in the 1944 Education Act of a group of difficult children whose problems would not respond to traditionally punitive techniques. Paradoxically the gradual, yet increasingly rapid escalation of special school facilities for such children since 1944 (see Chapter 2) has reflected both an increasing acceptance of this fact, which is surely encouraging, and an increasing demand that something be done to get difficult children removed from ordinary schools, which is not. John Hellier, the head of Brislington School, took the view that special educational treatment for maladjusted children was needed but should be provided wherever possible in the normal school, as did the heads of those primary schools which first established nurture and adjustment groups. Indeed, the unit for maladjusted children was preceded at Brislington by a special class for ESN(M) children; this was started because the head had been so impressed by the distress of one child who had been sent to an ESN(M) school.

Thus the motivation for special facilities for maladjusted children within ordinary schools was disenchantment with traditional child guidance support services and a growing awareness of the number of difficult or unhappy children whose needs were not adequately being met. This did not, however, imply rejection of the expertise of clinic staff, but acceptance of their help in setting up additional facilities within schools. The solution was to establish a sort of short-term mini special school within the ordinary school, or (in the West Sussex adjustment groups) a part-time special class with much of the general philosophy and aims of a special school. In each case the general aim – to provide special education for special needs – was laudable, but the more detailed objectives were perhaps constrained by the rather narrow concept of maladjustment from which they were derived.

The idea that a spin-off of the groups would be to benefit the classes from which maladjusted pupils had been removed (and their teachers) was recognised and accepted both at Brislington and West Sussex; similarly all the projects described in this chapter emphasised the unsatisfactory home background of the majority of children selected for the groups. David Davies, the teacher in charge of the Brislington unit for five years and now special education adviser for the county of Avon took this a step further by arguing that a unit's existence should teach the rest of the staff to work in a different way, to become more receptive to the advice of psychiatrists and educational psychologists, and to become 'readier to deal sensitively with regressive behaviour as the unit's members are fed back into normal classes' (Rowan, 1976).

Yet even this progressive and sensitive view skirts round the critical points: (*a*) that maladjusted behaviour can only result from an interaction between the child and other people with whom he comes into contact and (*b*) that many of the children who present problems at school do not do so at home (Rutter *et al.*, 1970). There is nothing inherently illogical or contradictory in holding the view that a child's difficult behaviour in school is precipitated by family circumstances even though it is not evident at home and his parents deny other problems, but before taking this position we must be absolutely certain that he is not reacting, logically or otherwise, against something he finds stressful or unpleasant at school Similarly, there is nothing inherently illogical in trying to provide a therapeutic educational milieu to alleviate problems which arise at home (especially when, as in the Brislington project and some at least of the ILEA nurture groups, there is a simultaneous attempt to work with the parents), but before doing so we should ask not only whether the treatment is appropriate to the 'illness' but also whether the illness is such as to alter the child's basic educational needs, since placing him in a full-time unit will necessarily restrict his curriculum.

Inevitably there will be a lot of compromise; some children will be unable to benefit from an ordinary curriculum because of their anxiety, self-consciousness or lack of confidence; the more restricted curriculum of a special unit will be a small price to pay if the alternative is at best to sit apathetically at the back of the room and worst to refuse to attend school at all. On the other hand, other children are able to benefit educationally from ordinary classes but present so many problems that they have to be removed for the benefit of their teachers and the rest of the class. To argue that the first group of children need to attend a special unit for their own benefit, while the second group need to be removed for the benefit of teachers and other children is to miss the more basic point that in both cases the children's behaviour is the product of the way they react to the ordinary classroom situation, and this poses the question: What is it about that situation which elicits this reaction? In some cases the answer may simply be, nothing, as the child's behaviour can clearly be seen as a direct response to stress outside school, though, as we argued earlier, this is by no means always the case. In principle, units can help children cope with the things they find difficult in ordinary classes, for example by developing the confidence of the timid, withdrawn child or by teaching the aggressive extrovert to redirect his energy into more socially acceptable channels; the success of various forms of treatment for maladjusted children was discussed in Chapter 4 and does not need repeating. The main point here is that this conceptual model – one of treating the child – implies dual standards for children and teachers, 'they' are the ones with problems, and 'we' are the ones who offer treatment.

The same attitude lies behind the frequent displacement of blame on to parents, and by parents on to schools. The fact that children do not behave in the same way at school as at home is one of the commonest sources of conflict between parents and teachers; the teacher thinks the worried parent is a 'whittler', or inadequate in her handling of the child, while the parent thinks that the complaining teacher is making unreasonable demands on the child or even victimising him. When the child is generally well-behaved ('normal') at school the teacher may think his parents are responsible for his disturbing behaviour at home, yet believe the reason for another child's worrying behaviour at school lies in the child's own problems, or at least in his family's. In other words, when there is disturbance in the child–family relationship the child is assumed to be the injured party, but when the problem is disturbance in the child–school relationship the school is assumed to be the injured party, with the assumption that the child (or his parents) have failed the system rather than that the system has failed to adapt to the child.

Stating the argument as baldly as this inevitably polarises the two points of view in a way that occurs only when parents and teachers reach breaking point; on the whole parents and teachers are willing and able to see each other's point of view. Nevertheless the extreme views of the last paragraph are quite frequently seen when parents seldom if ever meet their children's teachers, when the only meetings that take place are conducted in an atmosphere in which parents or teachers feel threatened and ill at ease, and when potentially embarrassing administrative decisions, such as a decision to suspend a child or request a special school place for him, have to be justified to parents or administrators. The point we wish to make here, though, is quite simply that the problem at home is neither the child nor his parents, at school neither the child nor the school nor class organisation; the problem lies in the interaction between the unhappy, angry or dissatisfied parties. Viewed in this way the concepts of blame and responsibility become inappropriate, since the question is no longer 'Who is to blame?', nor even 'Why does Jimmy do that?', but 'What are we *each* doing that contributes to this problem situation?' It is important not to misunderstand this argument, assuming it to be some kind of witch-hunt aimed at blaming teachers for the maladjusted behaviour of their pupils. The argument is not that maladjusted behaviour is often caused by the ways schools treat children, but rather that teachers perceive children's behaviour as maladjusted when they are anxious, unhappy or angry about the way they and the child are treating each other. The adult may insist that the problem lies only in the child's unreasonable behaviour yet behind his demand that the child should be helped (treated, punished, or just removed) is hazy recognition that the problem lies not simply in the child but in his and the child's interaction with each other; this is expressed in statements such as; 'Nothing I can do seems to make any difference', or; 'He's not like the others – he just flies off the handle when I praise him, and looks pleased when I punish him!'

The school's contribution in promoting social adjustment

This view that the informal label of maladjustment results from dissatisfaction on the part of teachers (or parents) about the way they and the child are interacting with each other has significant implications for the development of special educational provision for maladjusted children in ordinary schools. Unfortunately, it receives only a cursory nod in the Warnock Report (DES, 1978). It implies, for instance that the contribution to problem situations of the school's organisation and structure (as well as of individual teachers) should be recognised, and that a unit's diagnostic work should have implications for the education and management of problem children as and when they return to their ordinary classes. Before pursuing these points in the light of the explosion of sanctuaries, tutorial centres, sin-bins and other facilities within and outside ordinary schools, we should look more critically at the thesis that schools contribute significantly to their pupils' social and emotional adjustment. Sociologists have stressed that children spend less time at school than at home, or in the community; it is therefore absurd, the argument runs, to expect schools to have much influence on their pupils. If this somewhat nihilistic view is correct, teachers might as well stick to the three Rs, and special units might retreat into the clinical safety of a child guidance clinic orientation, with the explicit aim of treating abnormal children with the rather limited range of techniques available to individual and group therapists. Under this model the role of school psychological service or child guidance clinic personnel would be to advise special group teachers on the application of treatment techniques in schools; there need be no emphasis on influencing the teaching and organisation of the school as a whole since school is viewed as a largely neutral influence.

Few teachers would wish to claim that school can exert a greater influence than home on children's adjustment, but not even the most pessimistic would be happy about the idea that school is of negligible influence. They would be supported by the growing body of research in the last ten years which shows that a school does in fact exert a substantial influence on the lives and futures of its pupils.

Research carried out in one secondary modern school as a participant observer convinced Hargreaves (1967) that the school's policy of streaming led to the formation of two opposed sub-cultures. The higher stream boys not only took external examinations but were disproportionately represented in the school's sporting activities and shared attitudes compatible with those of their teachers; in contrast lower stream boys were prevented from taking external examinations and by the third year were adopting a self-protective and unified wall of opposition to the system which they felt had condemned them to failure. Hargreaves argued that the two opposing subcultures within the school resulted from the streaming system; the teachers at the school would presumably have argued the reverse case – that the existence of an anti-school subculture necessitated streaming for the benefit of the brighter and more cooperative children, but this view overlooked the uncomfortable fact that low stream boys in the first two years were not on the whole united in their opposition to the school's value system; this opposition arose from the recognition that they had been 'written off' as examination prospects. Hargreaves comments laconically: 'If the examination is the carrot by which we entice the horse to run, we should not be surprised if the horse stands still when we take the carrot away.' Other research (Douglas, 1964) had shown that high stream pupils improve their IQ test scores at each IQ level between the ages of eight and eleven, while lower stream children deteriorate in the same period; Hargreaves found an analogous polarisation into social and antisocial attitudes as boys in high and low streams progressed up the schools.

Participant observer studies have the strength of allowing a detailed investigation of the social relationships in one school. The picture which emerges achieves a degree of realism, impossible in a numerical survey. In a later book Hargreaves *et al.* (1975), describe in more detail the social interaction between pupils and teachers which results in certain children being labelled as difficult and consequently forming *themselves* into a deviant, anti-school subgroup. By its very detail, though, participant observer research cannot look closely at the progress of a large number of children in different schools. Hargreaves demonstrated some of the policies and attitudes contributing to maladjustment in one school (though he would not call it maladjustment but the ascription of deviance, regarding the formation of a pupil's subgroup as a self-protective device which was predictable and even healthy in the circumstances). On the other hand a detailed study of one school can no more justify extending the conclusions to all schools than a detailed study on one child can justify conclusions about the whole class; comparison of statistical evidence from several different schools can yield evidence that some appear to have striking success in certain areas.

The first person to provide statistical evidence that schools have an influence on whether or not their pupils become delinquent was Michael Power (1967; 1972; Phillipson, 1971). Power claimed to find large differences in delinquency rates between secondary schools which he could not attribute solely to differences in delinquency rates in the school's catchment area. He argued that some of the schools whose delinquency rates he studied may have helped to prevent delinquency while others may have actually contributed to its development. What features *within* the 'delinquogenic' school might contribute to delinquency *outside* it, Power did not know, and the Inner London Education Authority refused permission for further related research in its schools. In fact, Power's conclusions were attacked by Baldwin (1972) on the grounds that he did not adequately control for differences in catchment area, and research in other London schools by the Cambridge Institute of Criminology (Farrington, 1972; West and Farrington, 1973) indicated that high delinquency schools tended to admit more children who might reasonably be regarded as 'at risk' on the basis of evidence about their home district.

On the other hand Rutter's surveys in an Inner London Borough (Rutter *et al.*, 1975b) showed that schools with a high turnover of staff or pupils had high rates of behavioural deviance, and the same applied to schools with high absentee rates or a high proportion of children receiving free meals. However, the 'deviant' children in these schools were *not* always those receiving free meals; the association was just as strong when they were excluded from the analysis, indicating that the rate of deviance in children *not* eligible for free meals was associated with the proportion of children who *were* eligible. 'This suggests that, however it may be caused, it is something about the school itself that plays some part in the association with deviance in the children.'

The school characteristics associated with behavioural deviance were generally the same as those associated with specific reading retardation, though large classes were associated neither with this nor with behaviour problems. The adverse school factors associated with deviance in London were generally the same as in the earlier Isle of Wight study (Rutter *et al.*, 1970), but they were much more common in London. With one or two provisos, the same applied, as we saw in Chapter 2, to adverse family circumstances, so that Rutter and Quinton (1977) were able to conclude that 'whereas much has still to be learned about the mechanisms involved it may be concluded that the area difference in *child* psychiatric disorder is entirely explicable in terms of family and school conditions'. The real measure of a school's influence though came when pupils in the ILB study were followed up at the age of fourteen (Rutter, 1977). Using the fact that the findings at age ten gave a reasonably accurate prediction of adjustment at age fourteen, he calculated the proportion of deviant children expected in each school on the basis of the findings when they were ten. The results showed substantial differences between schools; taking extreme examples, twelve fourteen-year-olds were expected at one school but in fact only six were actually considered deviant, while at another school ten were expected but the number actually found was twenty-four. Rutter concluded that this pointed to the probability of school exerting a considerable effect on children's behaviour, and at the time of this book going to press a further project on the school factors contributing to good or poor adjustment was nearing completion.

One of the problems which confuses research into the effects of different schools on their pupils is the overlap in catchment areas and the system of parental choice whereby parents can opt for their children to attend a certain school. This issue formed the basis of criticism of Michael Power's work in Tower Hamlets, but did not apply to David Reynold's research in South Wales. He was able to study nine secondary modern schools in a socially homogeneous area which had no parental choice system (Reynolds, 1976). He was able to obtain details about attendance at each school, the number of first offenders in the juvenile court per annum, and the number of children obtaining places at the local technical college (generally regarded in the area as the key to an apprenticeship or craft training).

He found marked differences between the nine schools. While more than half the pupils at one school obtained places at the local technical college, less than 10 per cent did so from another; while one school had an average attendance rate of nearly 90 per cent, another school's was only 77 per cent. Moreover, these figures were remarkably stable from year to year, and the average did not mask major variations in the course of the six-year period. Even more important, there was no evidence that the high delinquency schools drew their pupils from the most highly depressed or impoverished areas, as Reynolds found little association between delinquency in the school and the proportion of the catchment area population in Social Classes 4 and 5, or in Social Class 5 on its own. He concluded that 'these nine schools therefore appear to be producing large differences in the rates of delinquency, truancy and academic attainment of their pupils, differences which do not appear to be significantly related to variations in the social background of the catchment areas from which the schools take their pupils'.

Differences in delinquency rates between schools with similar catchment areas were also found in a northern city (Finlayson and Loughran, 1976). Their study was of pupils' perceptions in high and low delinquency schools and showed that teachers in the low delinquency school were seen by their pupils as exercising their authority in a manner less hostile to the pupils than in the high delinquency schools even though the staff in one of the latter were seen as showing more concern and interest in their welfare than by pupils in the corresponding low delinquency school. This was consistent with Reynolds' (1976) suggestion that behaviour deteriorates 'when pupils and teachers refuse a truce'; if teachers become inflexible in their insistence on rules and regulations to which the children feel no intrinsic commitment there will be a gradual escalation in the use of coercive disciplinary techniques and a corresponding increase in the pupils' rejection to the teachers' expectations.

Another way of looking at the level of maladjustment in different schools would be to compare exclusion rates or rates of referral for special education. Unfortunately the latter are notoriously hard to obtain, and the one detailed psychiatric study of children excluded from school in this country (York *et al.,* 1972) did not report differences in prevalence between schools. On the other hand, Galloway (1976a) found in a northern city where secondary education had been reorganised into a comprehensive system that former selective schools tended to exclude more pupils for unacceptable behaviour than former non-selective schools. Further work still in progress, is showing marked variation in exclusion rates from school to school, which have remained fairly consistent over a four-year period and bear little observable relationship either to the size of schools or to their catchment areas.

Implications for the development and philosophy of special groups in ordinary schools

The research, then, is showing with reasonable consistency that there are social influences within schools which affect the prevalence of such indices of maladjustment as juvenile delinquency and truancy. Describing the difficult children in a school which regularly finds it necessary to exclude pupils for unmanageable behaviour as maladjusted, or behaviourally deviant, or psychiatrically disordered (the label depends largely on the academic training of the professional concerned) may arguably be technically accurate in the sense that the child's behaviour conforms to some arbitrary definition of abnormality, but it has no implications for treatment. For psychologists and education officers the problem is both ethical and practical. If the children concerned are removed to a special school they may well be happier and adjust more acceptably to school and to society, though as we saw in Chapter 3 the evidence for this is rather scanty. Yet to remove the children is to grant official recognition, in practice if not in theory, to the idea that the maladjustment exists only in the children, with the implication inherent in this assumption that no changes are needed in the school's organisation and attitudes. Further, if the latter undergo no constructive development they will presumably continue to assist unhappy, inadequate or unsuccessful parents in the production of more maladjusted children who in turn will become candidates for exclusion if they have not first obtained a special school place.

It is questionable whether the advisory and administrative branches of a local education authority should contribute to this process. Yet the other side of the picture is no brighter. If a local education authority's administration insists on a child's return to, or retention in, a school which firmly believes it can do nothing to help him there will inevitably be enormous stress on the school's teachers as well as on the child and his family. Compelling an unwilling school to keep a disturbing child is hardly the best way to encourage the flexibility of organisation and curriculum which will be needed if his needs are to be met more adequately; innovation and flexibility flourish in an atmosphere of confidence and cooperation, not anxiety and resentment.

Regarded in this context, the development of nurture groups and adjustment units for maladjusted children in ordinary schools can be seen not as a solution to the needs of these 'odd' children but as an additional facility closely integrated into the school's curriculum and pastoral care network. As mentioned already, the need for close cooperation between special group teachers and class teachers was emphasised in the earlier projects, but there was perhaps a less clear recognition of the possibility that some children might need admission to an adjustment group *because of,* rather than *in spite of* help they had already received within the school's pastoral care, teaching and disciplinary structure. Again, it is important not to misunderstand the implications in this suggestion. The implication is not that teachers should conduct a witch-hunt to discover whether they or their colleagues have caused or contributed to a child's maladjusted behaviour through unwise or insensitive handling, or poor organisation; the implication is that teachers should accept the extremely encouraging evidence about their influence on children's social and emotional adjustment and consequently be willing to consider the possibility of adapting the curriculum and their teaching methods to meet the needs of a disturbed child more successfully. If a unit for problem pupils gives them the breathing space necessary to carry out this reassessment it will justify its existence; if at the same time the teacher running it can form his own independent assessment of the child's needs and use this in working out a programme for his rehabilitation with his regular teachers, he will cease to be the custodian of a 'sin-bin' or class for 'nutty kids' as he starts contributing to the way difficult children are taught and handled in the school as a whole. More concrete examples of ways this can be done are discussed in detail in the next chapter.

Recent developments

Meanwhile we need to look at the expansion of special facilities for difficult children in the 1970s. This period has been characterised by rapid and far-reaching changes in the education services. The reorganisation of secondary education into a comprehensive system in all but a tiny minority of authorities, and a parallel reorganisation in many areas of primary education from traditional infant/junior schools into Plowden-type first and middle schools (DES, 1967) are among the more far-reaching. By upsetting the *status quo,* change creates uncertainty, with associated stress and insecurity; it is unfortunate that stress on teachers caused by rapid changes in the education system has been compounded by stress associated with equally rapid changes in society. The popular belief, fostered by a news-hungry media, that we are living in a uniquely violent era has little supporting evidence, yet many adolescents now feel freer to challenge adult opinions and rules, and measures of stress such as family breakdown are increasing. In this educational and social climate it is not surprising that underlying anxiety has found a legitimate outlet in widespread concern about problem children.

Debates on the subject at annual conferences of teacher associations have not always made edifying reading: at the 1977 conference of the National Association of Schoolmasters/Union of Women Teachers, one London teacher blamed the existence of problem children on 'a system rooted in soft psychology and permissive, progressive education arranged on production line principles – I mean comprehensives'. At the same conference a Leeds teacher told of one boy who had escaped from a reprimand from a teacher by leaping from a first floor window. The conference applauded when she said: 'Perhaps the solution would be to teach them on the fifth floor' (Lodge, 1977). The union's threat that 'where LEAs refuse to face the overwhelming evidence of severely disruptive behaviour we shall continue to exclude the militants', would perhaps have been rather more impressive if there was more evidence that the prevalence of exclusion declines as special centres are opened. At another national conference three years earlier (the 1974 conference of the Association of Assistant Mistresses) the damaging term 'sin-bin' was used to describe sanctuary units for disturbed children (Rowan, 1976).

As a result of genuine concern about the children in question, supplemented by political pressure from teacher unions, most authorities have now made some moves in the direction of special facilities for problem children (some would call them additional facilities) outside the traditional special school system. Warnock recommends that these should be regarded explicitly as part of the special education network (DES, 1978). In some cases this has taken the form of encouraging head teachers to start a sanctuary or adjustment group in their own schools; in others the Education Committee has opened special centres which draw children from any of the authority's secondary schools; in yet others a range of facilities is becoming available, both inside many ordinary schools and in special centres outside them. Rowan (1976) noted that children were always accepted for the outside units on the understanding that they remain on the roll of their ordinary school, to which they will return when and if possible. Unfortunately, return to school is all too frequently written off as impractical, though lip-service is generally paid to the idea. However, one notable exception where return is a *condition* of acceptance is described in the next chapter. As one might expect, the ideology and organisation of the burgeoning number of units which now exist in a majority of authorities are as varied as the names used to describe them, and the problems of the children for whom they cater. Apart from sanctuaries and adjustment groups, they are formally or informally known as Educational Guidance Units, Opportunity Classes (often for children with learning difficulties as well as behaviour problems), and Truancy Centres.

Their philosophies range from a social case-work orientated, non-directive, tolerant acceptance of the children and their problems to a rigorous application of behaviour modification principles derived from learning theory. Most of the centres outside ordinary schools admit disruptive children or truants but this is not always the case with units within ordinary schools, where the philosophy and admission procedures seem to vary even more widely. In some schools the unit was set up as an additional part of the school's disciplinary system; the threat of admission is intended to be a deterrent, and the regime is calculated to make the children wish to earn a speedy release. At other schools the unit accepts the most disruptive pupils, but admission is regarded as a privilege rather than a punishment and the emphasis is on treatment rather than punishment. At others still, actively disruptive behaviour is a disqualification for admission; this is dealt with by experienced staff imposing extra supervision on the disruptive pupils, while the special unit caters for school refusers, and withdrawn or neurotic children who might otherwise be submerged or overlooked in a large school.

The wide variation in philosophy and practice in the growing industry of problem children (the only growth area in British education in the second half of the 1970s) reflects not only the lack of any consensus among teachers, and between teachers and other professionals on the education or treatment of maladjusted children but also, more basically, about which children should be considered maladjusted in the first place; if, as some people would argue, mere 'disruptives' should not be regarded as maladjusted it might conceivably make sense to subject them to a strict and highly regimented environment from which they would seek to earn a speedy release by changing their ways. Intentionally or otherwise some local education authorities encourage this belief by insisting that all 'maladjusted' children are catered for in special schools for this category of handicap. The inconsistency can frequently be seen by looking at the ages of the pupils on admission to the different establishments; often special schools admit primary or younger secondary children while the 'disruptives' units admit older adolescents. Similarly the behaviour and backgrounds of children in special schools and special units lend no support to the idea that maladjusted children can be readily identified. The problems of children in units outside ordinary schools may be more intransigent than those of children attending the sanctuaries within their own schools, yet few psychologists would have much trouble in justifying a special school place for almost all children selected to attend any sort of unit on a full-time basis if they thought this recommendation either practical or desirable. This would not, of course, always be true in the cases of units which take a larger number of children on a part-time basis.

The choice, then, lies between accepting the principle that children accepted for the units are maladjusted and, more radically, refusing to describe *any* children, including those in special schools, as maladjusted on the grounds that the term has no clinical significance and is vague to the point of meaninglessness. The latter alternative is preferable. The question facing teachers and psychologists should not be whether a child is or is not maladjusted; in view of the confusion and disagreement about the nature of the term, the answer can only be arbitrary and idiosyncratic. Instead, the questions should be about the nature of the child's special needs, the ways he, his teachers or parents are causing difficulties for each other, and ways in which their respective expectations and needs can be modified and met. The main argument of the next chapter is that teachers have the knowledge and the ability to carry out this sort of assessment provided they are willing to adapt their practical and theoretical knowledge of the way children learn educational skills to the way they learn different patterns of behaviour.

Chapter 8

Innovations in the education of maladjusted children: II

A. Proving that change is possible

Introduction

In the last chapter we reviewed evidence that the number of maladjusted children in a school depends not only on the number of pupils who are at risk because of constitutional, family or social problems, but also on factors connected with the school's own organisation or attitudes. To put it more bluntly, there is growing evidence that some schools are succeeding in reducing the level of maladjustment among their pupils while others may even be increasing it. In the ILEA teachers' organisations and the administration at first reacted with such dismay and hostility to these findings that further research on the subject ceased. That anxiety was understandable and may have been caused by a failure in public relations on the part of the research team. Nevertheless, it can hardly be stressed strongly enough that the anxiety was misplaced; for the first time research was showing that school might influence the vital aspects of its pupils' lives over which popular sociological opinion believed that it could exert no influence.

This fatalism is seen in parts of the Plowden Report (DES, 1967) in this country and in the Coleman Report (Coleman, 1966) in the United States, both of which reflect the prevalent belief that differences in curriculum and methods have little impact on the overriding influence of home and community. The reason for the failure of these and similar studies to identify school factors which may influence the level of maladjustment was that they investigated aspects of school life and organisation which are certainly important, but probably do not have as much influence on attendance and behaviour as the social relationships and attitudes within the school. The size of class, for example, has been investigated extensively, with the consistent result that children in small classes do no better academically than those in large (Davie *et al.*, 1972). Similarly, size and age of school appears relatively unimportant compared with other influences such as high turnover of staff or pupils, or the internal organisation.

Although some research projects are currently trying to discover what it is about a successful school that contributes to its success there is not as yet any clear consensus. We have already seen that factors such as staff and pupil turnover were relevant both in London and the Isle of Wight (Rutter *et al.*, 1975b), and there is growing evidence about the importance of teachers' attitudes to their pupils (Hargreaves, 1967; Hargreaves *et al.*, 1975; Finlayson and Loughran, 1976; Reynolds, 1976). All the same, the evidence is still scanty and suffers from the additional limitation that it contains little guidance for teachers; they can take encouragement from the evidence that they *do* affect their pupils' attitudes and socio-emotional adjustment, yet be left wondering what changes in organisation and attitude are needed in their own schools; even if they feel clear about what changes are needed, they may still feel bewildered about how to achieve them. Here, however, we are helped by recent research on classroom interaction and behaviour modification.

Classroom interaction and behaviour modification

Behaviour modification is a generic term for an approach to treatment which focuses explicitly on the presenting problem, without assuming that it is caused by underlying conflicts which must be dealt with first. This approach uses a collection of techniques for achieving change in behaviour, and should always be based on a detailed analysis of how the different parties, for example child and teacher or child and other children, are interacting with each other and influencing each other's behaviour (Galloway, 1975, 1977).

While the studies described so far have concentrated on a descriptive (and sometimes statistical) evaluation of certain factors in schools, investigations on classroom interaction and behaviour modification have looked in much more detail at a smaller number of teachers and their classes, or more often at individual problem children in a classroom. The principles of behaviour modification have been applied with children of all ages and all sorts of difficulties, in special and ordinary schools. They have been used almost as often with children with learning difficulties as with behaviour problems. There is an enormous literature on their use with subnormal and autistic children, but here we shall concentrate on their application with pupils of near-average ability.

The use of behaviour modification has probably attracted more controversy than any other treatment technique. Much of the criticism has been ill-informed or misguided, as it has been based either on a basic misunderstanding of the principles involved or else on inappropriate application of them; it is always easy to criticise bad practice. As we shall argue in the course of this chapter, the *principles* of behaviour modification (which include the all-important assessment of teacher–child interaction which should form the starting point for every treatment programme) constitute no more than good and uncontroversial teaching practice. The reason for the controversy is not to be found in the underlying principles (though these have been savagely attacked) but in the obscure, mechanistic, jargon-laden way they have been described by the psychologists who first developed them. Teachers who can work successfully with problem children apply intuitively many of the principles and techniques which academic psychologists have developed under the title of behaviour modification; they have arrived at the same, or nearly the same, place by different routes, generally without recognising it.

To understand the reason for this we need to understand the origins of research on teacher–child or parent–child interaction and behaviour modification. We knew more than fifty years ago that there was a relationship between learning and phobias (Watson, 1924), yet until quite recently the predominant influence on treatment of all kinds was that of psychotherapy derived from the theories of Freud and other early psychoanalysts. The essential difference between behaviour and analytic therapy is that the psychoanalytic therapist is reluctant to accept at face value the symptom for which the child is referred. He believes there is an unconscious 'cause' to the problem and aims to help the child understand and accept his unconscious drives. For the psychoanalytic therapist it is irresponsible to treat the symptom directly since this will result in 'symptom substitution'; new, and possibly more dangerous symptoms will appear, as the underlying, and probably unconscious cause of the problem has not been treated. In contrast, behaviour therapists and behaviour modifiers claim there is little evidence for symptom substitution (Yates, 1970) and regard the presenting problem as *the* problem, denying the need to seek theoretical underlying conflicts. This is not to say that they ignore other factors; in fact as suggested earlier they are likely to plan effective treatment only if they first make a very detailed *behavioural* analysis of the problem. They look carefully at the child's behaviour and at the behaviour of the people around him – teachers, parents, peers – in order to understand what causes the problem. Having made this preliminary assessment they have to make an ethical decision as to what aspects of the adult–child interaction they should reasonably seek to change (Galloway, 1975). They then draw up a management programme in which they may see the child individually, but more often involve his parents or teachers as the main agents for change (O'Leary and O'Leary, 1972; Johnson and Katz, 1973).

Why, then, has behaviour modification aroused so much controversy? To start with, the pioneers in the educational treatment of maladjusted children were strongly influenced by psychoanalytic ideas, even though many of the techniques of group pressure which they used, such as self-government and shared responsibility (Wills, 1960; Shaw, 1965; Lennhoff, 1960), might well have received nods of cautious approval from an experimental psychologist with an interest in behaviour modification. The latter's concept of the direct treatment of symptoms struck at the heart of their theoretical value system. Even worse, many of the early behaviour therapists were experimental psychologists who sought to apply to children the principles of learning theory derived from the rat laboratory. (An excellent example of the way in which results of animal learning experiments led to the development of the first effective treatment for a psychotic illness in adults is given by Meyer (1973).) As a result they described their findings in the jargon of experimental psychology; children, like laboratory rats, were often referred to as Ss (subjects) and the teacher or psychologist as E (experimenter); the emphasis was on proving experimentally that behaviour could change in certain predictable ways; bad behaviour was encouraged ('reinforced') by teachers inadvertently paying attention to the wrong things, while good behaviour frequently received no reinforcement. An example of this is the child who has learnt that he can make his teacher stop whatever he is doing by standing up and starting to move around the classroom; the same child may have learnt that his teacher will ignore him when he sits quietly at his desk (perhaps the teacher has heaved a perfectly understandable sigh of relief that he is having an uninterrupted lesson for a change, and can therefore give other children some much needed attention).

David Wills (1960) refused to accept that a child is a problem, insisting that it is certain things he does which constitute the problem: 'I like you, but I don't like what you do'. Behaviour modification goes a stage further by insisting that the problem does not just lie in certain specifiable aspects of the child's behaviour – for instance his shouting out, his tearfulness, his nervousness, his aggression to other children – but *also* in the way other children and adults react to him. Thus Zimmerman and Zimmerman (1962), in one of the first detailed descriptions of classroom behaviour modification (in this instance a special class for disturbed children), showed that an eleven-year-old boy's spelling mistakes were not caused by his own lack of ability but by his teacher's tendency to concentrate on him when he made spelling mistakes. If she ignored him whenever he spelled a word incorrectly and reinforced him for spelling a word correctly by letting him help her do something enjoyable, he rapidly improved. With another child the preliminary analysis of his temper tantrums suggested that he was encouraged to throw tantrums by the attention lavished on him at the time by the teachers and helpers in the unit. When all adults were asked to take no notice of the boy when he threw a tantrum, he quickly stopped doing so, thus confirming the suggestion derived from learning theory that when reinforcement is removed, the behaviour will cease, or 'extinguish' to use the jargon phrase. It is worth noting that even in this early study the problem was tackled by removing its cause; some of the more extreme and ill-informed opponents of behaviour modification maintain that it only treats the symptoms, ignoring their causes. From the Zimmermans' study it should be clear that the aim here was to tackle problem behaviour by altering the interaction between child and teacher; the target behaviours were the spelling difficulty and the temper tantrums but the problem lay in the teacher unintentionally encouraging what she was trying to stop.

The Zimmermans showed the importance of understanding the interaction between children and their teachers when trying to deal with problem behaviour, and opened the way for further investigations on the teaching styles which reduce or contribute to maladjusted behaviour patterns. The early research was carried out under rigorous, not to say artificial, conditions in the United States but nevertheless substantially increased our understanding of classroom interaction. Hall *et al.* (1968b) studied the effect of their teachers' attention on disruptive and distractible six- and eight-year-old children. Independent observers kept records at regular intervals throughout the day on whether the children were concentrating on their work, whether and how the teachers were talking to them, and whether they were close to them at the time. After keeping these records for two weeks (a luxury only possible in a well funded research project) the records showed that the teachers attended to the children mainly when they were *not* concentrating on their work, even though the teachers were experienced. (Before criticising the teachers concerned it may be as well to ask whether any teacher can place his hand on his heart and deny that he frequently overlooks the disruptive child who is having an unusual 'good' day, seizing the chance to give the others some much needed attention but teaching the difficult child that good behaviour does not pay.) Hall and his colleagues discussed the results with the children's teachers, emphasising the principles of social reinforcement; they subsequently gave each teacher a signal whenever their child was concentrating on the task in hand, so that he or she could then be given some attention. A satisfactory level of concentration – 'study behaviour' in the jargon – was soon reached, and the research worker then stopped signalling to the teachers, with the result that the pupils' concentration quickly fell to its original level. When this was pointed out to the teachers, they were soon able to give the children attention for 'good' behaviour without the help of special signals. Important features of this early study were that it did not seem to interfere much with the teachers' ordinary activities, nor did it result in *more* attention for the difficult children; instead these pupils received *different* attention, and because of the sharp decrease in maladjusted behaviour their teachers had more time for constructive teaching.

In a similar study in the same year Madsen *et al.* (1968) systematically varied the teaching styles of two volunteer elementary (primary) school teachers in order to ascertain how different styles would affect the behaviour of three disruptive children. As in Hall's study, trained observers recorded the children's behaviour and samples of the teachers' behaviour. First the teachers were asked to give the class a clear set of rules, and draw attention to them at frequent intervals. Next they were asked to ignore unsatisfactory behaviour, and finally to give approval and attention for satisfactory behaviour. The results showed that rules on their own did not improve classroom control, and that ignoring unsatisfactory conduct was also not very effective unless it was combined with approval for satisfactory conduct. This might of course, have been predicted for two reasons: (*a*) observation of the teachers' behaviour showed that they had great difficulty in ignoring inappropriate behaviour, and (*b*) if disruptive behaviour is intended to attract attention it cannot be expected to disappear unless the child finds that he can obtain attention in other, more constructive ways. In a partial replication of Madsen's work, Harrop and Critchley (1972) found that two children aged five and nine improved, while a thirteen-year-old ESN girl deteriorated sharply in the experimental period and only improved to her previous state when the teacher reverted to his previous methods of control.

This raises several issues about the nature of classroom control in general and the management of maladjusted children in particular. In an earlier article Holmes (1966) had suggested that some reactions which teachers intend to be mildly, or even severely, punishing to children may in fact have the opposite effect. Obvious examples are public rebuke and corporal punishment, which can have the effect of strengthening a child's own 'tough' self-image and his status in an anti-school subgroup. The thirteen-year-old girl mentioned above did not respond to her teacher's praise – a fact which will cause no surprise to teachers of maladjusted children, who often regard adult approval as a threat.

The methods described so far rested on the incorrect premise that a teacher's praise always has greater reinforcement value than the disapproval which had previously maintained the maladjusted behaviour. Adult attention and friendship may pose an intolerable threat to the precarious defences of a child who has come to expect unreliable, inconsistent behaviour from adults; like the backward reader who refuses to try rather than risk further failure, such a child may regard the adult who seems to like him with hostility and suspicion. Thus the study of classroom interaction cannot logically be divorced from that of the 'reinforcement history' of individuals in the class. By the 'reinforcement history' we mean the influences in a child's background which have influenced the ways he responds to different circumstances. The child of an irascible but largely disinterested father and a depressed, exhausted mother may discover very early in life that if he is quiet ('behaves himself') he will be ignored – an unhappy state of affairs for most adults and unbearable for a pre-school child. On the other hand if he turns off the television while dad is watching his favourite programme or makes a determined effort to pull a pan of boiling water over himself while mum is cooking, he will receive a shout or a slap, which at least means his existence is being acknowledge and is therefore better than being ignored. This can easily generalise to his behaviour at school and establish a vicious circle in which punishment is an active incentive to further provocative behaviour, especially if the pupil comes to regard the adult world with hostility and suspicion like the child mentioned earlier. For the teacher, though, the problem lies in the obvious fact that the same behaviour can have different causes; exactly the same sort of provocative behaviour which we have just described may be motivated by a need for acceptance from other disruptive classmates. In this rather simplistic example the teacher will need to ask whether the child seems to be 'playing to the gallery', or appears relatively insensitive to the reactions of other children.

The great limitation of the American, and more recently the British, literature on behaviour modification is that the subject is too often presented as a collection of esoteric-sounding techniques, and not as the result of a careful study of the interaction between individuals in a classroom. Hall (1968b) O'Leary *et al.* (1969) and Harrop and Critchley (1972) described instances in which a mixture of praising appropriate behaviour while ignoring inappropriate behaviour was unsuccessful; this led to greater awareness of social influences within the pupils themselves, and to more emphasis on classroom organisation as a relevant influence. Thus, McAllister *et al.* (1969) found that the teacher of a class of sixteen- to nineteen-year-olds in an American High School tended not to identify students by name when asking them to stop talking; he gave no praise when they were not talking, and seldom carried out his threats. A combination of direct sharp rebukes to named pupils and explicit approval for the following reduction in talking out of turn had a dramatic effect. In contrast O'Leary *et al.* (1970) did not concentrate on group control in this way, but tested the idea that loud reprimands had the effect of increasing disruptive behaviour rather than reducing it. They asked teachers to use soft reprimands, audible only to the child they were addressing, and found that the level of maladjusted behaviour declined in most of the children, though there were exceptions with whom it had little or no effect.

We pointed out earlier that the study of classroom interaction cannot logically be divorced from that of the individual child and his background. The same applies, of course, to the teacher, as his reaction to different children is governed largely by his own previous learning experiences as a child, adolescent and adult; this is one of the reasons that teachers, like everyone else, differ so widely in the sorts of behaviour they find intolerable. Critical self-awareness is as important in the study of classroom interaction and behaviour modification as in any other form of work with maladjusted children. Children who do not respond to social incentives such as praise and disapproval may cooperate with a more direct approach. One approach which has been used extensively is to let children earn tokens for completion of work, or for suitable behaviour. The tokens can be exchanged for sweets, outings, toys, the right to take part in a popular activity and so on. O'Leary and Becker (1967) used tokens in a class of seventeen disruptive nine-year-olds; the tokens consisted of ratings from 1 to 10 placed in a small booklet on each child's desk and were awarded according to the extent they followed their teacher's requests. The ratings could be used to 'buy' things like sweets or comics at the back of the room. The use of 'token economies' in the classroom was reviewed by O'Leary and Drabman (1971); the intention is that the child's newly acquired educational skills and work habits will not depend on the tokens but can be maintained by other incentives such as the teacher's praise and approval. Thus tokens might motivate a backward reader to start learning, but once he has achieved a degree of success the intrinsic satisfaction of making progress and a wish to retain his teacher's approval should maintain his motivation without the need for tokens. In practice, though, children often relapse when the tokens are withdrawn; an even more practical objection is the reluctance of many teachers to use them on the grounds that children should not be 'bribed'. Tokens could be thought of as an exceptionally systematic, structured form of the incentives teachers give children anyway, necessary only when some artificial motivation is needed for an apathetic child or class. On the other hand, they have been used with considerable success not only in special school classes (O'Leary and Becker, 1967), but also in social education projects with delinquent adolescents (Fixsen *et al.*, 1973; Lane and Millar, 1977). However, the last two projects did *not* use the system indiscriminately for all children in the project, but drew up individual programmes for each child based on his needs. This is a point to which we shall return later in this chapter.

The difficulties in using tokens do not apply to another approach which lends itself particularly to use in relatively informal classrooms which have a wide variety of readily accessible activities. This is the 'reinforcement menu', derived from the Premack Principle (Premack, 1959). The principle, briefly, is that a popular activity, such as drawing, can act as an incentive for an unpopular activity, such as completing a maths assignment. It has been shown by animal psychologists that when something that is liked follows something that is disliked, the latter activity becomes less unpopular. The same has been shown in an ESN(M) school classroom where a list was made of things the girls enjoyed doing (the 'menu'); they could then choose one of the items on completion of their arithmetic work. Not only did the quantity and quality of the class's arithmetic improve, but the girls even started to enjoy the subject and some even selected it as a choice on the menu after completing a reading assignment.

Many experienced teachers could legitimately say, 'Yes, but we've been doing this for years and we certainly don't need a fancy name to describe it!' Others could equally legitimately argue that this approach requires a flexibility in classroom organisation which would totally disrupt teaching methods they have successfully developed over the years. Similarly, it is hard to see a reinforcement menu working in a secondary school where children have to move on to a different room at the end of the lesson. The point is that the difficult (or slow) child *must* have his choice on completion of his task; all too often it is only the bright and well-behaved child who finishes early and is allowed to do something enjoyable. The slow-learning or disturbing child who struggles to finish his work by the end of the lesson is easily overlooked, just because he has got to struggle to finish by the end of the lesson.

Difficulties in applying behaviour modification

At this stage we need to look more closely at some of the difficulties associated with the study of classroom interaction and behaviour modification in relation to difficult children. Many of these problems are just as evident in special schools as in ordinary schools. An immediate, and sometimes insuperable, difficulty in secondary schools is a logistic one, but paradoxically it underlines the central theme of the chapter that a child's problem does not lie exclusively in his own behaviour but should be examined in the light of his interaction with other people. The problem in secondary schools arises from the complexity of the timetable; each pupil generally has up to a dozen different teachers in the course of the week, and gathering them all together in one place at one time can be a formidable exercise. Yet when this formidable exercise is undertaken it very frequently reveals that the child behaves in quite different ways with different teachers. In a case history on a girl (Lillian) Galloway (1976b) describes how she was regarded as an enormous behaviour problem by inexperienced teachers but was pitied as a poor, timid, bullied little thing by their experienced senior colleagues. In fact her different behaviour with different teachers had the same result– she successfully monopolised their attention; with the young teachers she could do this by being a nuisance, but the general classroom control and discipline of the experienced staff was so good that she could only attract their sympathy by provoking boys into bullying her. The provocation, though, only came to light after the meeting at which it was decided that her interaction with other children should be watched more closely. In primary schools, where children remain with the same class teacher for all or most of the week, it is harder to illustrate how the teacher's behaviour affects that of the child. Sometimes a change of class results in marked improvement, but many heads feel that this undermines the confidence and authority of the child's present teacher, or fear that the other parents will demand a change of class if a precedent is created.

A more basic difficulty, however, is how to carry out the initial observations on which an analysis of teacher–child, teacher–class, or child–child interaction has to be based. The early American literature on behaviour modification was carried out in specially funded research projects which enabled trained observers to act as 'flies on the wall', sometimes for weeks on end. Incidentally, it has consistently been found that children fairly soon accept a non-participating observer as part of the furniture and behave as if he did not exist. Clearly, no such luxury is possible in an ordinary or even in a special school. Visiting psychologists can seldom spare more than a day (often less than half a day) for systematic classroom observation and this is probably insufficient time for the children to get used to his presence. Confident teachers who enjoy working as a team in an open-plan classroom can observe each other in a spirit of constructive criticism, yet comments from colleagues can easily be viewed as a personal criticism or a threat to one's own autonomy. Often the best that can be achieved is to ask the teacher of a difficult or disturbing child to keep brief but systematic records of certain clearly specified aspects of his behaviour. For instance, she may make a note each time he shouts out in the course of the lesson, or each instance of cooperative play with another child. The point of this is to obtain some sort of record against which to measure future progress, but it has the additional advantage of focusing the teacher's attention on different aspects of his behaviour. Harrop (1977) has pointed out that a number of problems seem to disappear at this stage – the child appears miraculously to improve. Exactly what changes occur is not clear, but it seems quite likely that the initial 'base-line' observations sensitise the teacher to aspects of his behaviour which she had previously overlooked, so that though neither pupil nor teacher have received any specific advice the child responds to the teacher's changed perceptions. The limitation of a teacher's observations of children in her own class is that they are too child-orientated and cannot easily take into account the teacher's own contribution to the interaction process. One teacher's solution – to ask children to keep records of *her* behaviour – is not likely to be widely accepted! (Students of the American learning theorist, B. F. Skinner, did something similar by testing his own theories on him; they are alleged to have found they could induce him to stand on a spot of his lecturer's platform which they had previously selected by coughing, shuffling papers and generally appearing disinterested whenever he moved away from it, and showing signs of eager, intelligent concentration when he moved towards it).

Yet although the initial observations are generally of the *child's* behaviour, the subsequent treatment programme is based on the principle that the *teacher's* reactions must change before the child's can. Probably the most widely misunderstood point about behaviour modification is that any change in a child's behaviour is secondary to change in the teacher's, a point which should be clear from every piece of research described so far, where the teacher was asked to alter his previous way of coping with disturbing children in his class. There are admittedly some forms of treatment where this principle does not altogether hold true; these are the programmes which consciously seek to teach children new skills, for instance how to cope with authority or how to tolerate failure or frustration, but these constitute new learning for the child, and the aim is to help him cope with the stresses he experiences from adults and from his peers. This implies that maladjusted children can be taught to become their own therapists, and is a point to which we shall return. However, when the aim is to help a class teacher educate difficult children more successfully by altering the destructively disruptive interaction between himself and them, it follows that *his* behaviour must be the first to change; the only alternative, as we have just noted would be for an outside 'expert' to teach the children how to avoid conflict with their 'difficult' teacher so that change in the latter's techniques and attitudes become secondary to that in his pupils!

B. Successful treatment – just good teaching?

What makes a successful teacher?

It might seem reasonable at this stage to ask when specialists in behaviour modification will get a blinding glimpse of the obvious and realise that almost by definition, all successful teachers and parents use at least some of the techniques which are presented in formalised, systematic ways in behaviour modification programmes. This is an argument whose validity was in fact recognised in the already quoted study by Hall and his colleagues (1968a).

They accepted that many teachers used these methods long before Skinner formulated the principles of operant conditioning in the experimental laboratory and tried to extend their use to the home and school. Nevertheless, very few teachers, even the most successful and experienced, are able to look at their own behaviour with sufficient objectivity to specify *what* they have done, and hence what an inexperienced colleague should do to achieve similarly acceptable standards of work and behaviour. All too often advice to probationer teachers and to students ranges from the banal to the platitudinous: 'it's just a matter of experience, you know', or 'crack down on them hard to start with and then you'll be able to let up'.

Hall argued that behavioural analysis (systematically analysing the behaviour of teacher and children) enables supervisors to teach students or probationers the skills of classroom management without recourse to the haphazard trial and error method which was all that had been available previously. Ward (1971) also points out that 'many young teachers develop idiosyncratic methods which can become highly effective over the years, and certainly work with the majority of children'. The problem, though, lies in the phrase 'over the years'; it is possible that the most rigid teachers are the disillusioned probationers, and some young teachers of tough classes either crack up before trial and error learning can take effect, or leave the profession, or return to the middle class fold where teachers, children and parents have a clearer image of their respective roles.

An interesting example of the way understanding the application of learning theory to teacher–child interaction can increase the effectiveness of senior staff is given by Ferster (1967). With a background in experimental psychology, mostly with animals, he observed a skilled and experienced therapist working with a very disturbed handicapped child. Afterwards he interpreted to her what she had been attempting in the course of the interview; she was astonished at the accuracy of his observations, exclaiming that it took years of practice to understand the interaction between therapist and child. This lady had always been more successful as a therapist than at sharing her own skills with less experienced colleagues. When she was able to develop a conceptual framework within which to describe what she was attempting. she became more effective as a supervisor.

Taking this argument a stage further, one of the aims of interaction analysis is to identify some of the features of a successful teacher which make him successful. More radically, another aim is to understand the sort of learning experiences (or to put it another way the sort of relationships and the sort of adult–child interaction) at home and at school which contribute to a reduction or an increase in the level of maladjustment. We can now see how classroom interaction and behaviour modification studies share common ground with the results of sociological research, for instance Reynolds's (1976) conclusion described in the last chapter that problems proliferate when teachers and children refuse to form a truce. A project which did have some success in identifying the features of teaching style which affected maladjusted children in ordinary American primary school classrooms was that of Kounin and his colleagues (1966). With the help of videotape recordings they showed that the teachers who were most successful in managing ordinary children were also the most successful with emotionally disturbed pupils. Moreover, the effect of a disturbed child on the rest of the class was closely related to the teacher's control over the rest of the class. Of special interest, though, was the discovery that techniques of handling bad behaviour had no observable effect on its incidence. (In contrast, Hall *et al.* (1968) found that the more times children were told to sit down, the more they spent standing up!) With only one teacher out of thirty in Kounin's study was there any close association between her technique for checking bad behaviour and the immediate success of her efforts. In contrast what Kounin awkwardly called 'teacher with-it-ness' *was* closely associated with good behaviour from both the emotionally disturbed and the normal pupils. By 'teacher with-it-ness' he meant variety in learning activities, recognising what was happening at a given moment, techniques for handling group movement around the classroom and so on.

Kounin's study has at least three important implications for an attempt to understand the needs of maladjusted children. First, he confirmed that even successful experienced teachers have little theoretical understanding of the principles of classroom control (shown by the lack of success of all but one teacher in their explicit efforts to control the children). Second, and more important, he showed the importance of the teacher's expertise in her subject; common sense would suggest that the teacher who is not competent in her subject, or has inadequate materials with which to teach it, will have discipline problems, yet this rather obvious fact is overlooked in much of the literature. Finally, and perhaps most important of all as far as this book is concerned, he provided further evidence that 'emotionally disturbed' (his term) and normal children do not form separate populations; the teaching styles which worked with the normal children also worked with the emotionally disturbed pupils. This hardly supports the all too prevalent idea among special school teachers that different, and special, qualities are required for their sort of work. Moreover, if it can be shown that the same sort of teaching skills and personal qualities are needed, a policy of segregating the most disturbing children into special schools of their own is hardly logical, especially as common sense is supported by research findings that children influence each other's behaviour. This is implicitly recognised in the widespread and sometimes justified concern about the effect of a maladjusted child on the rest of his class; the teacher's concern is partly that the difficult child demands an undue proportion of her time, and partly that other children may start to copy his behaviour. In fact, children copy 'good' as well as 'bad' behaviour, and if one unsettled and disruptive child has an undue influence on the others it may be that they feel there is a greater pay-off for disruptive behaviour, than for cooperation. This becomes not probable but inevitable where the teacher lacks confidence in her subject, or where she fails to notice and approve of effort and success.

Successful behaviour modification and successful teaching

The linguistic and scientific rigour of the early behaviour modification literature was perhaps justifiable when behaviour therapists were struggling to establish a new, reputable discipline distinct from analytically influenced psychotherapy. However, our understanding of the classroom (and playground) interation problems which result in a formal label of maladjustment has come a long way since the early 1960s when workers such as the Zimmermans (1962) took learning theory from the animal laboratory and into the classroom. Today the problem is not to locate books, articles and pamphlets on the treatment of disturbing children in their ordinary classrooms, but to select the most useful material from an extensive and expanding range (Galloway, 1977). The problem is not so much to demonstrate to a sceptical profession that change is possible, as to de-mystify behavioural analysis and modification and incorporate the underlying principles into a wider conceptual framework as part of an educational philosophy of practical value to a larger number of teachers. The need for this is indicated both by the widespread misunderstanding about the aims and methods of this approach, and also by a central limitation of the published work which has substantially contributed to the misunderstanding. It is probably already clear that the literature describes a large number of techniques for an even larger number of problems; unfortunately, however, more authors have described successful techniques than have investigated the much more difficult (and interesting) problem of choosing a technique after a careful analysis of the interaction between teacher, child and class. Most examples of effective techniques give brief descriptions of the teacher's management techniques, usually with an emphasis on how he creates his own problems, for example by giving general, non-specific instruction like 'Sit down 4f', or by failing to recognise positive aspects of a child's performance; fewer authors tackle the more fundamental question of how to make the preliminary assessment before selecting an appropriate method to remediate the interaction problem it reveals.

It is partly this failure, and partly the professional background of the psychologists who developed behaviour therapy in schools that has obscured the similarity between successful behaviour modification and good teaching. In fact the two should be recognised as one and the same thing, and until this is accepted there will be little chance of the underlying principles of teaching (and learning) being more widely used to help maladjusted children and their teachers in ordinary classrooms. Two examples which could come from any primary school classroom will illustrate our argument that effective behaviour therapy and effective teaching have a great deal in common:

1. Traditionally, teachers have used tests to assess their pupils' educational attainments and intellectual ability. Specifically, group intelligence and reading tests are still widely used. Unfortunately these have limitations:
   (a) they are insufficiently related to classroom activities; for instance, a child's ability to bark appropriately at the words in Schonell's Graded Word Reading Test (Schonell and Goodacre, 1974) is no guarantee that he will be able to understand them when he comes across them in his reading book;
   (b) they do not provide an adequate base from which to plan the child's future educational needs; for instance, a low score on a test of non-verbal reasoning has no clear meaning if the child is well within the average range in all his attainments;
   (c) they ignore other, equally important aspects of development such as social and emotional development. Many teachers therefore prefer 'criterion referenced' observation schedules such as the one developed by two psychologists in Croydon (Bryans and Wolfendale, 1973) which provide a focus and structure for their own observations. These observations are of specific, well-defined activities relating to different aspects of each child's overall development. As children progress through

the school their educational, social and emotional progress is monitored systematically, so that a cumulative record is built up of each child's strengths and weaknesses. When problems are revealed, more detailed observations are made, sometimes supported by diagnostic tests, in order to plan a compensatory programme.

Although not carried out in all schools, this is no more than good teaching practice. It bears a striking resemblance to the principles of behavioural analysis described in this chapter in that: (*a*) the emphasis is on observed activities; (*b*) the recording is systematic, and (*c*) it provides a base from which to plan further work with the child.

2. As teachers become more aware of the limitations of traditional reading tests, and even of the more detailed tests for diagnosing the reason for educational failure, they are increasingly recognising the possibilities of 'diagnostic teaching'. This is especially true in the field of reading, where the search for a genetically distinct syndrome of dyslexia has failed (Rutter and Yule, 1975) and emotional factors can overlap with perceptual problems. Taking a child with specific reading retardation as an example, a teacher may note that he makes an excessive number of reversals, and suspect that his retardation is related to visual sequencing problems. The teacher will provide a teaching programme which aims to improve this particular sub-skill. If the child's visual sequencing (left–right orientation) when reading does not improve the teacher will modify the programme; on the other hand, if it does improve, but his overall reading ability does not, the teacher will reject his original hypothesis and think again.

Again this second example is no more than sound practice, but the similarity to some of the behaviour modification programmes described earlier in this chapter is obvious; in each case the teacher is following a clearly defined programme which she modifies or alters in the light of experience. To put it slightly differently, we are arguing that behaviour analysis and modification are merely applying in the field of behaviour the same principles and skills which successful teachers have always applied, less systematically but not necessarily less effectively, in teaching more traditional educational skills. Behaviour therapy has, of course been applied to educational problems such as reading backwardness, but there is nothing about these programmes which is inconsistent with many traditional teaching methods. If our argument is valid, the main function of classroom interaction studies is to identify the skills which contribute to successful learning, in order to extend the principles that are effective with learning difficulties to include behavioural or emotional problems.

Thus the principal application of behavioural analysis and modification does not lie in developing a pool of techniques for coping with maladjusted behaviour but in providing a conceptual framework within which to approach problem situations. The same principles of systematic observation, carefully thought out planning of programmes, detailed monitoring of progress, and subsequent evaluation and (if necessary) modification of the current approach are intrinsic to activities as superficially diverse as teaching 'normal' children to read and altering the interaction between a teacher and an out-of-control class of sixteen-year-olds. One of these principles, as indicated above, is to seek to identify the underlying factors which contribute to successful classroom control and educational progress, or to put it another way, the skills which are found in the good teacher.

Opponents of behaviour modification (and regrettably some of its more evangelical advocates as well) often make the mistake of thinking that it concentrates only on removing deviant behaviour and by implication overlooks the 'whole child' so beloved of educational theorists (Quicke, 1976). This would be true of a programme based on a superficial statement of the problem, without an adequate analysis of the behaviour of the different people concerned; it is always easy to criticise bad practice, and behaviour modification has its fair share of bad practice. Yet closer observation will show the criticism to be invalid. If we take as an example observation-based assessment of a seven-year-old referred for his 'attention-seeking' behaviour and slow progress in reading we may find that the behaviour problem is maintained by his teacher's attention while his reading difficulty is not unrelated to the improbable, staccato, jerk-jerk chatter of the characters in his reading book, and his teacher's tendency to concentrate on other children in the infrequent moments when he does make a serious attempt to read. Both have implications for his future teaching and management, but these implications may well be secondary to more fundamental points about educational resources and classroom control. In other words, the initial assessment may demonstrate problems in the interaction between teachers and child, yet also show that these problems are caused by, or at least associated with, limitations in the materials available to the teacher, her basic knowledge about the subject she is teaching, and the way she tries to control *all* the children in her class. Far more than most other types of therapy, interaction analysis and behaviour modification demand a detailed understanding of the whole child and his relationship with his environment; without this understanding any programme aimed at specific problems in his behaviour will be largely a matter of chance since the planning has an inadequate theoretical basis.

The old clinic-based Child Guidance Service and many hospital based departments of child psychiatry were not so much limited by their narrow, psychoanalytically-influenced clinical orientation as by their failure to appreciate the significance of the social psychology (or sociology) of the school and classroom. Ullman (1973), an eminent American behaviour therapist, has argued that clinical psychology was once applied personality theory, progressed to applied learning theory, and is now becoming applied social psychology. The same could be said of educational psychology, except that the first progression would have been from clinic based testing to school based testing, and of the educational treatment of maladjusted children, except again that the first progression would have been from clinic-based psychotherapy to school-based psychotherapy.

Experienced teachers would rightly criticise a behaviour therapy programme which aimed to reduce *one* child's disruptive behaviour if several other children in the class showed similarly disruptive behaviour as a predictable result of, say, being expected to do work which was too difficult or sensing their teacher's lack of confidence in her subject; how many primary school teachers were never taught how to teach children to read in their colleges of education? Yet their criticism should not be directed at the underlying principles but at a bad application of them. If the same principles govern the monitoring of educational progress and the assessment of disturbing behaviour, then clinical advice and in-service courses which concentrate too heavily on the latter may be unnecessarily restrictive in the sense that they can too easily lead teachers to overlook the interaction between different skills as, for instance, in the example above of a child with a reading problem, and divisive in the sense that they foster the illusion that teachers of problem children need a set of skills which differs from the skills required by teachers of 'normal' children.

Conclusions

We have argued in this chapter that maladjustment can only be understood in its social context, and that the principles of behavioural analysis and behaviour modification provide an effective framework for first, understanding the needs of maladjusted pupils, and second, altering inappropriate, potentially destructive interaction between children and adults into a more positive constructive relationship. We are not arguing that behaviour modification is a solution to the problem of problem children, but rather that it provides a conceptual framework for illustrating the changes needed in the child, his family, and sometimes his school. The encouraging recent research showing that school does have a considerable influence on such crucial aspects of a child's life as his psychosocial adjustment and future employment prospects, quite apart from the influence of his family and social background, is further evidence of the need to understand the child in the light of the social relationships and attitudes at school, as opposed to assessing him primarily in terms of family relationships and some arbitrary definition of normality.

This is not in any way to deny or underestimate the significance of stresses at home or in the community, but if what happens at home can have a crucial influence on how the child develops outside home it would seem unreasonably modest of teachers to deny that what happens at school will have some influence on how he develops outside school. Teachers cannot have it both ways: if they wish to argue that home may have a beneficial or an adverse effect depending on the circumstances, it would be unreasonable to maintain that all schools conform to some uniform shade of rosiness which can only be beneficial. As we shall argue in the next chapter, special schools should have an important role in the education service by demonstrating the possibility of appropriate educational and social standards from children whose ordinary schools could not help them. The fact that other ordinary schools might well have offered appropriate help merely underlines this point.

Yet if we are thinking about improving the quality of education for *all* the maladjusted children described in the review of national surveys in Chapter 2, and not just for the elitist minority who conform to the criterion of dreadfulness or despair which qualifies them for a special school place, we have to think how ordinary schools can become more flexible. Special school placement becomes necessary when child and school are trapped in a vicious circle from which neither can break out. The adjustment groups, sanctuaries and special units in ordinary schools which we discussed in the last chapter can break this vicious circle by giving the child and his teachers a breathing space, a cooling off period in which both parties have time to readjust. In a rather different way, the same can be said of some of the behaviour modification programmes described in this chapter.

It would be accurate, but possibly misleading, to say that the aim of pastoral care in a school is to prevent a vicious circle of failure and frustration from becoming established. The danger here is the possible inference that pastoral care is in some way separate from the curriculum and other aspects of the school's organisation. Far from being separate from the curriculum there is a powerful argument that pastoral problems arise when the curriculum fails to meet children's needs; this should not be taken to imply that conflicts arising outside school are irrelevant, but rather that they should be taken into consideration when planning the curriculum. Good examples of the way children can be helped to face controversial or emotionally upsetting subjects, and to start discovering constructive solutions are the North West Region Curriculum Development Board's projects on health education and social education, and Peter McPhail's Schools Council Moral Education Project (McPhail *et al.*, 1972). Nevertheless, the issue goes deeper than the mere content of the curriculum, since few experienced teachers will deny that *what* is taught is sometimes less important than *how* the teaching takes place. None of the projects described so far have really tackled the crucial question why a child fails dismally at one school while its closest neighbour becomes a welcome sanctuary for the same child, as well as for most of its other disturbed children. Similarly, none of the projects has made any explicit attempt to alter problems within the school which contribute to a child's maladjustment. As we argued earlier, behaviour modification programmes generally operate by changing the teacher's behaviour, although the stated aim is to change that of the child. This inconsistency may result in behavioural programmes being more readily accepted in schools, but can hardly promote recognition of the principle that school curriculum and organisation may also contribute to the reduction or development of maladjustment. One project which has grasped this nettle with considerable success is the ILEA's Hungerford Educational Guidance Centre (Lane and Millar, 1977). The Centre caters for children with severe behaviour and learning difficulties, though not for learning difficulties alone. Most of the pupils have been on the verge of exclusion from their ordinary schools or have actually been excluded in the past. Nevertheless the centre offers short-term therapy by working closely with referring schools within a framework of 'contract therapy'. After initial assessment a 'therapy contract' is drawn up between school, child and centre, specifying what is to be changed, and what is to be done by each party to the contract. Thus things expected from the school are specified as clearly and in as much detail as the cooperation required from the child. The child is required to stick to his contract, and can see whether centre and school stick to theirs. Training and advice on the initial assessment and subsequent modification of behaviour problems is provided for the child's ordinary school teachers, while the children themselves are systematically taught how to cope with the situations which had previously led to confrontation.

The Hungerford Centre takes children from some of its surrounding schools, though not all are prepared to cooperate, but the director's emphasis on reversing 'the tendency of teachers (and behaviour modifiers?) to overvalue techniques and undervalue diagnosis' (Lane and Millar, 1977) has more general application. The diagnosis, or as Lane calls it 'functional analysis' is not an assessment of the child's psychopathology so much as a description of his behavioural and educational skills in the context of his interaction with adults and other children.

Chapter 9

The implications of integrating slow-learning and disturbing children in ordinary schools

Introduction

The National Association for Remedial Education opened its evidence to the Warnock Committee (DES, 1978) by criticising the committee as 'largely unrepresentative of the total needs of handicapped children in this country'. NARE made the point which this book has already made a number of times, namely that only 2 per cent of children receive their education in special schools or formally recognised special classes, as opposed to remedial classes, while as many as 15 per cent require special educational help.

Consequently 13 per cent of children in need are within the ordinary school system [NARE's evidence continued], and yet the Warnock Committee has almost no members with expertise or experience in dealing with children with learning difficulties outside the special school system. This is characteristic of the total outlook towards special education in the ordinary school. Every survey which has taken place, including the DES (1971) Survey pamphlet no. 15 has emphasised the lack of recognition of the need of these children except where they have been removed from the normal school system.

The Snowdon Working Party (National Fund for Research into Crippling Diseases, 1976) has argued that as the majority (i.e. the 13 per cent who have traditionally remained in ordinary schools) are less severely handicapped, the debate about the education of handicapped children should concentrate on the 150,000 or so who have been formally ascertained as needing special education, with consequent placement in a special school. To some extent this argument is valid for all categories of handicap, but it carried less weight with the intrinsically non-medical handicaps associated with ESN(M) and maladjusted children than with the more obviously medical handicaps. This is partly because the former are so much more prevalent and partly because, as we have already argued, the criteria for selection are so much less clearly defined. The boundary between children who find their way to special schools and the most difficult and educationally backward who remain in ordinary schools has always been more blurred with the ESN(M) and the maladjusted than with the other categories. It is possible that the influence of the schools' internal attitudes and organisation is greater with children who are constitutionally or temperamentally vulnerable to learning or behavioural disorders; nevertheless both the referral policy in schools and the assessmment policy of different psychologists are also relevant.

The growing demand for integration in the USA, Scandinavia and the UK has followed greater public awareness of the needs and feelings of disabled people, as well as increasingly vocal and articulate demands by the disabled themselves for a say in their own destiny. This is not, of course, to deny the debate's invaluable function in making the teaching profession and the general public more aware of disabled people as people. In 1944 the problem was to compel LEAs to provide *any* sort of education for the disabled, not to ensure that education of the same calibre as that previously available in special schools should now be provided in ordinary schools. There is a possible analogy here, developed in Chapter 10, between the move away from a tripartite selective system to a fully comprehensive system of secondary education in the 1960s and 1970s and the move towards integrated schooling for the handicapped.

In 1944 a war-weakened country could scarcely have afforded the upheaval involved in so revolutionary a change as a fully comprehensive secondary school system. The problem would not simply have been the shortage of trained teachers, nor the fact that those teachers who *were* theoretically trained had no experience to equip them for such a challenge, nor the enormous increase in the building programme which would have been needed to convert existing premises into the larger units necessary for a viable comprehensive school (with or without a sixth form). As important as any of these was the fact that public and educational opinion still laboured under the curiously naive and misplaced impression that if your parents could not afford to place you in an expensive public school, the next best thing would be a similarly elitist grammar school which would try (though less successfully, of course) to teach the same things in the same ways. In other words, with the country's essentially elitist outlook, a free and compulsory secondary education system was as much educational change as could be assimilated. (This is perhaps a bit too kind to early psychologists who uncritically and sometimes unscrupulously exaggerated the reliability of their 'scientific' IQ tests (Kamin, 1977).)

Pressure for comprehensive schools resulted from growing public recognition of the injustice and waste inherent in selection at the age of eleven. In other words, it reflected a change in public awareness and public attitudes while at the same time contributing to the process. Similarly, in many parts of the country the battle in 1944 was for provision for the handicapped, not for improvement of existing provision. It is only as the public has become more aware of, and sympathetic to handicap that there has been constructive critical discussion about the benefits of special schools. The process has been encouraged by pressure groups of parents of disabled children and of the disabled themselves (though as we have seen the ESN(M) and the maladjusted are under-represented), which have challenged the convenient and lazy pigeon-holing of children into categories. It is as well to recognise that members of disabled groups are now able to make their views heard precisely because of the education they received in post-1944 special schools. Yet in no way does this invalidate their claim that special education should progress from special schools to special facilities in ordinary schools; it merely underlines the argument that the demand for integrated special education is part of a wider, and irreversible, social and educational development.

Physical resources for a range of special educational provision

Sir Edward Britton (1977) points out that teachers regard Section 10 of the

1976 Education Act with apprehension. This is the section which lays down the principle that handicapped children should, when possible, be taught in ordinary schools. 'Nor', he comments, 'are their fears groundless. One chairman of an education committee has already expressed impatience for the operation of Section 10 on the grounds that his authority will then be able to save £2½ million by closing their special schools.' At a time of economic restraint, such unfortunate attitudes are perhaps to be expected from a minority of parsimonious authorities, but no one should need to stress that the demand for integration is characterised by a wish to extend and improve facilities for handicapped and unsuccessful children, not to save money at their expense.

If we return for a moment to the continuum of special educational provision described in Chapter 4, we have to ask what *additional* facilities should be made available in ordinary schools. We argued in Chapter 4 that the existing facilities contain an insufficient range of options, and that the options which do exist are insufficiently flexible to meet children's needs. Establishing special classes or units in selected ordinary schools is clearly a viable alternative to full-time special school placement with many physically handicapped children (Cope and Anderson, 1977). It is also a possibility with the ESN(M) and maladjusted, though both groups raise additional questions about the sort of educational philosophy and practice that an authority should encourage in its schools. Warnock refers to the need for 'functional unity' within the ordinary school if a policy of integration is to be successful.

The history of special education for children with learning and behaviour difficulties suggests that demand may often expand to exceed existing supply, though for the first time there has recently been evidence in a number of LEAs of a substantial reduction in demand for ESN(M) places. Whether it will be desirable to remove the slower and more disturbing children to a special unit in another ordinary school must clearly depend on what can be provided at the children's original school. In this connection, there is a real danger that an expansion of special provision in the form of units could further weaken the encouraging development of remedial and pastoral care facilities in many ordinary schools. Why should a head teacher allocate his scarce teaching and financial resources to problem children when there is a unit for them down the road at a neighbouring school? As the Scandinavian and American research suggests that many ESN(M) children do as well in their ordinary classes as in special schools, there is obviously a strong case for concentrating resources in the ordinary schools where they may benefit less backward and less disturbing children as well as the small minority who would hitherto have been selected for removal.

Another argument against special units for the ESN(M) and maladjusted can be made on practical grounds. Both common sense and psychological research suggest that children copy each other's behaviour, just as they copy that of their parents and, to a smaller degree, their teachers. Placing a lot of very difficult children together may thus be seen as a recipe for further disturbance. This is indeed one of the central problems in special schools for the maladjusted, where a common reason for refusing to admit a child is that 'we have already got too many aggressives, and they react on each other'. Unfortunately this observation has not always led the special school world to question the basic assumption that separate school buildings, activities and philosophy are necessary and desirable for maladjusted children. However, it is unlikely that many head teachers or ordinary schools will willingly accept an influx of maladjusted children into a unit which will be integrated with the rest of their school. They are only too aware of the influence which one difficult child can exert on other children, quite apart from the added tension for teachers, so are hardly likely to welcome an influx of 'problems' from neighbouring schools. This argument does not apply to the same extent with ESN(M) children, though even here it may well create problems as so many of the pupils selected for this form of special education come from homes with chronic social problems.

Although we have so far argued that priority should be given to supporting the ESN(M) and maladjusted in their ordinary school, there will perhaps be circumstances where this is impossible or impractical. The sort of resources required are discussed later in this chapter. At this stage we only need to point out that successful integration within the child's neighbourhood school requires a range and a flexibility of resources which can seldom be available in small primary schools, for instance with a two-form entry or smaller.

In areas where primary education is organised on the basis of a large number of small primary schools (as in many rural and some inner city areas) it may be justifiable to concentrate some, though not all resources on a special unit attached to one of the ordinary schools. However, it seems unlikely that this will result in genuine integration if the unit is regarded as a long-term educational alternative rather than as an opportunity to remediate specific problems. Thus, when a child enters the unit it should be with the clear expectation that he will be returning to his original school when he has mastered certain specified educational skills and has made sufficient social or emotional progress for a phased return.

One implication of this model is rejection of the DES categories of handicap as recommended in the Warnock Report (DES, 1978). It implies that in some areas there may be a case for a unit attached to an ordinary school, which admits children from a number of surrounding schools. Such a unit would act as a short-term treatment centre for children with a wide range of learning and behaviour problems; the overlap between the educational and behaviour problems of children in special schools for the ESN(M), the maladjusted, the so-called 'delicate', and schools for children with learning difficulties is considerable. If the objective of special educational treatment is successful integration within ordinary schools, the case against units based on the existing categories becomes virtually unanswerable. Handicapped children's obstinate refusal to be pigeon-holed into categories, combined with growing recognition that, irrespective of category, they have far more in common with each other and with non-handicapped children than they have which is different, are two of the prime reasons for the movement towards integration.

The same model could be applied in an existing special school which was willing to change its function to that of a generally short-term centre for children with a wide range of learning difficulties. Although it would lack the potential advantage of a base within an ordinary school it could have the advantage of utilising the buildings and skilled staff of existing schools and would save the expense of adding to or adapting an ordinary school to take a unit.

Whether based in an ordinary school unit or in a separate special school, this has implications which go far beyond rejection of the DES categories for the

ESN(M) and maladjusted. The wider the range of the children's difficulties, the greater the need for a staffing ratio which allows adequate differentiation between them. Especially when the aim is return to the referring school within a quite short space of time, perhaps a maximum of two years, neighbourhood special schools would need a more generous staffing ratio than that currently recommended by the DES (1973b). Further and equally important reasons for this are the amount of teachers' time needed for liaison with referring schools in planning a child's return, and also for supporting a child, and his teachers, after return. This is stressed in the Warnock Report, with recommendations for detailed discussions before admission, and for a senior teacher to take subsequent responsibility for the child.

Evidence on the effects of remedial teaching (reviewed in Chapter 4) suggests that short-term gains are not difficult to achieve, but that they are maintained only when adequate follow-up is provided. In the case of children returning from special schools or units, subsequent support is doubly necessary. The remedial programme must be reflected to some extent in the child's daily curriculum in his ordinary school, so that the progress already made, as well as the interest established, are not lost by default; in addition, return to a school in which you have previously failed carries obvious difficulties in its own right, and the child may need a good deal of support from trusted teachers in the unit or special school in the initial stages. This support is most likely to be helpful when there is a relationship of mutual respect between the ordinary and the special schools, based on working towards common goals. That, of course, will only be achieved when:

(a) the special school or unit teachers actively promote a policy of integration by fostering links with referring schools and involving them in every stage of the child's progress, if only through regular reports; and
(b) children passing through the 'special' provision are seen to have benefited from it.

If neighbourhood units or special schools for children with a wide range of learning difficulties should have a more generous staffing ratio than that currently recommended, what about staffing in ordinary schools which are not supported by a neighbourhood special school? We have already suggested that the sort of generic special provision described above may be more appropriate in areas where primary school organisation is based on a large number of relatively small schools while comprehensive secondary schools and larger primary schools might be expected, with appropriate support, to retain their ESN(M) and maladjusted children themselves.

Staffing, salaries and responsibilities

Perhaps the first point to be made here should be that a policy of integrating the slowest learners and most disturbing children cannot be based on the same mean-minded policy that has characterised the integration of physically handicapped children in ordinary schools, namely a hopeful optimism that the child will be assimilated without providing any of the additional resources available in a special school. Staffing is among the most crucial. In 1973 the DES issued a circular on staffing in special schools, in which the recommended staff–child ratio in schools for the maladjusted was 7:1, and in ESN(M) schools 12:1. For other categories of handicap the recommendations were similarly favourable. It should not be a matter for debate that ordinary schools which retain physically handicapped should receive recognition in their allocation of staff, yet it is quite clear that this has by no means always happened (Anderson, 1973).

The staffing problem for physically handicapped children in ordinary schools is simplified by the fact that these children are on the whole somewhat easier to identify than the ESN(M) and maladjusted. Yet even with physically handicapped children there are considerable problems in assessment, particularly in the 'borderline' group of children who might or might not have been selected for special education under the traditional separate special school system. There can be little doubt that recognising the presence of 'integrated' handicapped children in staffing levels will result in a considerable increase in the numbers of children for whom allowance is claimed.

A still greater problem is the overlap between categories of handicap. We know, for example that children with neurological lesions above the brainstem, such as epilepsy or cerebral palsy, are a good deal more likely to display behavioural disturbance than children whose lesions lie below the brainstem, as, for instance, in muscular dystrophy (Graham and Rutter, 1968b). In the case of the most difficult handicapped children, should staffing ratios be based on those for physically handicapped, or for maladjusted? There is obviously no immediate answer, though a great deal will inevitably depend on the sincerity of the individual LEA's desire to provide the best aspects of traditional special schools in its ordinary schools.

Another nettle which will have to be grasped concerns the procedures for identifying handicapped children in order that their presence may be recognised in staffing levels. If a central argument against traditional special schools is the stigma and negative labelling which results from attending them, it seems ironic that formal procedures may still be needed to 'identify' these children when they remain in ordinary schools. One possible solution is to adapt existing selection procedures (described in Chapter 1) so that for the purposes of staffing and capitation allowances, a child is considered to be handicapped when the authority receives a request from his head teacher, supported by an educational psychologist and school medical officer. This is basically what the Warnock Report recommends.

How handicapped children in ordinary schools should benefit from the additional resources granted to children with their handicap is also likely to arouse fierce discussion. The only way to *ensure* that the resources are allocated to the children for whom they are intended would be to provide them in a specially segregated unit, which rather misses the point of integration in the first place! On the other hand, it could be only too easy in a large comprehensive school for one additional teacher, appointed, perhaps, due to the presence of five or six maladjusted children, to be 'lost' in the timetable with only a marginal benefit to the children concerned.

This argument, however, misses the point that integration should be seen as a way of extending special education, beyond the elitist minority who have traditionally been placed in special schools, to help all the other less handicapped children who have physical or emotional problems, yet have always remained in their neighbourhood school. If the integrated children who would formerly have been in special schools benefit from friendship with their non-handicapped peers and enjoy the wider range of educational facilities in an ordinary school, it is only right that other, perhaps less handicapped, children should benefit from their presence.

Once there is an informal administrative procedure for identifying handicapped children, finding some formula for recognising their presence in staffing levels and capitation allowances (the sum of money allocated per pupil for books, equipment and so on) should not be insuperable. The capitation allowance could be adjusted upwards in recognition of the higher rate for a handicapped child, and the same principle could apply in allocating staffing levels. For instance, if a LEA bases its secondary school staffing establishment on a teacher–child ratio of 1:20, a child recognised as maladjusted would merit about three units (as the DES recommends a ratio of 1:7 for this category), or the equivalent of one-seventh of a teacher above establishment.

These suggestions apply to all categories of handicap, but as indicated already may present particularly severe administrative difficulties in the case of the ESN(M) and maladjusted. In Chapter 7 we reviewed evidence that the internal attitudes and organisation of a school contribute noticeably to its pupils' attendance rates and to their behaviour both inside *and* outside school. If research findings are correct that some schools protect their pupils from maladjustment or delinquency, while others may even do the reverse, it seems unfortunate, to put it mildly, that the most successful schools should be penalised for not having many maladjusted children, while the least successful are rewarded by the appointment of additional staff to help cope with the problems!

This may be an extreme example, but it is undoubtedly the sort of question which will be raised. To avoid it there could be a case for treating ESN(M) and maladjusted children in a different way to all the categories of physical handicap with regard to staffing support. LEAs might be able to work out some formula with the teachers' organisations whereby schools are given resources on the basis of an *estimated* number of children in need. The estimate would be based on local and national research on the prevalence of severe learning difficulties or behavioural disorders in urban and rural areas. The same principle has already been used in the allocation of additional resources to schools in so-called 'educational priority areas' (DES, 1967) and later to schools of exceptional difficulty. In these cases priority was determined by an agreed formula based on several measures of disadvantage in the catchment area.

So far we have concentrated on the allocation of staffing and financial resources to ordinary schools as an integral part of any trend towards integration. In the climate of anxiety and suspicion engendered by talk of dismantling, or at least changing the function of, the traditional special school system, an equally important issue will be the career structure for teachers in special education. At present teachers receive an allowance for teaching in special *schools,* but few LEAs have seen their way clear to paying the same allowance to teachers of handicapped children in ordinary schools; it does not even appear to be common practice for teachers in special units for problem children, let alone for teachers of remedial classes, to receive the special schools allowance. It is in fact quite possible for teachers in ordinary schools to receive the special schools allowance; Goodwin (1978) has noted that in

Leicestershire this payment was common. In 1975, for example, three teachers in the High School at Countesthorpe and two in the Upper School were in receipt of a special schools allowance, mainly in recognition of their work with ESN(M) and maladjusted children who might otherwise have attended a special school. The formal criterion for receipt of the allowance was that the teachers concerned should spend at least 80 per cent out of their time teaching children with an IQ of 80 or less.

There are arguments, however, against extending the special schools allowance to teachers in ordinary schools. To do so could be divisive within ordinary schools by creating resentment between staff who receive it and staff who do not, even though they may be doing an equally stressful job of work, or have equally good qualifications and experience. Further, there will always be a suspicion (however unworthy or unjustified) that receiving the special school's allowance might be regarded as an alternative to promotion within the current salary structure. This could easily place at a disadvantage the careers of teachers who receive the special schools allowance, while remaining on Scale 1 or 2 of the current salary structure, compared with colleagues who have already risen to Scales 3 or 4. Integration should enable special education and mainstream education to learn from each other; experience in special education should be seen to enhance prospects of promotion to the most senior positions; anything in the salary structure that might possibly restrict career prospects would discourage some of the most able young teachers from seeking experience in the special education field.

In addition to its potentially divisive effect if paid to teachers of handicapped children in ordinary schools, the special school allowance is already divisive in splitting the career structures between special schools and ordinary schools. It is unfortunately all too common to hear teachers in special schools say that they cannot return to the ordinary school system without taking an unacceptable drop in salary. The implication is that the teachers concerned would be unable to obtain a sufficiently senior post in an ordinary school to compensate for loss of the special school allowance.

It is worth asking why the special school allowance is paid. If to attract recruits into an exceptionally demanding aspect of education, it should presumably also be paid to teachers of the most difficult and much larger classes in ordinary schools, and even to those who are responsible for teaching to university entrance standard. The allowance might be paid in recognition of additional skills, experience and training needed for work with the handicapped, or else in recognition of the exceptionally demanding, stressful and difficult nature of the work. Against the latter, the special school day is shorter, the classes smaller, the ancillary and professional support services better, and the money available for equipment normally more generous than in the mainstream. Against the former, ordinary school staff receive salary recognition in the form of special responsibility posts above the bottom scale of the salary structure for duties which are particularly onerous, or which require special skills. There is no reason why a separate model should be applied to special education.

The special school allowance has outlived its usefulness, but should only be abolished in favour of a system which will attract able teachers into special education while facilitating an interchange of personnel and ideas with the rest of the education system. Even more than physically handicapped children, the

ESN(M) and maladjusted need experienced and resourceful teachers with a background of successful work with ordinary children.

Recognising that the children have special needs should not be allowed to obscure the fact that they have far more in common with the majority than they have which is different. It follows that the salaries offered should be at a competitive point within the ordinary salary structure. This implies a change in the present unsatisfactory position in some secondary schools, where the head of the remedial department (often only one teacher, and sometimes even a part-timer) is paid less than the head of any other subject department. Later in this chapter we shall see that the head of the remedial department's responsibilities should in fact exceed those of the traditional subject departments, since curriculum planning requires the ability to help subject teacher colleagues adapt their materials and methods to suit the slow-learning or behaviourally disturbed child. They should therefore be paid at least as much, and their posts should carry commensurate status within the school. In an integrated policy of special education there is no place at the head of a department for the dedicated teacher whom head teachers 'call the "salt of the earth" and keep on scale one for ever' (Galletley, 1977). Similarly, it would be taken for granted that all teachers of handicapped children (whether physically handicapped, ESN(M) or maladjusted) should have adequate experience and ability to justify at least a Scale 2 post, from which they might progress to more senior positions within the special education field, or to other posts in the mainstream. For instance, some experience with exceptionally difficult children after two or three years ordinary classroom teaching might prove an ideal stepping stone to a more senior post with responsibility for extending and coordinating the pastoral care responsibilities of class teachers in a secondary school. With such a policy the special school allowance should become redundant.

Yet as Warnock argued (DES, 1978), this does not mean that special schools will become redundant, however far the LEA carried its policy of integration. In fact, the more handicapped children are integrated within ordinary schools the more their teachers will need access to practical guidance and advice from colleagues with more extensive experience. This is a role which special schools are seldom filling at present. It is a role which will place them firmly within the mainstream of the education system, even though they may remain in their present physically separate premises. It will be an enormously challenging role. They would admit the most difficult children – those with the most severe learning difficulties, and those who were too disturbed or disturbing to benefit from a well developed policy of special education in the ordinary school. Yet because part of their function would be to demonstrate the principles, methods, curriculum and materials for use with these end-of-spectrum children, they would have to justify their existence by their results. Basing a resource bank of equipment in a special school, as suggested by Warnock, would enable visitors to see it in use, or at least enable the special school teachers to explain how they use it with their children.

This is a function which could, of course, be filled by the neighbourhood special school suggested earlier. That this is not an unrealistic objective is seen by the success of some special units for 'disruptive' teenagers and for truants. Not only do the children attend regularly, but they achieve an acceptable standard of work. However, it is not enough for remaining special schools to demonstrate that they can achieve a degree of success where others have failed; they also need to be able to show colleagues in the referring schools *how* they have succeeded, and to help them to see what changes may be needed in order to help similar children in the future. Needless to say, superimposing an advisory or supportive role on top of the teaching role will require exceptionally mature and able teachers. On the other hand, the senior teachers in all schools have precisely this sort of responsibility to their colleagues at an informal level; the head of the department is expected to help and advise less experienced colleagues in problems arising from subject teaching, while someone else may be approached for help and advice about a disciplinary or pastoral problem. How well this informal support system works in an ordinary school depends largely on the quality of relationships between staff. How well it would work at a more formal level for mainstream staff visiting a special school would also depend on the quality of relationships between the two.

In-service education and support services

Integrating the majority of ESN(M) and maladjusted children as well as the physically handicapped as proposed so far in this chapter would require an extension of present in-service education facilities. In addition, initial training should contain greater emphasis on understanding and recognising the needs of the handicapped as individuals. Getting able-bodied students to negotiate their way around college buildings in a wheel chair would be a useful start, and could be followed by a similar session making students more aware of the difficulties faced by partially sighted or partially hearing children. A tutor skilled in the use of role play could bring home far more dramatically than any lecture the effect of negative expectation ('We mustn't expect too much of him') and derogatory labelling ('he's mad, sir, really mad!') on ESN(M) and maladjusted children.

At initial training level the aim should not be to give factual information about handicap, so much as to reduce the fog of emotion and misunderstanding that surrounds it. For students to reach university or college without ever having met, or even spoken to, a mentally or physically handicapped contemporary is restricting for the handicapped; it is also limiting for the non-handicapped by creating social barriers which exaggerate the significance of the handicap, and hence perpetuate it. The handicapped should be spared the additional problem of overcoming the anxieties of ordinary people. Some of the fears which ordinary school teachers express about integration might be reduced by an imaginative course on handicap during their initial training.

A trend on in-service courses run by universities and LEAs is for greater integration between special education and the mainstream. Thus the divide is increasingly on an 'ages and stages' basis, catering for different age groups in contrast to the traditional category-based course on, for instance, 'The maladjusted child'. This trend enables teachers, in secondary maladjusted schools for example, to attend courses on pastoral care, while their colleagues in ESN(M) schools are able to benefit from courses on remedial teaching. It is hard to see how a separation between special and ordinary education has ever been justified on many in-service courses in topics such as literacy, the teaching of reading or early maths, developing observation skills and so on. Even though ESN(M) and maladjusted children need more gradual or more structured teaching methods, the processes involved are essentially the same. However, this is not to deny the need for more specialist advanced courses. Warnock's recommendation of a specialist qualification for teachers responsible for children with special needs should be pursued.

A principal emphasis on children's needs instead of on children attending a particular type of school has an additional advantage beyond the obvious one of helping teachers to see different ways of adapting their approach to a subject to the needs of different children. Holbrook (1965), for example, has shown how the slowest children in a low stream in a secondary modern school can be encouraged to write vivid, imaginative poetry. A versatile teacher of an 'A' stream class in a traditional grammar school might use similar principles to achieve similarly stimulating results, but he would set about arousing his pupils' interest in different ways. If one function of in-service courses is to introduce teachers to new skills and new ideas, another is to encourage their flexible use. There is always a danger that the advantages of experience may be offset by unnecessary resistance to ideas introduced by younger recruits to the school's staff.

The development of integrated advisory and support services goes alongside a trend towards integration in in-service education. The majority of LEAs have always appointed advisers for special education. In some areas they are known as inspectors, but were appointed locally and not by the DES as is the case with Her Majesty's Inspectors of Schools (HMI). Among other things, the function of advisers in LEAs is to ensure that the authority's schools reach at least the minimum standard which the public has a right to expect. The change in name from inspector to adviser reflects a change in emphasis from the inspectorial role to one which requires closer cooperation with schools and gives them a greater responsibility for helping teachers with curriculum development projects. An adviser for primary education might, for example, at any one time be working with groups of teachers on projects as diverse as home–school liaison, the choice and introduction of a new approach to the teaching of reading, or the introduction of environmental studies into the junior school curriculum.

In addition to an advisory role for specific aspects of the curriculum, reflected in the appointments of advisers for a particular subject, they have more general responsibilities for investigating complaints on behalf of the authority, and, in certain circumstances for representing the school's point of view to the authority's administrative branches and vice versa. Hence a head teacher's request for an additional member of staff for some exceptional purposes, such as establishing a special group for difficult children in an ordinary school, will probably already have been discussed with his school's adviser, but will almost certainly be referred to him by the central administration if it has not. Similarly, an application for a special grant to cover the cost of some remedial reading equipment or of some audiovisual aids for the modern language department will probably be referred to the appropriate adviser for his comments. In many cases the school may actually approach the adviser direct, since they are allocated a sum of money annually for curriculum development.

The appointment of an adviser for special education should in theory facilitate the extension of special education into the ordinary school network. In the continuum of special education provision proposed in this book, it is clear for two reasons that the majority of his work would be with teachers in ordinary schools: first, the majority of handicapped children would be educated in ordinary schools, and second the remaining special schools would be staffed by teachers who would themselves have an advisory role.

Regrettably this is not yet the widely accepted role for advisers in special education; in many areas their work is still overwhelmingly orientated towards special schools rather than towards special education. This results partly from the great divide between special schools and the mainstream, which perpetuates the myth that children in special schools are a race apart from their peers in ordinary schools, even though the same myth created the division in the first place. Equally important is the sheer administrative burden of supervising the full range of special schools, each with its own unique range of medical and, to a slightly lesser extent, educational problems.

This burden would certainly be increased by a trend towards integrated facilities for the handicapped, but would be enormously reduced by integrating the bulk of the genuine advisory (as opposed to administrative) case load for special education within the rest of the advisory service. An adviser for primary maths, for instance, would then be expected to offer a service to teachers in ESN(M) or maladjusted schools, perhaps by introducing different approaches or methods and helping to work out how these may be adapted to the children's needs. The fact that his own background was within ordinary schools would be an advantage rather than the reverse, since it could act as a stimulus to special schools or units, keeping them up to date with current policy and practice.

The credibility of advisers and educational psychologists with teachers has never been high. For special school advisers the credibility gap is particularly wide, since they have seldom had experience in more than one sort of special school: 'How can Mr X with his background in physical handicap, possible have anything useful to tell us about meeting the needs of our ESN(M) children, let alone about how we should teach them to read?' On the other hand, if Mr X's experience is in overcoming all the problems involved in introducing a special unit for physically handicapped children into an ordinary school, he may well be able to help in the introduction of units for children with different handicaps, and even in issues such as integrating the work of a traditionally separate remedial department into the rest of the school. Many of the fears and anxieties will be the same; experience in one setting can help you to anticipate and avoid problems in another. Similarly, an adviser with extensive experience in the teaching of reading and development of literacy should be able to establish his credibility in the special education field by demonstrating his ability to apply his knowledge in a flexible way, according to the needs and skills of the children or teachers concerned.

A move towards integration from the LEA's advisers makes sense from educational and administrative points of view. Implicit in such a move is the assumption that the adviser for special education would be appointed as much for his ability to promote closer cooperation between the traditional special school and ordinary school networks as for his successful record in special education as such.

The move towards integration is already influencing the work of advisers, and also has implications for the other support services of the LEA. The ones principally concerned here are the psychological service, the education welfare service, the careers service and the school health services. Of these the two which have traditionally had greatest involvement both in developing special education facilities and in the selection and review of children are the psychological service and the school health service, whose present responsibilities in the selection process were described in Chapter 2. With few exceptions educational psychologists offer a service to a range of schools which includes primary, secondary and special. In the larger LEA services which followed local government reorganisation in 1974 it is often possible for educational psychologists to be allocated to special schools according to their interest and experience. This does not altogether overcome the unfortunate state of affairs in many of the former small authorities, in which one or two psychologists struggled to offer something useful to all the ordinary and special schools in the district. The principal problem was not so much that they lacked experience with all age groups in each category of handicap as that the massive caseload forced them to rely on assessment techniques which were of doubtful scientific validity and less educational relevance. The present situation does not altogether overcome this problem because it still puts great pressure on psychologists to process the referrals to and from special education. They might be more usefully employed in projects to extend the authority's range of special education in ordinary schools than in acting as administrative agents within the present system.

Nevertheless, psychologists could not avoid administrative responsibilities even in the highly integrated special education network proposed in this chapter. As we argued earlier, the development of better facilities for ESN(M) and maladjusted children in ordinary schools requires the allocation of additional teachers and other resources; educational psychologists cannot hope to avoid responsibility for advising on how these should be allocated. In the same way, the school health service will always have an important responsibility for advising on the need for welfare staff or specialist medical equipment for physically handicapped children.

A more basic requirement for all the support services, though, is to ensure that they cooperate with each other in providing groups of schools with a network of advisory services. If the same people covered both the special school or units and the schools which send children to them, they should be able to encourage communication between special and ordinary schools, using the resources of each to meet the needs of individual children before their problems become acute.

A network of support services working together also has many of the strengths of the old child guidance clinics, without their limiting isolation. In the traditional child guidance clinic a psychiatrist, or less frequently psychologist, could offer the child treatment, while a psychiatric social worker did case-work with his parents, more often his mother. In the network of support services suggested here there would be a greater range, and consequently greater flexibility. When the child's problem appears to be associated with problems in the organisation or teaching methods in his class at school, perhaps because a teacher in his probationary year needs more guidance and support, the educational psychologist or adviser should be able to tackle the problem at source. Conversely, if the child's problem results from some distressing events at home such as parental separation and consequent financial problems, it should be possible for the team to combine factual advice on welfare benefits with short-term counselling or case-work to help the child and family over the crisis period.

This team work would, of course be strengthened by development of the education welfare service, the branch of the LEA which is responsible for school attendance. Work currently in progress in Sheffield is showing a high level of possible psychiatric disorder in the mothers of persistent absentees from school (based on the results of a health questionnaire which inquires about symptoms associated with stress). There is also evidence that up to 40 per cent of the children who are persistently absent from school may often remain at home because of anxiety about their parents' health. It goes almost without saying that attendance problems are often found among the slowest and most difficult children who come from homes with a variety of social or psychiatric problems – in other words the sort of children who are most likely to be referred to ESN(M) and maladjusted schools. In view of the profound effects of a decision to take legal action against a child or his parents (a decision which can result in the child spending many years in care) one hopes that more LEAs will start to implement the recommendations of the Local Government Training Board (1972) on the role and training of educational welfare officers. Under the chairmanship of Professor Ralph, this report recommended that a social work qualification should constitute the basic training for members of the service. If implemented in full, the service would be able to take its place in the network of support services described in this chapter, providing a range of skills to families and to schools, ranging from social case-work and advice on welfare benefits, to detailed discussion of the implications of a child's problems at home for his management at school.

The careers service too would develop its role in an integrated network for ESN(M) and maladjusted children. At present careers officers often go to an immense amount of trouble to obtain suitable employment for pupils leaving special schools or centres. Indeed an argument which is not infrequently used to persuade parents to accept a special school place for their child is the improved employment opportunities which this will entail.

Careers officers have an almost unique view of the products of the education system, and are additionally aware of the occasional mismatch between the real or imagined needs of employers and the skills and attitudes with which young people actually leave school. They also often suspect what Reynolds (1977) has claimed in Wales, that schools vary considerably in their success in equipping young people to obtain and hold down a job after leaving. Inevitably there will always be some inconsistency between what schools teach and what employers want; from the pronouncements of some employers it sometimes seems as if they regard the school's function as turning out a compliant, unquestioning work force who will uncomplainingly carry out monotonous jobs in unpleasant conditions from decade to decade, conveniently overlooking the fact that the radical changes of the last thirty years in society and in schools have implications for personnel management in industry.

As a link between school and employers, with a broader view than is usually possible for the careers specialist on a secondary school's staff, the careers' service is aware of problems which arise both from school leavers' attitudes towards school or work and from their more measurable educational attainments. As such he should be well placed to discuss with head teachers and other members of the support services any more general issues which might have implications for school policy or organisation; he may also be able to enlist their help for young people with problems that have remained unrecognised by the school and the other support services.

Close coordination will be needed if the network of support services is to operate effectively. It would be all too easy to establish a multi-disciplinary team on paper which in practice continued to operate as a collection of individuals. This does not necessarily imply that the team should have a director in the manner of some child guidance clinics, but rather that there should be regular arrangements for members to meet, plan their approach to different problems and coordinate their activities. There would be an obvious danger of spending time in meetings that might more profitably be spent in schools or with clients (Fiske, 1977); yet if different members of the team are to use their individual skills most effectively, avoiding wasteful duplication of effort, they will need to make time to meet each other.

Implications for the curriculum

It will already be clear that a policy for integration of ESN(M) and maladjusted children will have important implications for the curriculum in ordinary schools. These implications extend beyond the needs of the small number of children concerned to include the much larger number of slow-learning and disturbing children who have traditionally remained in ordinary schools.

One of the most basic problems is one which has legitimately concerned many opponents of integration. This is the interaction between the formal curriculum and the 'hidden curriculum'. The formal curriculum is merely what is covered in the syllabus for each subject, while the hidden curriculum includes everything which is *not* formally taught, but which is nevertheless picked up in the form of attitudes and behaviour. Since much of what is taught formally is forgotten as quickly as it is learnt (how many readers of this book who have done no maths since 'O' level can remember how to work out the circumference of a circle?), the hidden curriculum is perhaps of even greater importance. A chain-smoking senior teacher who preaches a doctrine of love in Assembly and subsequently canes every child he catches smoking will succeed only in teaching attitudes which he deplores. Similarly, no amount of skilled teaching in the school's remedial department or in its special group for problem pupils will lead to real social mixing if the classes concerned are merely tolerated with resignation by the school's senior staff. In other words, successful integration requires that the school's ethos – reflected in the hidden curriculum – caters as fully for the educational and social needs of its slowest and most disturbing members as those of its brightest and most cooperative examination candidates.

Acceptance as defined here is only likely when all the senior teachers responsible for coordinating work in their respective subjects accept the need to modify the syllabus and materials of their subject to cater for slow or retarded children. Materials for backward readers, for instance, require both conceptual and linguistic modification, as was argued in Chapter 6. Too often discussion of this point remains fixed at the level of selecting an appropriate reading scheme or range of reading books for use in remedial reading groups. What happens for the rest of the school day when the child returns to his ordinary class is left largely to chance, though there is generally an effort to see that he returns for lessons such as PE or practical activities when his educational backwardness does not create a handicap.

Yet even if backward children are retrained in remedial classes for all lessons except those which require little reading or writing ability, it does not overcome the problem. They still need a range of materials for use with the full range of subjects. Moreover, these materials must be directly related to the activities of ordinary classes at the time; if they are not, the opportunity for children to return to their ordinary class, progressing gradually up the continuum of special educational provision as envisaged in Chapter 4, will be severely restricted. Building up such a range for each of the basic primary school skills and for each of the subject areas in secondary schools must clearly involve active cooperation between the 'remedial' specialist and his teacher colleagues.

In spite of the wealth of material on the market for backward readers, relatively little of it caters explicitly for young people in secondary schools, and much less for teaching them maths, geography, social studies, technical drawing and so on. The lack of published resources underlines the need for detailed planning within the school. If the head of the secondary school remedial department is to influence the way his colleagues cater for slow learners in their respective subjects, his own teaching commitment will have to allow him time to attend curriculum planning meetings in each of the main subject departments. The same principle applies in primary schools, even though the division into subject specialities is much less clearly defined. The class teacher will also need time to help in adapting materials and equipment, in the way that already happens in the best special schools and remedial departments.

There is an analogy in the relationship envisaged here between the head of a remedial department or special unit for difficult pupils and his class teacher and subject teacher colleagues, and the relationship suggested earlier between the special education adviser and his other adviser colleagues. In both cases the specialist uses his own particular skills and knowledge in order to help his colleagues plan more effective work for the children concerned. The distinction recognises that ESN(M) children need to learn many of the same things as other children, but that the curriculum and materials need to be adapted for them. The principles involved in this are common to all subjects, even though the methods differ. The remedial specialist, whether adviser or teacher, can no more hope to cater for all subject areas than the French teacher can hope to teach science. In primary schools, where children spend most if not all their time with their class teacher, this problem is not obviously so acute. Nevertheless if the needs of slow-learning children are to be met in more constructive ways than the full-time remedial class which makes individual learning difficult and can only cater for a minority in the first place, it is essential that the routine in-service education of class teachers should include more practical experience in adapting their regular work to the skills of the less successful and more difficult child. In practice this is extremely difficult; for example, simplifying material for a humanities course so that all the children can read most of it is as time-consuming as it is difficult. A slightly different approach is to rely more heavily on individual and group projects whose complexity is determined by the pupils' ability, but this too requires time, effort and flexibility.

The relevance of school organisation

The same principles of communication between specialist teachers and class teachers and of flexible use of generous resources applies to planning work with maladjusted children. These children are almost invariably 'found' at school – very few are referred for problems at home, even though epidemiological research suggests that as many parents as teachers are worried about their children's behaviour. Their behaviour is allegedly abnormal, yet the emotions of anger, fear, anxiety and so on are normal ones; the 'abnormality' is only that they are expressed in a school setting which cannot tolerate them. As we argued in Chapters 7 and 8, whether a child shows 'maladjusted' behaviour depends not only on the child and his family but also on his school; maladjustment is a description of a disturbing interaction, and you cannot have an interaction to which only one person – the child – contributes.

Reynolds's (1977) work suggests that expanding a school's middle management structure of year-tutors, counsellors and so on will not necessarily result in any fundamental improvement in attitudes or adjustment. Similarly, expansion of 'caring agencies' such as educational psychology or educational welfare will not on its own be a solution. (The suggestions for the organisation of these agencies earlier in the chapter did not necessarily require an expansion of numbers.) Rather than creating additional facilities for these children, we might seek to support the class teachers with whom they spend most of their time. Stress for teachers and children can often be reduced in a number of small but important ways. Thus if one teacher has the same class for the last lesson at the end of each day in the week it hardly needs saying that he may be disappointed by their inattention and may consequently complain of maladjusted behaviour. Similarly, allowing inadequate time between lessons in a large secondary school makes the irritant of lateness inevitable. Teachers with responsibility for pastoral care, and educational psychologists, might be better employed in identifying the sources of friction than in patching up the results.

Nevertheless, a number of children will need additional support to that of their class teacher, and some teachers will need support in their dealings with certain pupils. Some children, for instance, who are living in difficult circumstances at home may benefit from a sanctuary unit that provides 'tea and sympathy'. Other disruptive pupils may need a withdrawal room where they must work on their own. A feature of this could be the detailed monitoring of children referred to the withdrawal room, *and* of the teachers who frequently send children to it, so that advice and help can be given at an earlier stage; pastoral care is not just for children! At the level of school organisation, some schools may need a clearer, or a more flexible, policy about such matters as uniform, and to ensure that the policy is followed. It is worth noting in passing that the more rules a school has, the easier it is for children to break them. Similarly, if a lot of problems are occurring at relatively unsupervised times such as the lunch break, it may be worth altering the timetable so that not all children and teachers take their lunch break at the same time, thus reducing the opportunity for problems arising from lack of supervision and associated boredom.

The ideas suggested here are based firmly on the assumption that so-called maladjusted children have the same needs as ordinary children. They may need additional support and supervision, but proposing a radically different educational philosophy to meet their needs is not only unnecessary but counter-productive.

Trends in assessment

Providing integrated support services and an integrated curriculum for ESN(M) and maladjusted children carries important implications for their initial assessment and subsequent review. We have already discussed the limitations of the standard tests of intelligence and educational attainment. They only investigate a narrow range of skills, they are not very reliable even in this limited respect, they are insufficiently related to the child's ordinary classroom work, and they provide little or no basis from which to plan remedial work (Galloway, 1977). Consequently many teachers are turning to 'criterion referenced' observation schedules in which the teacher's systematic observation of the child's development provides the basis for assessment.

It is not hard to see how this is consistent with a move towards integrated facilities in which the remedial department has a central role in adapting the conceptual and linguistic level of the ordinary curriculum to the needs of individual children. You cannot fit the curriculum to children's needs unless you have first assessed the nature of those needs. Standard intelligence and attainment tests will give you a number in the form of IQ or reading age for the purpose of comparison with a national sample, but will not tell you whether a group of children will be able to cope with a particular book, nor the level of complexity they will be able to manage in different areas of the curriculum. In aspects of assessment and curriculum planning there is no substitute for systematic observation, backed up when necessary by diagnostic tests and by assessment of the reading level required for the books in current use in the school (Gilliland, 1972).

Work with parents

Teachers are generally well aware of parents' anxieties when their children are failing to make progress. Unfortunately neither ESN(M) nor maladjusted children as a group are characterised by close cooperation between home and school. In the case of maladjusted children poor parent–child relationships are often the presenting problem, while the social problems within homes of many ESN(M) children can create considerable barriers. The Warnock Committee's recommendations (DES, 1978) that parents be seen as partners are of immense importance here.

That the barriers can be overcome is evident from the thriving parents' groups in some special schools, though even here they are not in a majority. When children are failing educationally or presenting severe problems in their behaviour, conflict is almost built into the home–school relationship and can only be avoided by a high level of understanding on the part of the teachers. This constitutes a real obstacle to integration; after months or years of failure or complaints in an ordinary school parents are often quick to grasp the chance of a new start in a special school and subsequently resist suggestions that their child might be ready to leave.

The problems involved in establishing a cooperative relationship with the parents of ESN(M) and maladjusted children are, however, the same whether they are in a special school or in the mainstream. The fact that relationships frequently break down in ordinary schools is in part the result of their lacking suitable provision for the child, and in part the relative inexperience of their teachers in working with parents who are often anxious, inarticulate, and burdened with feelings of guilt because they feel personally responsible for their child's problems. For a policy of integration to be successful, the teachers responsible for handicapped children, particularly the ESN(M) and maladjusted, should have specific in-service training in contact with parents. They will also need to be fully aware of the range of statutory and voluntary agencies which exist to help families and children in difficulty.

Implicit in close cooperation between parents and school is an explicit statement of what the school is doing to help the child. Too often special school is held out as a source of 'help'. Frightened of being thought uncooperative, embarrassed by the trouble their child has caused, and intimidated by the education department's impersonal bureaucracy, few parents are bold enough to ask what he is to be helped to do, by whom, when, why and with what prognosis. Similarly, return to ordinary school is often held out as a possibility 'if he makes progress', but few parents demand to know *what* progress is required for this to happen, and fewer still ask how many children have returned to ordinary schools in the past two years. One wonders whether the answers to these questions, if asked, might influence their decision.

However carefully teachers, school medical officers and educational psychologists try to explain what is involved in special education, there is always a strong probability of misunderstanding when parents are anxious, resentful or generally ill at ease. It would be helpful if they could be given a simple written statement of the administrative procedures, together with their own legal rights in the process. If this written statement could be supplemented by a straightforward explanation of the reason for their child's proposed transfer to a special school or unit, together with the circumstances under which return to ordinary school will be considered, further misunderstanding might be avoided.

At present special education sometimes seems to parents rather like the thin end of the wedge; they agree to their child entering a special school because he cannot read, but two or three years later when he is reading fluently they are told that he must stay there because he is lacking in confidence socially! Under the present segregated system of special education a parent can agree to special education for one reason, yet find that he faces insuperable administrative and legal barriers when this reason is no longer relevant and he wishes his child to return to an ordinary school. If the original reason is still relevant, for instance if the child is still not reading, the difficulties are even greater. The parent who says 'Jimmy might as well go back and fail in an ordinary school as in the special school where he has already been failing for two years – at least he won't be teased by other kids for going to the "daft" school', is not likely to attract much sympathy. All the same, it is hard to deny that he may have a point. In the more flexible, integrated system proposed in this chapter, such problems would be reduced; an offer of help at one point in the continuum of special educational help should not constitute such an irrevocable step, and should be based on a more explicit statement of the aims and objectives for each individual.

Chapter 10

Conclusions: special education for all who need it – in ordinary schools?

Summary of arguments for and against ordinary schools and special schools

At this stage it would be worth summarising some of the respective strengths and limitations of teaching children with problems in ordinary schools (Britton, 1977). On the credit side ordinary schools hold less social stigma than special schools. However much we may deplore it, this is still a major problem and is probably more acute for the ESN(M) and maladjusted than for other categories; it is one thing to be placed in a special school because you are spastic by an accident of birth, but quite another to be placed there because you are 'daft' or a 'nutter'. As we have already pointed out, slow-learning and disturbing children can also be stigmatised in ordinary schools, but this seldom extends into the community to the same extent as special school placement.

Ordinary school placement entails no potentially traumatic change of school, and contains better specialist facilities such as libraries, gymnasium, and science and language laboratories. The teachers on the whole have better promotion prospects (except in the smaller primary schools) and have more specialised teaching skills, particularly in secondary schools where specialisation is inevitable. This is not to deny that special school teachers have specialised skills and knowledge, only that the smaller staff cannot have the same range of subject teaching skills as an ordinary school. The ordinary school also provides an opportunity for ESN(M) and maladjusted children to learn to work and play with more able children – critical social skills, without which their later employment prospects must be severely limited. There is a further advantage for the ordinary children in the opportunity integration offers their teachers in helping them develop an attitude towards the less fortunate which is based on understanding and helpfulness rather than pity and ignorance. In the long run this must be crucial in altering society's attitude towards handicap.

Arguments against ordinary schools are that the premises are often unsatisfactory and would cost too much to modify. This, though, applies more to medically handicapped children than to the ESN(M) and maladjusted. More important, many teachers are not aware of the special needs of slow-learning and disturbing children, and a few are actively unsympathetic. Teasing by other children, combined with persistent failure resulting from an unsuitable curriculum can rapidly undermine a child's confidence and cause behaviour problems in addition to the original learning difficulty. In addition, the other children can suffer when too much of the teacher's attention is devoted to the ESN(M) or the maladjusted.

Whether or not these arguments are valid depends not on whether there is a policy of integration, but on how it is carried out. In the last chapter we discussed some of the necessary conditions for it to be successful. Nevertheless, detailed planning cannot hope to prevent all problems, merely to anticipate some of them.

In support of special schools, it can be argued that the buildings are more suitable, though again this is less often the case for the ESN(M) and maladjusted than for other categories of handicap; that there is more specialist equipment, and that the staff are more skilled in meeting their special needs. Following on from this, the curriculum can be designed to meet the needs of the children concerned, and not merely adapted to them as may be the case in an ordinary school. The withdrawn, timid child can be protected, and social and sporting activities can be provided for similarly handicapped children who could not hope to compete on equal terms in an ordinary school. Scarce ancillary professions such as specialist medical personnel, speech therapists, physiotherapists, even psychotherapists, can be concentrated on one centre where they can help the maximum number of children without wasting time on travel. A spin-off from all this could be an improved advisory service for parents, except where the special school is so far from their homes that they cannot easily reach it without special help.

Against special schools, the problem of selection is a crucial argument. The cut-off point has to be drawn somewhere, and there must always be a grey area in which the decision to apply for a special school place or to recommend that the child remains in an ordinary school depends largely on the idiosyncracies of the psychologist and ordinary school head teacher. This problem is most severe in the case of ESN(M) and maladjusted children; as we have already argued a number of times the selection criteria are notoriously opaque for these children, in borderline cases depending almost as much on the skills and attitudes of their existing teachers as on their own personal or educational problems. Yet selection is also a problem for physically handicapped children, since physical handicap cannot be equated with educational handicap. A paraplegic child in a spacious secondary school may well have fewer educational difficulties than a child with slight damage to the tendons of his right hand, who as a result cannot keep up with his class's written work.

Further arguments against special schools are travelling distances, the shorter day, and the fact that in country areas they sometimes have to be residential. Parents can be lulled into complacency, confident in the teachers' assurance that their child is doing well; he may be in comparison with other handicapped children, but he will eventually have to live in a non-handicapped world. Connected with this is the risk of special schools becoming overprotective and underdemanding, especially when they cater for the whole age range. Moreover, the research on the influence of teachers' expectations on pupils' progress (Pidgeon, 1970; Rosenthal and Jacobson, 1968) raises the obvious possibility that special schools may create self-fulfilling prophecies. A child is sent to a school for maladjusted children because he shows maladjusted behaviour, so if he does not show maladjusted behaviour he will be something of an oddity in the school; expectancy effects operate on children as well as adults. This could be one reason why the number of children returning to the mainstream from special schools for the maladjusted appears to be fewer than the number we might expect on the basis of evidence from studies of the spontaneous improvement of behaviour problems.

As we implied earlier, the arguments in favour of special schools and against ordinary schools have to be considered in the light of the quality of education which each can offer to handicapped children. Whether or not a special school or an ordinary school is better for a particular child depends not on any theoretical arguments for or against integration, but on the facilities available in each. If the facilities in ordinary schools are as good as those in the existing special schools, there can be no argument for retaining the special schools. As we argued in Chapter 1, certain needs cannot easily be met in special schools; the most obvious examples are the need to learn to live with non-handicapped children and an opportunity to acquire a mature acceptance of one's handicap.

The 'elitism' of special schools

We saw in Chapters 2 and 3 that special schools for children with learning or behavioural difficulties cater for no more than 2 per cent of all children, while up to a further 13 per cent remain in ordinary schools. Although, strictly speaking, the 1944 Act did not require selection for secondary education, selection was the logical result of the available buildings and resources at the time. After the war there was a plentiful supply of large, cheap houses, previously used for evacuees, which could easily be converted into special schools. It is worth considering for a moment the similarity between arguments in favour of retaining selection at eleven for grammar schools and arguments in favour of a separate special school system. Every one of the arguments listed above in favour of special schools was also used with varying degrees of emphasis in the campaign to retain grammar schools. More skilled staff, specialist teaching facilities, more suitable curriculum, protection from ridicule by other, less intelligent, children, opportunity for social activities with similarly able children, concentration of resources (though in this case teaching resources rather than those of ancillary professions), were all used in the battle to support the elitist grammar school system. Now that this particular battle has been lost, apart from an insignificant rearguard action, the same arguments have been taken off the shelf, dusted and polished up to support selective special schools.

In the same way, the arguments against selection in secondary education are strikingly similar to those against special schools. The traditional test-based criteria were inaccurate and unreliable, the grammar school system was socially divisive, the academic hothouse atmosphere was unrelated to real life, the 'failures' in secondary modern schools regarded themselves as failures and consequently performed like failures, and so on.

There is another and more disturbing similarity between the campaign to retain grammar schools and the pressure groups against integration in special education. A suspicion which was often felt but less often openly expressed was that the teachers and governors of grammar schools wished to retain their independent elitist status in order to preserve their own career structure and the individuality of their schools; this was not quite the same thing as saying that they should be retained for the service they offered the pupils. It was not an entirely unworthy argument. There were undoubtedly a number of teachers who had made valuable contributions in the selective school setting, yet doubted their own ability to succeed in a mixed ability comprehensive school; if you think you are giving a valuable service you fight to retain it.

It is noticeable that the strongest pressure groups in favour of integration are those of parents and of the handicapped themselves, though as we have already seen the ESN(M) and the maladjusted are uniquely conspicuous by their absence. Conversely, the strongest pressure groups against integration have tended to be those of teachers in special schools. It is laudable that they should fight to retain what they think is valuable, but there may sometimes be a suspicion that anxiety about the world outside is not confined to the children leaving special schools. The expertise and experience of teachers in special schools might be better used in pressurising their LEA to extend the same staffing and financial support for similar children in ordinary schools, thus not only ensuring that integration will be successful for the children who might otherwise have been selected for special schools, but also that the improved facilities benefit other children as well.

Special education for all who need it

Whether or not a child is handicapped depends on what society expects from him. A slightly shortsighted boy in western society has a visual defect, but this certainly does not constitute a handicap. A similarly shortsighted child in a nomadic bushman family in Southern Africa would be severely handicapped; he could not carry out the tracking and hunting duties required of men in his society. The analogy with special education is clear. Whether a child is considered handicapped, and consequently needs to be removed for more specialised help, depends on his ability to meet the expectations of his ordinary school, which in turn depends on what it has to offer and what it expects.

We argued in the last chapter and in Chapter 4 that a range of facilities is needed to form a coherent network capable of catering for all children with special needs. In this context, the controversy between integration and segregation becomes inappropriate since different needs will be met at different points on the continuum, with flexible interchange between them. At present, although special schools and ordinary schools can learn a lot from each other, they seldom find an opportunity to do so. The scope for mutual stimulation and assistance will be realised when there is flexible interchange between the different points on a continuum of special education facilities, the majority based in ordinary schools, and between the separate facilities and the mainstream.

Integration will certainly become an administrative and educational fact rather than the politico-educational theory, which it is at present; the trend is reflected in Section 10 of the 1976 Education Act, and can no more be reversed than the move away from selection in secondary education can be reversed. As it becomes an accepted fact, it will become more obvious to the majority of teachers, doctors and educational psychologists that the same principles and philosophy apply to special education as to the education of any other children.

In the divisive days of the eleven-plus examination primary schools went to immense trouble to ensure that children who stood any chance of 'passing' received every encouragement and opportunity. The result was that the least able or least experienced teachers were often required to teach the slowest and most difficult children. In this climate special school places were a necessity. On the credit side, primary schools demonstrated a willingness and ability to attend to special needs, even if these special needs were of the restricted kind needed to score high marks in the curious questions dreamed up by the architects of the local eleven-plus examination. In just the same way, grammar schools never failed to attend to the special needs of their most able pupils – those who could realistically aim for a university place, preferably at Oxbridge.

Our argument is not that primary school head teachers who went to such lengths to cater for the special needs of potential eleven-plus successes were wrong to do so, nor that the grammar, and comprehensive, school staff who went, and go, to such lengths to cater for the special needs of potential university candidates were wrong to do so. In most cases they were putting themselves to a lot of trouble in order to give the children and young people concerned the best opportunity in life. Parental pressure was undoubtedly a feature but it would be cynical and uncharitable to consider it the principal influence. In any case, this is not the point; whatever their motivation, schools have always shown their capacity for adapting their curriculum, timetable and organisation to the needs of their most able children.

In the political, economic and social climate of the late 1940s and 1950s it did not appear feasible for schools to devote the same energy and resources to the needs of the majority, let alone the needs of the problem children minority, as to the needs of the few high-flyers. From the 1960s onwards parents have become more articulate, more demanding; politicians have become increasingly critical of the inequalities in our education system. Finally, though by no means least, teachers have recognised the exciting possibilities if they are permitted the resources to cater for the special needs of all children and not just those of the most gifted minority.

What was demonstrated by some of the best features of the selective secondary education system was that schools could provide special education of a high quality. This was not, of course confined to primary and grammar schools, since many secondary modern schools refused to write their pupils off as failures and achieved impressive results.

The movement towards integration has ostensibly been motivated by dissatisfaction with the separate special school system. Parents, former pupils, and sometimes teachers, have identified weaknesses in the system and demanded to share the opportunities of their local comprehensive school. Yet this movement could never have attracted widespread attention and support, reflected for instance, in the appointment of the Warnock Committee, without a converging change of attitude in the ordinary system. This change has seldom been identified explicitly with the special schools controversy, but is nevertheless central to it. The abolition of selection in secondary education both reflected and contributed to a wider feeling among politicians and the general public that second-class education was unacceptable in modern society.

In spite of the misconceptions of a few of the early comprehensive school head teachers, the objective was not to bring grammar school education in reach of the majority; the limitations of the philosophy and practice of the former grammar schools have formed books of their own. Rather the objective was to introduce a broader, more flexible curriculum in which *all* pupils could achieve their full potential without the administrative strait-jacket of a system that regarded the majority as 'non-academic' and allocated resources accordingly.

The relevance of this to the debate about the future of special schools is that the prevailing political and educational climate in this country is now demanding that ordinary schools should give the same attention and resources to the special needs of all their pupils as they have traditionally given to the minority. Within individual schools this is reflected in more flexible timetables which allow children of average general ability to develop their special aptitudes in a way that was seldom possible twenty years ago. It is also reflected in the resources allocated to classes for children with learning difficulties, which are now seldom left to inexperienced probationers or teachers whose heads wish to protect them from other classes. As a result, schools have increasingly come to recognise their ability to provide special education for the least able children as well as the most able. It is this, as much as the drop in the birth rate over the last few years, which has led to a decline in numbers at ESN(M) schools in some authorities. Teachers who have worked hard and successfully with a dull child in his early school years are no longer willing to accept unquestioningly the opinion of a psychologist or doctor that he would be better off in a special school.

The contribution of ESN(M) and maladjusted children to educational practices

Public discussion about handicapped children centres on how their needs can be met. This is both natural and right, but tends to overlook one of the most basic human needs, namely our need to feel that we are making a useful contribution to the society in which we live. For the handicapped, educationally backward or behaviourally difficult child this is particularly important. Imaginative teachers have always been able to find ways for the slowest and most difficult children to contribute to school activities. Yet there is another level at which slow learning and disturbing children contribute to educational practice in a school. On the whole, children are conformists and will make the worst systems work. Children who fail make us rethink our current ideas and, hopefully, improve on them.

Reading schemes in primary schools are a good example. The jerk-jerk language of some of the most popular schemes is far removed from the linguistic experience of any children. Yet schools continue to buy these schemes in their thousands. That they succeed in teaching the majority of children to read is in part a tribute to the skill of teachers in arousing children's enthusiasm for rather uninteresting material, and in part a reflection of children's enthusiasm for clearcut, teacher-directed activity. Their willingness to sit for hours doing mechanical sums is another example of this.

Given the willingness of most children to adapt enthusiastically to almost any system, teachers have little incentive for critical analysis of current practice. The incentive must either come from within, or be imposed from without by that small minority who challenge the system, either by failing to learn, or by refusing to conform to the school's traditional set of rewards and sanctions. ESN(M) and maladjusted children challenge our ideas about normality, and thereby force us to ask questions about the sort of education we are providing for the majority. A jerk-jerk reading scheme, for example, can hardly be linguistically inappropriate for slow-learning children without also being linguistically inappropriate for all other children. If the slowest and most disturbing children need something with more intrinsic interest, more closely related to general literacy skills, the same must presumably apply to all the others as well. To summarise, the average child can benefit from the presence of the slow learning because the teacher has to take special care to ensure that she gets her lesson across.

Retaining ESN(M) and maladjusted children in ordinary schools presents a challenge to their teachers, yet paradoxically may help them to raise the overall quality of education for all children. The brightest children in a school have always forced their teachers to re-examine their curriculum and teaching methods, with consequent benefits for the majority. The same applies at the other end of the intellectual and behavioural continuum. With gifted children it is not a simple matter of raising the expectations and standards for the majority; nor, most emphatically, is it a matter of lowering the prevailing standards and expectations to cater for the slowest and most difficult children. Rather the presence of exceptional children, whether gifted or handicapped, forces us to make the curriculum more flexible so that it can adapt to the varying needs of the children concerned. More fundamentally, their presence makes us ask whether the context and the teaching method for each subject area is consistent with what we are really trying to do. Are the most widely used reading schemes, for instance, consistent with the development of literacy? If the answer is negative for the exceptional children who have challenged the system, the same is likely to apply to the majority.

Catering for similarities

Much concern about integration has concentrated on the ability of ordinary schools to cater for the differences between children. Quite understandably, teachers have questioned whether the special needs of handicapped children can be met in the mainstream. Although ESN(M) and maladjusted children appear at first sight more like children in ordinary schools than their peers in schools for all other categories of handicap, doubt about the ability of mainstream schools to cater for their particular needs has been even greater than with physical handicaps. The reason probably lies in the fact that they have generally been referred to a special school after a period of failure in an ordinary school. Concern is obviously justified if the ordinary schools do not receive sufficient support and encouragement to adapt their curriculum and pastoral care organisation to the needs of their slower and more disturbing pupils.

Here, however, we need to look at this question from a different angle: special schools, by definition, cater primarily for differences from the norm; are ordinary schools capable of catering for all the characteristics which dull and difficult children, as well as all physically handicapped pupils, have in common with the majority? In the last chapter we discussed the sort of support which would enable ordinary schools to cater for differences; recognising similarities is another matter altogether, and in many ways a more difficult one; precisely because ESN(M) and maladjusted children challenge our ideas about normality, the temptation to 'integrate' them in full-time 'remedial' classes or special units for difficult pupils is hard to resist.

Grouping is necessary for certain activities. Gifted mathematicians, for instance, need the stimulus that comes from working together on projects which would be beyond their classmates; similarly children retarded in reading need attention for their particular difficulty. The danger is that recognition of differences will blind us to the much greater similarities between children. A still greater danger is that the school's own organisation and curriculum contributes to the very difficulties it tries to solve. The 'C' stream pupils of a grammar school were often regarded as unintelligent, uncooperative failures – and regarded themselves as such – just as the 'remedial' classes in some theoretically unstreamed comprehensive schools are regarded today. Children must learn to cope with failure, yet failure should be a constructive learning experience rather than a threat imposed from outside. For the majority of ESN(M) and maladjusted children failure is a threat imposed by adults, at worst to be accepted with weary resignation, and at best, rejected with angry rebellion.

For a school to cater successfully for the similarities between children, its ethos must be one in which all children feel they have something to contribute, and are given an opportunity to contribute it. Catering for similarities does not simply imply token integration in PE and other 'non-academic' activities. It implies a practical recognition that all children, from the most gifted to the least able, come to school for the same basic experiences. The topics covered in the traditional curriculum constitute one set of children's experiences at school; these, in fact are the ones in which grouping by ability may sometimes be necessary. Equally important, and interrelated, are communicating thoughts and feelings with other children and with adults, working and playing cooperatively, recognising and exploiting their own particular abilities, and preparing them for the next stage in their life.

When we consider how little of what we were formally taught in school, especially secondary school, we can actually remember, it is clear that the learning experiences which last are the ones covered by the school's 'hidden curriculum', the attitudes and ideas which determine what sort of place the school is. In other words the most important learning experiences are the ones which ESN(M) and maladjusted and physically handicapped children share with all other children. The characteristics which distinguish them are in a minority.

In Chapter 7 we reviewed some of the recent research which shows that schools, contrary to popular sociological opinion, have a significant influence on their pupils' social adjustment both within and outside the school itself. It has been shown in more than one area that whether a young person finds himself in front of the juvenile court may depend not only on his home, his personality and where he lives, but also on which school he attends. It seems possible that this research is merely describing in quantifiable form the effect of what might more subjectively be called the school's ethos. Full social integration at the level of friendship between handicapped and non-handicapped children cannot be achieved by a politico-administrative decision to implement a policy of integration. It depends on the relationships and attitudes in ordinary schools. Here, again, we see how the basic needs are shared by all children. The minority of schools whose internal relationships are characterised by disputes between the staff and by unresolved friction between pupils and teachers have a 'hidden curriculum' which prevents them from recognising what handicapped and ordinary children have in common. This may only be saying that handicapped children do best in schools with good relationships; nevertheless as banal a fact as this does carry important implications both for the siting of special units in ordinary schools and also for the choice of school when a child is to be fully integrated into ordinary classes. A further implication is that the financial incentives to accept handicapped children should be sufficiently attractive to act as a positive inducement for schools to re-examine their existing policies and practices.

Integration and public relations

Section 10 of the 1976 Education Act (the section which requires a change of emphasis towards ordinary schools for the education of handicapped children) was passed by Parliament in spite of a notable lack of enthusiasm from the Department of Education and Science. Section 10 came on to the Statute Book because Members of Parliament were persuaded of the injustice and arbitrary nature of selection processes. A further motive may perhaps have been a desire to anticipate, or even influence, the findings of the Warnock Committee.

No one really believes now that the country will return to selection in secondary education. The uproar that would greet a return to selection would make the rearguard action of a few authorities to retain grammar schools and the eleven-plus exam seem like an insignificant squawk. The political, social and educational pressure against selection is now irreversible; the question which needs answering in the next two decades is not so much whether comprehensive schools can cater for gifted children as effectively as the former grammar schools, but whether children who are outstandingly gifted in certain specific skills may need some additional stimulus to what can be provided in a comprehensive school, let alone in a grammar school. Recognising that talented musicians, for example, need the added experience of playing in a county, or even national youth orchestra does not invalidate arguments against selection for secondary education as a whole. In the same way, recognition that an ESN(M) or maladjusted child has certain special needs which cannot all be met within his ordinary school does not invalidate the arguments against educational segregation in a full-time special school.

The movement towards integration is at an earlier stage than the movement towards comprehensive secondary schools, yet is no more reversible. An effect of Section 10, when implemented, will be to make parents more aware of the possibility that their children's needs should be met in an ordinary school. They will be less likely to acquiesce without protest in the recommendation of doctors and educational psychologists, backed up by education officers. The groups which will fight hardest for the right to an ordinary school education, or at least to a special unit in an ordinary school campus, are those which have traditionally formed self-help groups of parents and handicapped adults, namely the medical handicaps and the ESN(S). Coming largely from Social Classes IV and V on the Registrar General's classification the ESN(M) and maladjusted have attracted relatively little public and political support.

A revealing measure of the integrity of LEAs will be the degree to which they encourage their psychologists and head teachers to inform the parents of dull and difficult children for whom alternative placement is being considered about the existence of Section 10 and about the limitations of separate special school placement. Of course the decision to request special education is in theory always made in the child's interests. In practice, we have argued repeatedly in this book, the decision is often made in the interests of the referring school. For ESN(M) children the primary motivation in referral is frequently the perfectly understandable anxiety of the class teachers about their progress; with maladjusted children the same applies, but in both cases there is additional anxiety about their effect on other children in the class. In such cases, transfer to a special school is motivated as much by concern for the welfare of the teachers and children in the referring school as by any objective assessment of the good it will do the child.

Removing a child for the benefit of others rather than for his own is often justifiable; what is not justifiable is to tell his parents that the transfer is being requested for his benefit. We constantly underestimate the intelligence and reasonableness of parents, and never more so than when the parents come from Social Class V and have a problem child. A variety of methods is available for persuading parents to accept special school places. Ironically, many of them are also laudable examples of good practice; enabling parents and child to visit a potential school, meet the teachers and talk to the children, is an obvious example. Inevitably, though, they are given one-sided information which gives them a feeling of optimism about the results of special education which is unjustified by the research. Nor do they generally have any chance to realise that if the LEA's resources for special education were allocated towards special help in ordinary schools, as opposed to full-time treatment in special schools, their child might well require no change of school.

If integration requires LEAs to provide in ordinary schools the best aspects of what has traditionally been provided in special schools, it will not be a cheap alternative to special schools. Some of the necessary resources were described in the last chapter, from which it will be clear that an enormous amount of thought and planning must precede an equally large injection of money to provide the resources for it to succeed. We should be clear about what is involved here. Parliament passed Section 10 against the advice of the Department of Education and Science. It follows that Parliament should vote money to implement this policy, if necessary against the advice of the Treasury. The obvious retort: 'If you believe Parliament will do that you'll believe anthing!' should not obscure the deeper implication: if provision of additional facilities to integrate ESN(M) and maladjusted children is not only right for the children concerned, but also of benefit to the many other dull and difficult children who do not quite qualify for these labels, then it is worth fighting for.

Physically and severely mentally handicapped children already have active pressure groups of parents to ensure that their needs are not neglected in the accelerating trend towards integrated education. Lacking such well-established parent pressure groups, the ESN(M) and maladjusted are represented mainly by professional associations of special school teachers who not unnaturally have mixed feelings about integration if this may mean the closure of their schools. Yet the issue can be stated quite boldy: can integration be undesirable if it means introducing the best special school characteristics into the curriculum – and the atmosphere – of ordinary schools? Certain educational needs such as mixing with ordinary children cannot easily be met in special schools; conversely, there are none which cannot in principle be met in ordinary schools, though considerable change in the curriculum and organisation may be needed. For instance, much thought must be given to the provision of the protective function of special schools for the insecure, anxious child, though some of the special groups described in Chapter 7 have gone some way in providing this.

However understandable anxieties about integration may be they should not be allowed to conceal the central argument. This is not about integration or segregation as two mutually incompatible alternatives, but about providing a range of resources for the education of ESN(M) and maladjusted children. The majority of these should be based within ordinary schools, though a small number of separate establishments might still be needed. Ideally, these would act as intensive short-term centres to deal with specific difficulties, and to act as sources of inspiration to the much larger number of teachers in ordinary schools or in special units attached to ordinary schools. The political controversy should not focus on the sterile dichotomy between special schools and ordinary schools, but on the resources and facilities which are needed in order to meet children's needs in their neighbourhood schools. The best possible demonstration of professional confidence, integrity, and ultimately competence would be for the support services and the teachers' organisations to rise above their short-term anxieties by uniting to press for these resources at local and national levels.

References

Abbreviations

Brit. J. Educ. Psych.	British Journal of Educational Psychology
Brit. J. Psychiat.	British Journal of Psychiatry
Bull. Br. Assoc. Behav. Psychother.	Bulletin of the British Association for Behavioural Psychotherapy
Educ. Res.	Educational Research
J. Appl. Behav. Anal.	Journal of Applied Behavioural Analysis
J. Child Psychol. Psychiat.	Journal of Child Psychology and Psychiatry
Sp. Ed. Fd. Tr.	Special Education : Forward Trends
Ther. Ed.	Therapeutic Education
Times. Ed. Supp.	Times Educational Supplement

Ainsworth, S. H. (1959) *An Explanatory Study of Educational, Social and Emotional Factors in the Education of Mentally Retarded Children in Georgia Public Schools,* Athens: Univ. of Georgia (quoted in Osterling, 1967).

Anderson, E. M. (1971) Making Ordinary Schools Special: Report on the Integration of Physically Handicapped Children into Ordinary Schools in Scandinavia, *Guide-lines for Teachers,* no. 10, London: College of Special Education.

Anderson, E. (1973) *The Disabled Schoolchild: a study of integration in primary schools,* London: Methuen.

Ascher, M. (1970) The attainments of children in ESN schools and remedial departments, *Educ. Res.,* **12,** 215–19.

Balbernie, R. W. (1966) *Residential Work with Children,* Oxford: Pergamon.

Baldwin, J. (1972) Delinquent schools in Tower Hamlets I. A critique, *British Journal of Criminology,* **12,** 399–401.

Bank-Mikkelson, N. E. (1974) *The Principle of Normalisation,* Stockholm: National Board of Social Welfare.

Bennett, A. (1932) *A Comparative Study of Subnormal Children in the Elementary Grades,* New York (quoted in Osterling, 1967).

Berger, M., Yule, W. and **Rutter, M.** (1975) Attainment and adjustment in two geographical areas: II. The prevalence of specific reading retardation, *Brit. J. Psychiat.,* **126,** 510–19.

Binet, A. and **Simon, T.** (1914) *Mentally Defective Children,* London: E. J. Arnold.

Birch, L. B. (1950) The improvement of reading ability, *Brit. J. Educ. Psych.,* **20,** 73–6.

Blatt, B. (1958) The physical, personality and academic status of children who are mentally retarded attending special classes as compared with those who are mentally retarded attending regular classes, *American Journal of Mental Deficiency,* **62,** 810–18.

Board of Education (1934) *Report of the Committee of Inquiry into Problems Relating to Partially Sighted Children,* London: HMSO.

Board of Education (1938) *Report of the Committee of Inquiry into Problems Relating to Children with Defective Hearing,* London: HMSO.

Board of Education and **Board of Control** (1929) *Report of the Joint Departmental Committee on Mental Deficiency,* London: HMSO.

Boxall, M. (1973) Nurture groups, *Concern* 13, 9–11.

Brickman, W. W. (1967) *Denmark's Education System and its Problems,* Washington: US Dept. of Health, Education and Welfare.

British Psychological Society (1976) Summary of evidence presented by the B.P.S. to the Inquiry into Special Education set up by the DES, *Bulletin of the British Psychological Society,* **29,** 1–6.

Britton, E. (1977) Is the integration of special schools irresistible? *Education* (Supplement), 4 November, iii–iv.

Bryans, T. and **Wolfendale, S.** (1973) *Guide-lines for Teachers,* Croydon: Reading and Language Development Centre.

Burden, R. (1977) What's in a name? Some reflections on the possible consequences of labelling children educationally subnormal, *Association of Educational Psychologists' Journal,* **4,** no. 5, 37–42.

Burn, M. (1964) *Mr Lyward's Answer,* London: Hamish Hamilton.

Burt, C. (1937) *The Backward Child,* London: Hodder & Stoughton.

Cashdan, A. and **Pumfrey, P. D.** (1969) Some effects of the remedial teaching of reading, *Educ. Res.,* **11,** 138–42.

Cassidy, W. M. and **Stanton, J. E.** (1959) *An Investigation of Factors Involved in the Educational Placement of Mentally Retarded Children,* Columbus: Ohio (quoted in Osterling, 1967).

Cassidy, W. M. and **Stanton, J. E.** (1961) *An Additional Phase of an Investigation of Factors Involved in the Educational Placement of Mentally Retarded Children,* Columbus: Ohio (quoted in Osterling, 1967).

Chamberlain, J. (1973) Mentally handicapped children in ordinary schools. Learning Together, Paper No. 3; unpublished paper presented at conference run by the Campaign for Mental Handicap, April 1973.

Charity Organisation Society (1893) *The Epileptic and Crippled Child and Adult. A report on an investigation of the physical and mental condition of 50,000 school children, with suggestions for the better education and care of the feeble minded children and adults,* London: Swan-Sonnenschein.

Chisholm, B. J. (1977a) Remedial help within non-streaming, *Forum for the Discussion of New Trends in Education,* **20,** 24–6.

Chisholm, B. J. (1977b) Provision for deaf children in the Scandinavian countries, unpublished M.Sc. thesis, Division of Education, Univ of Sheffield.

Cleugh, M. F. (1957; 2nd ed, 1968) *The Slow Learner,* London: Methuen.

Coard, B. (1971) *How the West Indian Child is Made Educationally Sub-normal in the British School System,* London: New Beacon Books.

Coleman, J. S. (1966) *Equality of Educational Opportunity,* Washington: Office of Education.

Cooling, M. (1974) Educational provisions for maladjusted children in boarding schools, M.Ed. thesis, Birmingham University.

Cope, C. and **Anderson, E.** (1977) *Special Units in Ordinary Schools: an exploratory study of special provision for disabled children,* London: Univ. of London, Inst. of Ed.

Critchley, C. (1969) An experimental study of maladjusted children, M.A. thesis, Liverpool University.

Curr, W. and **Gourlay, N.** (1953) An experimental evaluation of remedial education, *Brit. J. Educ. Psych.,* **23,** 45–55.

Davie, R., Butler, N. and **Goldstein, H.** (1972) *From Birth to Seven,* London: Longmans.

Department of Education and Science, (1966) *The Health of the School Child, 1964—65,* London: HMSO.

Department of Education and Science (1967) *Children and their Primary Schools* (The Plowden Report), London: HMSO

Department of Education and Science (1971) *Slow Learners in Secondary Schools* (Education Survey no. 15), London: HMSO.

Department of Education and Science (1973a) *Special Education: a fresh look,* Reports on Education no. 77, London: DES.

Department of Education and Science (1973b) Staffing of Special Schools and Classes, Circular 4/73, London: HMSO.

Department of Education and Science (1974a) *Educational Statistics for the United Kingdom,* London: HMSO.

Department of Education and Science (1974b) *Integrating Handicapped Children,* London: HMSO.

Department of Education and Science (1975) The Discovery of Children Requiring Special Education and the Assessment of Their Needs, Circular 2/75, London: DES.

Department of Education and Science (1976) *A Language for Life* (The Bullock Report), London: HMSO.

Department of Education and Science (1978) *Special Educational Needs* (The Warnock Report), London: HMSO.

Department of Health and Social Security (1968) *Report of the Committee on Local Authority and Allied Personal Social Services* (The Seebohm Report) London: HMSO.

Douglas, J. W. B. (1964) *The Home and the School,* London: MacGibbon and Kee.

Dugdale, R. L. (1877) *The Jukes: a study in crime, pauperism, disease and heredity.*

Dunn, L. M. (1968) Special education for the mildly retarded – is much of it justifiable? *Exceptional Children,* **35,** 5–22 (reprinted in W. G. Becker, (ed.) *An Empirical Basis for Change in Education,* Henley-on-Thames, Science Res. Associates).

Education Act (1921) 11 and 12 George V, Ch. 51, London: HMSO.

Education Act (1944) 7 and 8 George VI, Ch. 31, London: HMSO.

Education Act (1976) Elizabeth II, Ch. 81, London: HMSO.

Education Department (1898) *Report of the Departmental Committee on Defective and Epileptic Children,* London: HMSO.

Education (Handicapped Children) Act (1970) Elizabeth II, Ch. 52, London: HMSO.

Eisenberg, L., Conners, K. and **Sharpe, L.** (1965) A controlled study of the differential application of out-patient psychiatric treatment for children, *Japanese Journal of Child Psychiatry,* **6,** 125–32.

Elementary Education Act (1870) 33 and 34 Victoria, Ch. 75, London: HMSO.

Elementary Education Act (1876) 39 and 40 Victoria, Ch. 79, London: HMSO.

Elementary Education Act (1880) 43 and 44 Victoria, Ch. 23, London: HMSO.

Elementary Education (Defective and Epileptic Children) Act (1899) 62 and 63 Victoria, Ch. 32, London: HMSO.

Elementary Education (Defective and Epileptic Children) Act (1914) 4 and 5 George V, Ch. 39, London: HMSO.

Ellenbogen, M. L. (1957) A comparative study of some aspects of academic and social adjustment of the two groups of mentally retarded children in special classes and in regular grades (quoted in Osterling, 1967).

Farrington, D. (1972) Delinquency begins at home, *New Society,* 14 September.

Ferster, C. B. (1967) Perspectives in psychology: **XXV.** Transition from animal laboratory to clinic, *Psychological Record,* **17,** 145–50.

Finlayson, D. S. and **Loughran, J. L.** (1976) Pupils' perceptions in high and low delinquency schools, *Educ. Res.,* **18,** 138–45.

Fisher, G. (1977) Integration at the Pingle School, *Sp. Ed. Fd. Tr.,* **4,** no. 1, 8–11.

Fiske, D. (1977) Week by week, *Education,* 25 November.

Fixsen, D. L., Phillips, E. L. and **Wolf, M.** (1973) Achievement place: experiments in self-government with pre-delinquents, *J. Appl. Behav. Anal.,* **6,** 31–47.

Fogelman, K. (1976) *Britain's Sixteen Year Olds,* London: National Children's Bureau.

Galletley, I. (1976) How to do away with yourself, *Remedial Education,* **11,** 149–51.

Galloway, D. (1975) A behavioural approach to treatment, *Therapeutic Education,* **3,** no. 2, 23–31.

Galloway, D. M. (1976a) Size of school, socio-economic hardship, suspension rates and persistent unjustified absence from school, *Brit. J. Educ. Psych.,* **46,** 40–7.

Galloway, D. M. (1976b) *Case Histories in Classroom Management,* London: Longmans.

Galloway, D. M. (1977) Application of behavioural analysis and behaviour modification in school psychological service practice, *Bull. Br. Assoc. Behav. Psychother.,* **5,** 63–6.

Garnett, J. (1975) A curriculum for less able children, unpublished ACE course dissertation, Oxford University.

Garnett, J. (1976) 'Special children' in a comprehensive, *Sp. Ed. Fd. Tr.,* **3,** no. 1, 8–11.

Gilliland, J. (1972) *Readability,* London: Hodder & Stoughton.

Goldstein, H. *et al* (1962) *Early School Development of Low I.Q. Children.* A study of special class placement, Interim Report, Illinois: Univ. of Illinois (quoted in Osterling, 1967).

Goodwin, C. A. (1974) Leicestershire: Countesthorpe College, *Remedial Education,* **9,** 16–18.

Goodwin, C. A. (1977) Special education for the mentally handicapped child in Denmark, Sweden and Norway, unpublished report to Action Research for the Crippled Child.

Goodwin, C. A. (1978) Personal communication.

Gorrell-Barnes, G. (1973) Work with nurture-group parents, *Concern,* **13,** 13–16.

Graham, P. and **Rutter, M.** (1968a) The reliability and validity of the psychiatric study of the child: II. Interview with the parent, *Brit. J. Psychiat.,* **114,** 581–92.

Graham, P. and **Rutter, M.** (1968b) Organic brain dysfunction and child psychiatric disorder, *British Medical Journal,* **3,** 695–700.

Graham, P. and **Rutter, M.** (1970) Selection of children with psychiatric disorder, in M. Rutter, J. Tizard, and K. Whitmore (1970) (eds) *Education, Health and Behaviour,* London: Longman.

Great Britain (Statutes) See under name of Act of Parliament; e.g. Education Act (1944).

Grunewald, K. (1974) *The Mentally Retarded in Sweden,* Stockholm: Swedish Inst.

Hall, R. V., Panyan, M., Rabon, D. and **Broden, M.** (1968a) Instructing beginning teachers in reinforcement procedures which improve classroom control,*J. Appl. Behav. Anal.,* **1**, 315–22.

Hall, R. V., Lund, D. and **Jackson, D.** (1968b) Effects of teacher attention on study behaviour,*J. Appl. Behav. Anal.,* **1**, 1–12.

Hargreaves, D. H. (1967) *Social Relationships in a Secondary School,* London: Routledge & Kegan Paul.

Hargreaves, D., Hestor, S.K. and **Mellor, F. J.** (1975) *Deviance in Classrooms,* London: Routledge & Kegan Paul.

Harrop, A. (1977) The vanishing problem, *Bull. Br. Assoc. Behav. Psychother.,* **5**, 51–5.

Harrop, A. and **Critchley, C.** (1972) Classroom management and deviant behaviour, *Behaviour Modification,* November, 6–9.

Haskell, S. and **Pauli, M.** (1975) Visits to Resources Centres and Special Institutes for the motor handicapped and mentally retarded children in Norway, Sweden and Denmark, unpublished report to Action Research for the Crippled Child.

Holbrook, D. (1965) *The Secret Places,* London: Methuen.

Holmes, D. S. (1966) The application of learning theory to a school behaviour problem: a case study, *Psychology in the Schools,* **3**, 355–9.

Hood-Williams, J. (1960) The results of psychotherapy with children: a revaluation, *Journal of Consulting Psychology.,* **24**, 84–8.

Inner London Education Authority (1965) *Survey into Progress of Maladjusted Children,* London: ILEA.

Inner London Education Authority (1968) *The Education of Immigrant Pupils in Primary Schools,* Report 959, 12 February.

Inner London Education Authority (1970) Literacy Survey (mimeographed report).

Johnson, C. A. and **Katz, R. C.** (1973) Using parents as change-agents for their children: a review, *J. Child Psychol. Psychiat.,* **14**, 181–200.

Johnson, G. O. (1961) A comparative study of the personal and social adjustment of mentally handicapped children placed in special classes with mentally handicapped children who remain in regular classes, Syracuse: New York (quoted in Osterling, 1967).

Johnson, G. O. (1962) Special education for the mentally handicapped: a paradox, *Exceptional Children,* **29**, 62–9.

Joint Council for the Education of Handicapped Children (undated) *Integration or Segregation? A false alternative,* London: JCEHC.

Jones, C. (1978) Personal communication.

Jones, N. (1973) Special adjustment units in comprehensive schools: I Needs and resources. II Structure and function, *Ther. Ed.,* **1**, no. 2, 23–31.

Jones, N. (1974) Special adjustment units in comprehensive schools: III Selection of Children, *Ther. Ed.,* **2**, no. 2, 21–6.

Jordan, A. (1959) Personal-social traits of mentally handicapped children, in T. G. Thurstone (ed.) *An Evaluation of Educating Mentally Handicapped Children in Special Classes and in Regular Classes,* Univ. of North Carolina (quoted in Osterling, 1967).

Jorgensen, I. S. (1973) *Special Education in Denmark,* Copenhagen: Min. of Ed.

Jorgensen, I. S. (1975) *Education Clinics in Danish Special Education,* Copenhagen: Min. of Ed.

Jorgensen, I. S. (1976) *Segregated versus Integrated Education,* Copenhagen: Min. of Ed.

Kamin, L. J. (1977) *The Science and Politics of I.Q.,* Harmondsworth: Penguin Education.

Klemm, L. R. (1891) *European Schools,* New York: D. Appleton.

Kounin, J. S., Friesen, W. V. and **Norton, E.** (1966) Managing emotionally disturbed children in regular classrooms, *Journal of Educational Psychology,* **57**, 1–13.

Labon, D. (1973) Helping maladjusted children in primary schools, *Ther. Ed.,* **1**, no. 2, 14–22.

Lane, D. A. (1977) Aspects of the use of behaviour modification in secondary schools, *Bull. Br. Assoc. Behav. Psychother.,* **5**, 76–9.

Lane, D. A. and **Millar, R.** (1977) Dealing with behaviour problems in school: a new development, *Community Health,* **8**, 155–8.

Lane, H. (1928) *Talks to Parents and Teachers,* London: Allen & Unwin..

Lansdown, R. (1970) *Day Schools for Maladjusted Children in the London Area,* Assoc. of Workers for Maladjusted Children.

Laslett, R. (1977) *Educating Maladjusted Children,* London: Crosby Lockwood Staples.

Lemert, E. M. (1967) *Human Deviance: social problems and social control,* Englewood Cliffs: Prentice Hall.

Lennhoff, F. E. (1960) *Exceptional Children,* London: Allen & Unwin.

Levitt, E. E. (1957) Results of psychotherapy with children: an evaluation, *Journal of Consulting Psychology*, **21**, 189–96.

Levitt, E. E. (1963) Psychotherapy with children: a further evaluation, *Behaviour, Research and Therapy*, **1**, 45–51.

Local Government Training Board (1972) *The Role and Training of Education Welfare Officers*, London: Dept. of Education and Science.

Lodge, B. (1977) Call to isolate the classroom thugs, *Times Ed. Supp.* 15 April.

Lovell, K., Byrne, C. and **Richardson, B.** (1963) A further study of the educational progress of children who had received remedial education, *Brit. J. Educ. Psych.*, **33**, 3–9.

Lovell, K., Johnson, E. and **Platts, D.** (1962) A summary of a study of the reading ages of children who had been given remedial teaching. *Brit. J. Educ. Psych.*, **32**, 66–71.

Lunacy (Consolidated) Act (1890) 53 Victoria, Ch. 5, London: HMSO.

Lyons, S. (1976) The mentally handicapped child: experiences of integration in an infant school, unpublished paper (personal communication).

McAllister, L. W., Stachowiak, J. G., Baer, D. M. and **Conderman, L.** (1969) The application of operant conditioning techniques in a secondary school classroom, *J. Appl. Behav. Anal.*, **3**, 277–85.

McFie, B. S. (1934) Behaviour and personality difficulties in school children, *Brit. J. Educ. Psych.*, **4**, 30–46.

McMullan, T. (1969) quoted by V. Makins, (1975) in *The Story of Countesthorpe*, *Times Ed. Supp.*, 23 May.

McPhail, P., Ungoed-Thomas, J. and **Chapman, H.** (1972) *Moral Education in the Secondary School*, London: Longman.

Madsen, C. H., Becker, W. C. and **Thomas, D. R.** (1968) Rules, praise and ignoring: elements of elementary classroom control, *J. Appl. Behav. Anal.*, **1**, 139–50.

Mental Deficiency Act (1913) 3 and 4 George V, Ch. 28, London: HMSO.

Meyer, V. and **Levy, R.** (1973) Modification of behaviour in obsessive-compulsive disorders, in H. E. Adams and I. P. Unikel (eds) *Issues and Trends in Behaviour Therapy*, Springfield, Ill.: Charles C. Thomas.

Milner, M. (1938) *The Human Problem in Schools*, London: Methuen.

Ministry of Education (1945) *The Handicapped Pupils and School Health Service Regulations* (S.R. and O. no. 1076), London: HMSO.

Ministry of Education (1953) Circular 269, The School Health Service and Handicapped Pupils Regulations, London: Min. Ed.

Ministry of Education (1954) *Training and Supply of Teachers of Handicapped Pupils,* Fourth Report of the National Advisory Council on the Training and Supply of Teachers, London: HMSO.

Ministry of Education, (1955) *Report of the Committee on Maladjusted children* (the Underwood Report), London: HMSO.

Ministry of Education (1958) *Report of the Chief Medical Officer for the Years 1956—57*, London: HMSO.

Ministry of Education, (1959) *The Handicapped Pupils and Special Schools Regulation* (S.I. no. 365), London: HMSO.

Ministry of Education, (1961) Circular 11/61, Special Educational Treatment for Educationally Sub-normal Pupils, London: Min. of Ed.

Morris, J. M. (1959) *Reading in the Primary School*, London: Newnes.

Morris, J. M. (1966) *Standards and Progress in Reading*, Slough: NFER.

Mullen, A. and **Itkin, W.** (1961) Achievement and adjustment of educable mentally handicapped children in special classes, and in regular classes. Chicago (quoted in Osterling, 1967).

National Board of Education (Sweden) (1975) *LSA 73; Curriculum for Special Schools for the Mentally Retarded.*

National Fund for Research into Crippling Diseases (1976) *Integrating the Disabled: Report of the Snowdon Working Party*, Horsham: NFRCD.

Neale, M. D. (1958) *Neale Analysis of Reading Ability Manual*, London: Macmillan.

O'Leary, D. K. and **Becker, W. C.** (1967) Behaviour modification of an adjustment class: a token reinforcement system, *Exceptional Children*, **33**, 637–42.

O'Leary, K. D., Becker, W. C., Evans, M. B. and **Saudergas, R. A.** (1969) A token reinforcement programme in a public school: a replication and systematic analysis, *J. Appl. Behav. Anal.* **2**, 3–13.

O'Leary, K. D., Kaufman, K. F., Kass, R. E. and **Drabman, R. S.** (1970) The effects of loud and soft reprimands on the behaviour of disruptive students. *Exceptional Children*, **37**, 145–55.

O'Leary, K. D. and **Drabman, R. S.** (1971) Token reinforcement programmes in the classroom: a review, *Psychological Bulletin,* **75,** 379–98.
O'Leary, K. D. and O'Leary, S. G., (eds) (1972) *Classroom Management,* New York: Pergamon.
Osterling, O. (1967) *The Efficacy of Special Education,* Uppsala: Scandinavian Univ. Books.
Phillipson, C. M. (1971) Juvenile delinquency and the school, in W. G. Carson and P. Wiles, (eds) *Crime and Delinquency in Britain: sociological readings,* London: Martin Robertson.
Pidgeon, D. A. (1970) *Expectation and Pupil Performance,* Slough: NFER.
Pollack, M. (1972) *Today's 3 Year Olds in London,* London: Heinemann.
Power, M. J., Alderson, M. R., Phillipson, C. M., Schoenberg, E. and Morris, J. M. (1967) Delinquent schools, *New Society,* 19 October.
Power, M. J., Benn, R. T. and Morris, J. M. (1972) Neighbourhood, school and juveniles before the Courts, *British Journal of Criminology,* **12,** 111–32
Premack, D. (1959) Towards empirical behaviour laws: I. Positive reinforcement, *Psychological Review,* **66,** 219–33.
Preston, P. (1975) Infant Rating Scales. Personal communication.
Pringle, M. L. Kellmer (1961) The long-term effects of remedial treatment: a follow-up study, *Educ. Res.,* **4,** 62–6.
Pringle, M. L. Kellmer, Butler, N. and Davie, R. (1966) *11,000 Seven Year Olds,* London: Longman.
Pritchard, D. G. (1963) *Education and the Handicapped 1760—1960,* London: Routledge & Kegan Paul.
Quicke, J. C. (1976) Behaviourism and education: a critique, *Assoc. Educ. Psychologists J.* **3,** no. 8, 8–16.
Reynolds, D. (1976) When pupils and teachers refuse a truce: the secondary school and the creation of delinquency, in G. Mungham and G. Pearson, (eds) *Working Class Youth Culture,* London: Routledge & Kegan Paul.
Reynolds, D. (1977) The sociology of schooling and the absent pupil: the school as a factor in the generation of truancy, in H. C. M. Carroll (ed.) *Absenteeism in South Wales: studies of pupils, their homes and their secondary schools,* Swansea: University College, Faculty of Education.
Robins, L. N. (1966) *Deviant Children Grown Up,* Baltimore: Williams & Wilkins.
Rosenthal, R. and Jacobson, L. (1968) *Pygmalion in the Classroom,* Holt, Rinehart & Winston.
Rowan, P. (1976) Short-term sanctuary, *Times Ed. Supp.* 2 April, 21–4.
Royal Commission in the Care and Control of the Feeble Minded (1908), *Report,* London: HMSO, 8 vols.
Rutter, M. (1965) Classification and categorisation in child psychiatry, *J. Child Psychol. Psychiat.,* **6,** 71–83.
Rutter, M. (1967) A children's behaviour questionnaire for completion by teachers: preliminary findings, *J. Child Psychol. Psychiat.,* **8,** 1–11.
Rutter, M. (1972) Critical notice *(Childhood Behaviour and Mental Health,* ed. M. Shepherd, B. Oppenheim, and S. Mitchell, London: Univ. London Press), *J. Child Psychol. Psychiat,* **13,** 219–22.
Rutter, M. (1977) Prospective studies to investigate behavioural change, in J. S. Strauss, H. M. Babigian, and M. Roff, (eds) *Methods of Longitudinal Research in Psychopathology,* New York: Plenum Publishing.
Rutter, M. and Graham, P. (1968) The reliability and validity of the psychiatric assessment of the child: I. Interview with the child, *Brit. J. Psychiat.,* **114,** 563–79.
Rutter, M., Lebovici, S., Eisenberg, L., Snerzevskij, A. V., Sadoun, R., Broke, E. and Tsun, Yi Lin (1969) A triaxial classification of mental disorders in children, *J. Child Psychol. Psychiat.,* **10,** 41–61.
Rutter, M., Tizard, J. and Whitmore, K. eds (1970) *Education, Health and Behaviour,* London: Longman.
Rutter, M., Yule, W., Berger, M., Yule, B., Morton, J. and Bagley, C. (1974) Children of West Indian immigrants: I. Rates of behavioural deviance and of psychiatric disorder, *J. Child Psychol. Psychiat.,* **15,** 241–62.
Rutter, M. and Yule, W. (1975) The concept of specific reading retardation, *J. Child Psychol. Psychiat.,* **16,** 181–97.
Rutter, M., Cox, A., Tupling, C., Berger, M. and Yule, W. (1975a) Attainment and adjustment in two geographical areas: I. The prevalence of psychiatric disorder, *Brit. J. Psychiat.,* **126,** 493–509.
Rutter, M., Yule, B., Quinton, D., Rowlands, O., Yule, W. and Berger, M. (1975b) Attainment and adjustment in two geographical areas: III. Some factors accounting for area differences, *Brit. J. Psychiat,* **126,** 520–33.

Rutter, M., Yule, B., Morton, J. and Bagley, C. (1975c) Children of West Indian immigrants: III. Home circumstances and family patterns. *J. Child Psychol. Psychiat.*, **16**, 105–23.

Rutter, M., Graham, P., Chadwick, O. F. D. and Yule, W. (1976) Adolescent turmoil: fact or fiction, *J. Child Psychol. Psychiat.*, **17**, 35–56.

Rutter, M. and Quinton, D. (1977) Psychiatric disorder – ecological factors and concepts of causation, in H. McGurk, (ed.) *Ecological Factors in Human Development*, Amsterdam: North Holland.

Sampson, O. C. (1975) *Remedial Education*, London: Routledge & Kegan Paul.

Schonell, F. J. and Goodacre, E. (1974) *The Psychology and Teaching of Reading*, Edinburgh: Oliver & Boyd.

Scottish Education Department (1975) *The Secondary Education of Physically Handicapped Children in Scotland*, Edinburgh: HMSO.

Shaw, O. (1965) *Maladjusted Boys*, London: Allen & Unwin.

Shearer, E. (1967) The long term effects of remedial education, *Educ. Res.*, **9**, 219–22.

Shearer, E. (1977) Survey of ESN(M) children in Cheshire, *Sp. Ed. Fd. Tr.*, **4**, no. 2, 20–2.

Shepherd, M., Oppenheim, B., and Mitchell, S. (1971) *Childhood Behaviour and Mental Health*, London: Univ. of London Press.

Shields, R. (1962) *A Cure of Delinquents*, London: Heinemann.

Shuttleworth, G. E. (1888) The education of children of abnormally weak mental capacity, *Journal of Mental Science*, **34**, 80–4.

Stenholm, B. (1975) *The Teaching of Children with Educational Difficulties and Handicaps in Sweden*, Stockholm: Swedish Inst.

Stott, D. H. (1963) *The Teaching of Children with Educational Difficulties and Handicaps in Sweden*, Stockholm: Swedish Inst.

Stott, D. H. (1963) *The Social Adjustment of Children*, 2nd edn, London: Univ. of London Press.

Stott, D. H. (1971) *The Bristol Social Adjustment Guides*, London: Univ. of London Press.

Terman, L. M. and Merrill, M. A. (1960) *Stanford Binet Intelligence Scale: Manual for the Third Revision, Form L—M*, Boston: Houghton-Mifflin.

Thompson, D. and Jones, C. (1974) Towards integration, *Sp. Ed. Fd. Tr.*, **1**, no. 1, 29–31.

Thurstone, T. G., ed. (1959) *An Evaluation of Educating Mentally Handicapped Children in Special Classes and in Regular Classes*, Univ. of North Carolina (quoted in Osterling, 1967).

Tisdall, W. (1962) The efficacy of a special class program on the productive thinking ability of educable mentally retarded children, PhD. thesis, Univ. of Illinois.

Tizard, J. (1973) Maladjusted children and the child guidance service, *London Educational Review* **2**, 22–37.

Tobin, D. and Pumfrey, P. (1976) Some long term effects of the remedial teaching of reading, *Educational Review*, **29**, 1–12.

Tuckey, L., Parfit, J. and Tuckey, R. (1973) *Handicapped School Leavers*, Windsor: NFER (NCB report).

Tuckwell, P. (1976) Handicap in infant schools, *New Psychiatry*, **3**, no. 14, 16–18.

Ullman, L. P. (1973) Perspectives in experimental clinical psychology: one view, in H. E. Adams and I. P. Unikel, (eds) *Issues and Trends in Behaviour Therapy*, Springfield, Ill.: Charles C. Thomas.

Valentine, H. B. (1951) Results of remedial education in a child guidance centre, *Brit. J. Educ. Psych.*, **21**, 145–9.

Ward, J. (1971) Modification of deviant classroom behaviour, *Brit. J. Educ. Psych.*, **41**, 304–13.

Watson, L. (1973) *Child Behaviour Modification: a manual for teachers, nurses and parents*, New York: Pergamon.

Watson, J. B. (1924) *Psychology from the Standpoint of a Behaviourist*, Philadelphia: Lippincott.

Watson, P. (1973) Stability of I.Q. of immigrant and non-immigrant slow-learning pupils, *Brit. J. Educ. Psych.*, **43**, 80–2.

Watts, J. (1976) Personal communication.

Wechsler, D. (1949) *Wechsler Intelligence Scale for Children (Manual)*, New York: The Psychological Corporation.

Wessman, L. (1976) *Normalisation and Integration*, Stockholm: National Swedish Board of Education.

West, D. J. and Farrington, D. (1973) *Who Becomes Delinquent?* London: Heinemann.

Wills, D. (1941) *The Hawkspur Experiment*, London: Allen & Unwin.

Wills, W. D. (1945) *The Barns Experiment*, London: Allen & Unwin.

Wills, W. D. (1960) *Throw Away Thy Rod*, London: Gollancz.

Wills, W. D. (1971) *Spare the Child*, Harmondsworth: Penguin Books.

Wilson, M. D., Evans, M. B., Dawson, R. L. and **Kiek, J. S.** (1977) Disturbed children in special schools, *Sp. Ed. Fd. Tr.*, **4**, no. 2, 8–10.

Wright, D. M., Moelis, I., and **Pollack, L. J.** (1976) The outcome of individual child psychotherapy: increments at follow-up, *J. Child Psychol. Psychiat.* **17**, 275–85.

Wrightstone, J. *et al* (1959) *A Comparison of Educational Outcomes under Single Track and Two-Track Plans for Educable Mentally Retarded Children,* New York (quoted in Osterling, 1967).

Yates, A. J. (1970) *Behaviour Therapy,* Toronto: Wiley.

York, R., Herron, J. M. and **Wolff, S.** (1972) Exclusion from school, *J. Child Psychol. Psychiat.*, **13**, 259–66.

Yule, W. (1973) Differential prognosis of reading backwardness and specific reading retardation, *Brit. J. Educ. Psych.*, **43**, 244–8.

Yule, W. (1976) Critical notice *(Taxonomy of Behaviour Disturbance,* ed. D. H. Scott, N. C. Marston and S. J. Neill, London: Univ. of London Press) *Ther. Ed.*, **4**, no. 1, 45–7.

Yule, W., Rutter, M., Berger, M. and **Thompson, J.** (1974) Over- and under-achievement in reading: distribution in the general population, *Brit. J. Educ. Psych.*, **44**, 1–12.

Yule, W., Berger, M., Rutter, M. and **Yule, B.** (1975) Children of West Indian immigrants: II. Intellectual performance and reading attainment. *J. Child Psychol. Psychiat.*, **16**, 1–17.

Zimmerman, E. H. and **Zimmerman, J.** (1962) The alteration of behaviour in a special classroom situation, *Journal for the Experimental Analysis of Behaviour,* **51**, 59–60.

Index